The Vanishing Word

Focal Point Series
ReViewing the Movies:
A Christian Response to Contemporary Film
by Peter Fraser and Vernon Edwin Neal

Christians in a .com World:
Getting Connected Without Being Consumed
by Gene Edward Veith, Jr. and Chris Stamper

Called to Womanhood:
A Biblical View for Today's World
by Beth Impson

God at Work:
Your Christian Vocation in All of Life
by Gene Edward Veith, Jr.

FOCAL POINT SERIES

Gene Edward Veith, Jr., general editor

The Vanishing Word

The Veneration of Visual Imagery in the Postmodern World

Arthur W. Hunt, III

CROSSWAY BOOKS

A DIVISION OF
GOOD NEWS PUBLISHERS
WHEATON, ILLINOIS

The Vanishing Word

Copyright © 2003 by Arthur W. Hunt, III

Published by Crossway Books
  a division of Good News Publishers
  1300 Crescent Street
  Wheaton, Illinois 60187

Cover design: David LaPlaca

Cover photo: PhotoDisc™

First printing, 2003

Printed in the United States of America

Unless otherwise indicated, Scripture quotations are taken from the King James Version.

Scripture quotations indicated NKJV are taken from *The Holy Bible: New King James Version,* copyright © 1982 by Thomas Nelson, Inc. All rights reserved. Used by permission.

Library of Congress Cataloging-in-Publication Data
Hunt, Arthur W., 1960-
   The vanishing Word : the veneration of visual imagery in the postmodern
world / Arthur W. Hunt, III.
      p. cm. — (Focal point series)
   Includes biographical references and indexes.
   ISBN 1-58134-404-X (pbk. : alk. paper)
   1. Visual communication. I. Title. II. Series.
P93.5 .H86   2003
302.23—dc21   2002152922

VP		13	12	11	10	09	08	07	06	05	04	03
15	14	13	12	11	10	9	8	7	6	5	4	3	2	1

To
Sheila

*"Thus men forgot that All deities reside
in the human breast."*

*William Blake,
"Marriage of Heaven and Hell"*

BLAKE HAD IT HALF RIGHT. ALL DEITIES RESIDE IN THE
HUMAN BREAST EXCEPT FOR ONE.

Contents

Acknowledgments

For about a decade now I have been thinking about the subject matter of this book. I owe a great debt to Neil Postman whose own books set me on a path of contemplation about the relationship between media technologies and American society. Especially enlightening was an article entitled "She Wants her TV! He Wants His Book!" which first appeared in *Harper's Magazine* (March 1991) and was based on a lively conversation between Postman (pro-print culture) and Camille Paglia (pro-TV culture). This book is really an extension of that conversation as seen through the eyes of a conservative evangelical.

I am not the only Christian who has addressed the problems of an image-oriented culture. Gene Veith has done so in a number of his books, particularly *Reading Between the Lines*, *Modern Fascism*, and *Postmodern Times*. I am grateful to Dr. Veith not only for the insights found in these books but also for his work as general editor of this series. When I learned that it was Dr. Veith who would be looking at my scribbles, it was a personal confirmation that God was in this project.

I would like to thank Crossway—my first choice of publisher—for seeing the need to address the issue.

Portions of *The Vanishing Word* have previously been published in *Christian Research Journal*, and I would like to acknowledge my gratitude to both Hank Hanegraaff and Elliot Miller for their willingness to engage the readers of the *Journal* with some of my concerns.

Finally, I would like to acknowledge Rick Sprouse, Bill Bowen, and James McDonald for reading my drafts, giving helpful comments, and listening to me without once saying, "You're not going to talk about the TV thing again, are you?"

CHAPTER ONE

Introduction: Tomorrowland

It's a wonderful world. It may destroy itself but at least you'll be able to watch it all on TV.

BOB HOPE

ALTHOUGH OUR COMMUNICATION TECHNOLOGIES DAZZLE US, THEY ALSO HAVE THE POTENTIAL TO UNRAVEL US, AND TO MAKE US A BEWITCHED PEOPLE.

෨

In the early 1960s, Orlando was a crossroads community of citrus groves, farmland, and swamps. Back then one could buy an acre in Orange County for about two hundred dollars. So when Walt Disney bought forty-six square miles worth, the citizens of Orlando must have mused how life would be different under the shadow of Mickey Mouse. However, the dreamer from Hollywood was not content to just build another theme park; he was ready to try his hand at building an elaborate city of the future. Upon the Florida flatland, Walt Disney envisioned a "City of Tomorrow," where dirt, disease, and poverty would be nonexistent; a nuclear-powered metropolis, controlling its own climate and recycling its own waste; a radiant web of white pods connected by silent transit systems. He quietly asserted that the city would be paid for from the profits of his new Disney World.[1] Only a handful knew the scope of Disney's City of Tomorrow and how it came to dwarf all other projects on his drawing board. Walt Disney never saw his utopia because he died in 1966, just after construction began in Orlando. Disney's successors, more concerned with the bottom line, settled for what is now the present-day EPCOT. Heirs of the Disney dynasty thought it more prudent to follow the tried formula of entertaining crowds with fantasy rides. The City of Tomorrow evolved into an expanded entertainment haven. Other parks followed. Today Metro Orlando receives more than forty-five million visitors a year. Almost all of us, at one time or another, have made a pilgrimage to one of central Florida's amusement meccas.

The development of Orlando allegorizes the changes taking place in our own culture. Like Walt Disney's successors, we also have thrown off our modern visions of utopia for an easier, more attainable, fun land. Orlando serves as an emblematic gauge of an image-driven public, dependent upon movies, television, and video games. Of course, the *theme* of Orlando's theme parks is primarily a reflection of the film industry. The Magic Kingdom, MGM Studios, and Animal Kingdom largely exist because of the movies they mimic. Universal Studios created their theme park especially for children and adults who would pay good money to swim with Jaws, fly with E.T., or fight side by side with the Terminator.

THE AGE OF THE IMAGE IN A
TECHNO-WONDERLAND

It does not take a social scientist to tell us that our culture has an insatiable appetite for visual stimulation. Within the last several years Disney and others have devoted their energies into creating virtual-reality rides, even procuring NASA rocket scientists to design image-enhanced simulators. This is not to say America has given up on space exploration, only that there seems to be more profit in applying our hologram-like technology toward amusing consumers. In promoting Orlando's new Island of Adventure, Steven Spielberg predicted that "virtual reality will live up to its name for the first time in the next ten years . . . because you'll be surrounded by images. . . . You'll feel the breezes. You'll smell the smells. . . . Yet when you stand back and turn on a light to look at where you've been standing, you're just in a dark room with a helmet on."[2] Spielberg claims that those in today's generation demand reality in their high-tech recreations. The dinosaurs must have wet noses and look like they have been rolling in the dust all day or they just will not do. Entertainment engineers know that the level of electro-sophistication possessed by young media connoisseurs is so keen that the thrill once provided by a wooden roller coaster is now antiquated.

Virtual reality's popular appeal has been augmented by advances in technology. And it is technology with which America has had an ongoing love affair. Historically the affection Americans have bestowed upon technological advancement has been rooted in a progressive spirit—a type of secular Manifest Destiny that sees any innovation as providential. Technology, progress, and the future are all synonyms in contemporary American culture. Technology has allowed us to live longer, has made us more comfortable, and has made us rich. Virtual reality is deemed good because it represents progress. The same can be said for the invention of television or the computer or the washing machine. To deny such technological providence is anathema.

A celebration of technological progress is enshrined at one particular attraction in Disney World's Tomorrowland—General Electric's Carousel of Progress. The ride is a cute summary of America's technological love fest. Touring Tomorrowland is like walking around in the future wearing Jules Verne spectacles. Perhaps the first to describe eco-tourism, Verne would have been delighted with Disney World. This is true not only because Disney made a film and a ride featuring *20,000 Leagues Under the Sea*, but also because Jules Verne shared Walt Disney's obsession with technology and the future. The Carousel of Progress traces a hundred years of progress as tourists relax in a sit-down, revolving theater. In the background we hear voices singing, "There's a great big beautiful tomorrow, shining at the end of every day." The show focuses on a family's history through time, showing all the conveniences made possible by innovations in electricity. There is a father, mother, daughter, son, grandfather, grandmother, and a silly cousin named Orville. The ride scoots you from the past and into the future with a historical panorama of our most remarkable household inventions. What is so intriguing about the show is that every family in every generation looks the same—always laughing and enjoying each other's company. Only the inventions have been changed. The message we walk away with is that technology is neutral and only serves to make us happier.

TECHNOLOGY IS NOT NEUTRAL

Contrary to popular thinking, technology is not neutral. It has the propensity to change our beliefs and behavior. For example, any historian will tell you that the printing press hurled Europe out of the Middle Ages and into the Protestant Reformation. When Johann Gutenberg introduced movable type in the fifteenth century, a whole new world opened up—liberty, freedom, discovery, democracy. The Bible became available to the people. Martin Luther called the invention of the printing press the "supreme act of grace by which the gospel can be driven forward." Europe was set on fire. People were thinking, arguing, creating, and reflecting. The printing press allowed ideas to be put in black and white so that anyone could analyze or criticize them. To a great extent, America was born out of a print-oriented culture.

What most often escapes our notice in public discussions is how new technologies create unintended effects. In this sense, technology is a mixed blessing to societies, whether the machines of warfare, transportation, or communication media. What Jules Verne knew, and what Walt Disney might not have cared to know, was how the future could have a dark side. Jules Verne understood the biases of technology, that technology had the capacity to change us or even destroy us. Because Captain Nemo feared the *Nautilus* would fall into the wrong hands, in the Disney movie he blew it up, along with the island that sheltered its mysterious secrets. Nemo's periscope might not have been able to rotate all the way around, but he was not too far off the deep end to fathom the depths of human depravity. Nemo would have agreed with King Solomon, who wrote, "Lo, this only have I found, that God hath made man upright; but they have sought out many inventions" (Ecclesiastes 7:29). (Although Leonardo da Vinci contrived a submarine three hundred years before the birth of Jules Verne, it is an interesting fact of history that the great inventor suppressed it because he felt it was too satanic to be placed in the hands of unregenerate men.[3])

Glitzy machines have a way of mesmerizing us so that we do not think about the unintended consequences they create. Our situation today is very much like a train that we have all boarded with enormous enthusiasm. With great splendor the train embarks from the station while we cheer, "Onward! Forward!" The train picks up speed, and we all shout, "Progress! Prosperity!" Faster and faster the wheels turn. With tremendous velocity the train races down the track. "Faster! Faster!" we yell. But we don't even know where the train is taking us. We don't know where it is going. It is a mystery train. Jules Verne and Walt Disney were able to make fantasizing about the future a commodity, which we have ingested right on up through George Jetson cartoons and more. For a hundred years we have anticipated the twenty-first century in visions of rockets, gadgets, and push buttons. But the new millennium has arrived. The future is here.

HISTORY'S TESTIMONY TO THE BIAS OF TECHNOLOGY

Technology's inherent bias to mold belief and behavior can be detected in two particular inventions of the twentieth century— atomic weaponry and the automobile. "Nuclear fission is now theoretically possible," wrote Albert Einstein in a 1939 letter to President Franklin Roosevelt explaining the power unleashed when the nucleus of a uranium atom is split. Fearing the Germans were close to the same discovery, Roosevelt authorized the Manhattan Project to develop an atomic weapon. Five years later the bomb was ready. The decision to use the bomb followed two other possible alternatives. One option involved impressing the Japanese into surrendering by dropping it in some unpopulated wooded area. The idea was that the Japanese would run over, see the big hole, and give up. However, President Truman's advisers preferred a more tangible target. A second alternative was to invade Japan, but the casualties for such a plan were estimated to be over the million mark.

John Costello says some scientists on the Manhattan Project had doubts about the "genie of technological destruction their work had uncorked."[4] James Franck, chairman of a committee on the bomb's "social and political implications," warned of the problems of international control and the danger of a precipitating arms race. His report claimed that the Japanese war was already won and that Japan was on the brink of being starved into surrender. Truman's advisers ignored Franck's report, urging the President to drop the bomb on a large city with a legitimate military target. Hiroshima had an army base and a munitions factory. Truman was confident. The President knew what kind of weapon had been handed to him after the first atomic explosion in Alamogordo, New Mexico, earlier that summer. Costello notes that an "irreversible momentum" to use the bomb superseded all other alternatives. Truman felt the bomb "would save many times the number of lives, both American and Japanese, than it would cost."[5] One of Truman's generals later observed, "He was like a little boy on a toboggan."[6]

Shortly after eating their breakfast on August 6, 1945, the inhabitants of Hiroshima noticed an object floating earthward. It probably reminded them of an episode a few days earlier when a flock of leaflets fluttered to the ground warning of an imminent attack upon their city. The message could not have been too surprising. They knew a war was on, and the enemy was winning. The bulk that pulled the sail to earth that morning weighed four tons and cost four million dollars to develop. The last memory held by curious gazers was a solitary flash of light. Once detonated, the light rippled from the center of the city, puffing to dust houses, bridges, and factories. The explosion killed one-third of Hiroshima's three hundred thousand residents instantly. Another bomb killed eighty thousand three days later, in the same manner, at Nagasaki. Over the next five years, five hundred thousand more would die from the effects of radiation exposure. Today nuclear weapons are forty times more powerful than the Hiroshima bomb.

Truman's decision to use the bomb no doubt saved millions of lives. But it was a bargain with the devil. The trade-off for having developed a machine of mass destruction yesterday is living with the threat of being blown to little bits tomorrow. For over half a century the world has lived under the shadow of a potential nuclear disaster. Techno-enthusiasts are incessantly expounding what a new machine can do *for* us, but little deliberation is ever afforded as to what a new machine will do *to* us. Technological advancement always comes with a price, to which history is more than willing to disgorge examples.

Henry Ford once confessed, "I don't know anything about history."[7] The comment was made to the radical journalist John Reed, who had an instinctive nose for revolutions in the making. Ford's revolution was fashioned on the automobile assembly line. So passionate was Ford about his own revolution of manufacturing Model T's, says Roger Burlingame, that he once threatened to fire any patriotic employee who chose to leave work and answer President Wilson's call to help guard the Mexican border when skirmishes erupted there. The *Chicago Tribune* soon after accused Ford of being an "ignorant idealist" and "anarchist." Ford thought otherwise and sued the *Tribune* for a million dollars. In trying to prove that Ford was indeed ignorant, lawyers for the *Tribune* asked him questions about the American Revolution. Ford had trouble explaining the basic fundamentals of American government. He did not know what part Benedict Arnold played in the war. When asked, "What was the United States originally?" Ford tersely replied, "Land, I guess." Ford would go on the record for pronouncing to the world, "History is more or less bunk." The sympathetic jury did not find the world's greatest industrialist ignorant, nor an anarchist. But neither could the jury find the *Tribune* reckless. The verdict required Ford to pay six cents in damages.[8]

Perhaps had Henry Ford known his history a bit better, he would have foreseen the social effects of the automobile. Although the automobile awarded us the commute and the family motor vacation, it also assisted in severing community and family ties like no other invention of its time. In the days when carriages were still hooked to horses, it was not uncommon to find, in any town across America, large front porches with people actually sitting on them, chatting with neighbors. The essence of this forgotten phenomenon is recorded in the famous *Middletown* study:

> In the nineties [1890s] we were all much more together. . . . People brought chairs and cushions out of the house and sat on the lawn evenings. We rolled out a strip of carpet and put cushions on the porch step to take care of the unlimited overflow of neighbors that dropped by. We'd sit out so all evening. The younger couples perhaps would wander off for half an hour to get a soda but come back to join in the informal singing or listen while somebody strummed a mandolin or guitar.[9]

The *Middletown* study focused on a typical American community in the 1920s. The researchers selected the town of Muncie, Indiana, termed "Middletown" because they viewed it to be the closest representation possible of contemporary American life.[10] Halfway into the 1920s it could be said that the "horse culture" in Middletown had trotted off into the sunset. The horse fountain at the courthouse square dried up, and possessing an automobile was deemed a necessity of normal living. In his book *The Rise of Selfishness in America*, James Collier says the car soon became a way for youth to escape authority. It allowed young couples to pair off. It was, in effect, a portable living room for eating, drinking, smoking, gossip, and sexual immorality.[11] Of thirty girls brought before the Middletown juvenile court charged with "sex crimes" within a given year, nineteen of them were listed as having committed the offense in an automobile.[12] When Henry Ford formulated the assembly line, he probably did not envision himself as a villain to virginity. Nevertheless, in making the automobile a commodity, he moved courtship from the parlor to the backseat.

It is not the purpose here to suggest that we stop developing instruments of war or permanently park our cars. These are not the rants of a technophobe. However, few of us in the information age ever stop to consider this truth: *For every expressed purpose a technology is designed to serve, there are always a number of unintended consequences accompanying it.* Tomorrowland poses a host of challenges that gadget masters are not likely to point out. And one of the most significant challenges that should concern us is what repercussions will transpire as America shifts from a print-oriented culture to an image-oriented one. Although our communication technologies dazzle us, they also have the potential to unravel us, and to make us a bewitched people.

THE ADVENT OF TELEVISION

The first American commercial TV broadcast occurred at New York's World's Fair on April 30, 1939. Television was the technology for the next generation, showcased in an exposition offering a gleaming glimpse of the future. The fair's theme was "Building the World of Tomorrow," the optimistic secular gospel Walt Disney later embraced as a major element in his own theme parks. A guidebook promoted the fair as the "stupendous, gigantic, super-magnificent . . . greatest-show-on-earth."[13] The 1939 World's Fair was the culmination of a decade-long aesthetic enchantment with technology. David Gelernter, author of *1939: The Lost World of the Fair*, writes:

> Nonetheless 1939 was a profoundly religious age, and its religiosity shows in the way it treated technology. It was not reverent. Rather it was spiritual; art made technology beautiful, made technology speak to the public not only pragmatically but emotionally. Art ministered to technology. Artists in the 1930s (not

all but many) were technology's priesthood. As a consequence art found itself embroiled alongside technology and the future.[14]

At the physical center of the fair stood a towering three-sided obelisk, and next to it an immense white sphere. Facing the dominating structures, President Roosevelt announced, "I hereby dedicate the World's Fair, the New York World's Fair of 1939, and I declare it open to all mankind!"[15] The President's image was dispersed from aerials atop the Empire State Building in a live broadcast by NBC. A week earlier, David Sarnoff had dedicated the RCA building in television's first news broadcast. His words were highly insightful: "It is with a feeling of humbleness that I come to this moment of announcing the birth in this country of a new art so important in its implications that it is bound to affect all society."[16]

Yes, it was *bound* to, which, no doubt, was the underlying basis of Sarnoff's humility. Also reflecting upon the impact of television at the time was the fair's science director, Gerald Wendt, who wrote that "democracy, under the influence of television, is likely to pay inordinate attention to the performer and interpreter rather than to the planner and thinker."[17] This is perhaps the first insight that television would not be a conducive medium for serious discourse. Wendt apparently understood that even if television was utilized for the "public good," thinking could never be a performing art. But these kinds of debates would have to be postponed. *Life* magazine observed how the fair "opened with happy hopes of the World of Tomorrow and closed amid war and crisis."[18] Four months after television's first commercial broadcast, Hitler invaded Poland.

The 1950s have been coined "the Golden Age of Television," but since the days of *I Love Lucy* our tube time has roughly doubled. Americans had little difficulty in accommodating the television set into their homes early on. But it wasn't too long after television's debut that the set prodded its way into the living room, replacing the older focal points of the fireplace and piano. (The practice of burning Yule logs on the television screen during

IMAGE   PERFORMER/INTERPRETER
WORD   PLANNER/THINKER

Christmas Eve began as early as 1950,[19] which some may see as evidence that television shied away from intellectual material in its programming from the very beginning.) Current estimates confirm that the television screen is flickering about forty hours a week in the average household. A study conducted at the end of the century showed that 65 percent of children over the age of eight have a TV set in their bedroom, which stays on even during meals, and that 61 percent of parents have absolutely no rules about viewing habits.[20] Mini-van manufacturers now use the built-in TV as a selling point in their commercials. We are given images of the happy vacationing family, perhaps touring a national park out West. The parents up front are smiling because a pop-in video has pacified the children behind them. Just outside the window is a once-in-a-lifetime panorama, but the kids are not paying attention to it. *The Rugrats* are much more interesting.

DUMBING DOWN FOR THE TWENTY-FIRST CENTURY

There is a big difference between processing information on a printed page compared with processing data conveyed through a series of moving pictures. Images have a way of evoking an emotional response. Pictures have a way of pushing rational discourse—linear logic—into the background. The chief aim of television is to sell products and entertain audiences. Television seeks emotional gratification. As a visual medium, television programming is designed to be amusing. Substance gives way to sounds and sights. Hard facts are undermined by stirring feelings. Important issues are drowned out by dramatic images. Reason is replaced by emotion.

In a national literacy study issued by the U.S. Department of Education in 1993, almost half of the adults performed within the lowest levels of literacy proficiency.[21] It is quite remarkable that although school is compulsory for all children in this country up into the high school years, a large chunk of the population is functionally illiterate. Such a statistic means that almost a majority of us have difficulty "using printed and written information to function in society, to achieve one's goals, and to develop one's knowledge and potential."[22] The Barna Research Group reported that the first half of the 1990s saw a dramatic drop in reading for pleasure. In 1991, 75 percent of adults claimed to read for pleasure in the course of a week. In 1994, the figure fell to 53 percent.[23] Barna says more people are using the library for alternative media (compact discs, audiocassettes, videos) rather than checking out books, and that a marked decline in reading is one of the fastest-changing behaviors within the last two decades.[24]

Robert Zich, a special-project czar to the Library of Congress, predicted that the great national libraries and their buildings will go the way of the railroad stations, that we will soon be going to the library as we now go to a musty museum.[25] Thomas Jefferson correctly theorized that an educated populace would safeguard democracy against the onslaughts of tyranny; but had he foreseen the invention of television he might have remarked, as religious philosopher Søren Kierkegaard did a century and a half ago: "Suppose someone invented an instrument, a convenient little talking tube which, say, could be heard over the whole land. . . . I wonder if the police would not forbid it, fearing that the whole country would become mentally deranged if it were used."

The term *dumbing down* is somewhat of a cliché; nevertheless, it is an accurate expression to describe what is happening to our public conversations. We have come to expect to be spoon-fed our news in bite-sized nuggets. Newspapers, which must compete with television to keep off the media's extinction list, have shortened the length of their stories and added attention-getting graphics. The major newsweeklies have also gone through a metamorphosis. Since 1985, *Time*, *Newsweek*, and *U.S. News & World Report* have redesigned their layouts to explode out at you. Where once an article might have run a thousand words, the length of an average story is now less than 750.[26]

The fact that we are on the threshold of a bold new image-cognizant and asinine era is evidenced on today's political terrain as well. Being a professional wrestler has recently been shown to be an effective technique for capturing the attention of the electorate.

For all practical purposes, it worked for Jesse "The Body" Ventura, who promised that if elected governor of Minnesota, he would rappel from a helicopter onto the statehouse lawn. (I have personally always categorized a professional wrestler as an individual who shouts and spits red-faced threats into a television camera after a round of grunting and gyrating playacting.) So, why did the good people of Minnesota elect Jesse Ventura as their governor? Did they temporarily lose their minds? Left-leaning cartoonist Garry Trudeau entreated the question of how a "land of small farmers, Norwegians, Lutherans, taciturn, slow-moving, buttoned-up, sensible types" could elect such a guy. In one *Doonesbury* strip Ventura says, "Everyone's bored. I'm like free cable."

Traditionally, distinguished persons of achievement constituted the candidate pool for political office. Now we must add celebrities. Daniel Boorstin says the hero, who once distinguished himself with noteworthy achievements, has now been replaced by the celebrity, distinguished solely by his image.[27] Something changed in American political life ever since the Nixon-Kennedy televised debates. Some say Nixon lost the presidential election to Kennedy because he was not telegenic enough. Quite possibly that is why Abraham Lincoln could not be elected President if he were running for office today.

Not only is our political landscape in flux, but Christianity also seems to be experiencing a type of remodeling, especially inside its sanctuaries. Generation Xers are hungering for a new style of worship that bares a closer resemblance to MTV than to their parents' old-time religion. In an opening address at the 1999 Southern Baptist Convention, Paige Patterson urged his audience to be careful of "twelve-minute sermonettes generated by the 'felt needs' of an assembled cast of postmodern listeners augmented by drama and multiple repetitions of touchy-touchy, feely-feely music."[28] The president of the nation's largest Protestant denomination was alluding to a new style of worship where congregants "come as they are," whether it be in jeans, shorts, or T-shirts. (One church in Virginia Beach had to alter this policy, when soon

after a waterfront sign was erected, visitors started showing up in
their bathing suits.) Drama, dance, video clips, rock and roll, TV
talk show formats, and eating in the services are just some of the
elements of the growing "worship renewal movement," where
people attend church much in the same manner as they watch
Wheel of Fortune. A critical examination would indicate that the
movement is a by-product of a culture that has been weaned on
television.

Omens like these made George Barna conclude that
Americans today are intellectually and spiritually frivolous:

> In this age, we find that Americans have been seduced by breadth
> rather than depth, by quantity rather than quality, by style rather
> than substance. It is the rare person who reads publications that
> require reflection; instead, the likes of *People, Sports Illustrated*
> and *TV Guide* dominate the newsstands. Harlequin novels and
> pop psychology reign at the bookstore. Conversations about the
> weather and the Super Bowl are more common and more intense
> than those about values and meaning in life. The political
> "wanna-bes" who prevail are most often those who offer super-
> ficial solutions to complex social problems, those who are the
> most photogenic or silver tongued, and those whose background
> is innocuous enough that the media cannot dredge up a scandal
> or otherwise assassinate their character.[29]

Culture critic Neil Postman begins his book *Amusing
Ourselves to Death* by contrasting two fictional prophecies—
Aldous Huxley's *Brave New World* and George Orwell's *1984*.
Of course, Orwell feared that we would be overcome by a
tyranny that would take away our freedoms—Big Brother look-
ing over our shoulder. Huxley feared that we would be ruined
by what we came to love. In *1984* books are banned. In *Brave
New World* no one wants to read a book. In one novel, Big
Brother suffocates civilization with a forceful hand. In the other
novel, civilization comes to adore its technologies so much that
it loses the capacity to think, preferring rather to be entertained.
Postman says that when we become "distracted by trivia, when

BREADTH   QUANTITY   STYLE   IMAGE
DEPTH   QUALITY   SUBSTANCE   WORD

cultural life is redefined as a perpetual round of entertainments, when serious public conversation becomes a form of baby-talk, when, in short, a people become an audience and their public business a vaudeville act, then a nation finds itself at risk; culture-death is a clear possibility."[30]

Here we are now, hitchhiking on the information highway. The computer has ushered us into the information age. In a decade or so television and the computer will probably merge into one technology. It is highly likely that "text" will be de-emphasized in whatever form electronic media take in the future. This is altogether frightening. For if it was a *logos*-centered culture that helped to produce our Protestant heritage, as well as American democracy itself, what will be the birth child of the continuing devaluation of the written word?

The devaluation of the word and its hostile supplanting by the image is a direct assault upon "the religion of the Book." In accordance to this thought, we are all in danger of becoming pagans. Not *just* pagans, but mindless and defenseless pagans who would prefer to have someone tell us how to think and behave. The possibility of tyranny still exists for us today because we have lost the biblical and mental defenses to arm ourselves against demagoguery. Our children are not being equipped to spot counterfeit leaders who would lead us astray with an overabundance of pathos. Kenneth Burke told us that one reason we should study Hitler is to "discover what kind of medicine this mad-man has concocted, that we may know, with greater accuracy, exactly what to guard against, if we are to forestall the concocting of similar medicine in America."[31] I want to show in the following pages how *Tomorrowland has the potential to become a total triumph for idolatry.*

Paganism never really died in modern western culture; it was only restrained. American Protestantism effectively suppressed many pagan forms up until the twentieth century; but the advent of image-based media has brought forth a revitalization of the pagan gods in popular culture. Sex, violence, and celebrity, which are so pervasive in the media, conform to a pagan ideal. Ignoring

ENTERTAINED

THINK

history's warnings of technology's tendency to change us, we have blindly boarded a glitzy train with a one-way ticket to Digit City. Like Pinocchio, we are being hoodwinked into making a journey to Pleasure Island, and we could, quite possibly, share the same fate as those laughing donkeys.

Realizing I am not the first to suggest that we are entering a high-tech version of the Dark Ages,[32] I have labored to provide a fresh perspective on an important topic. The book is designed to be historical as well as critical. The Judeo-Christian heritage, which characteristically has been *word*-dependent, is contrasted with paganism, which typically has been *image*-dependent. I will show how the Dark Ages in Europe illustrate what can happen when a culture lapses from the written word. I will then describe how the invention of the printing press launched three successive word-based movements: the Protestant Reformation, Puritanism, and the beginnings of the American experiment. However, the effects of these movements, embodied in Victorianism, were frustrated in the twentieth century with the entertainment values of the new electronic media. This is not to minimize the influence of individuals like Darwin, Freud, and Dewey. These men provided the philosophical excuse to drop moral restraints. I will go on to argue that the *image* has supplanted the *word*, inciting pagan forms to resurface. I suggest that the emergence of postmodernism is actually a by-product of two tandem occurrences—the rapid rise of the image and the denunciation of objectivity exemplified in the death throes of modernism. The traditional conventions of worship are being obliterated as we speak, and our church services are being shriveled to shallow spectacles. A church cut from its word-based heritage and a nation stripped of word-based modes of learning do not have the rhetorical or mental resources to guard against despotism. *The Vanishing Word* advances the proposition that our image-saturated culture is at risk of being preyed upon by a tyrant in waiting. Finally, several remedies will be suggested for our idolatrous predicament.

The Word
versus
The Image

֍

CHAPTER TWO

Tables of Stone

And he gave unto Moses, when he had made an end of communing with him upon mount Sinai, two tables of testimony, tables of stone, written with the finger of God.

—Exodus 31:18

THERE EXISTS A LONG-STANDING AND IRRECONCILABLE TENSION BETWEEN THE WORD AND THE IMAGE.

ꙅ

After seeing Pharaoh and his chariots swallowed by the Red Sea, you would have thought the message was clear: Jehovah is not a God to mock. The Israelites not only watched the Egyptian army drown in a crushing torrent of water, but they witnessed, firsthand, the systematic dilapidation of one of the mightiest empires on earth. The ten plagues were more than a means to get the people out of the land—all that affliction was an affront against Egypt's gods and the Nile's fertility. Once out of Egypt, it took three short months for the massive Israelite throng to reach Sinai. A living column of fire had conducted them through the desert to a place where God would say, "Will you go into a covenant with Me? Will you be My people?" The children of Israel had heard the thunder. They had smelled the smoke. They had felt the ground shake beneath their feet. But when Moses came down off the steamy mountain, there, in the middle of the camp, was a golden calf.

Idolatry is a seductive thing. To the ancient pagan mind, says Camille Paglia, nature and God were melded together. "In the beginning was nature."[1] Pagan rituals embroiled nature's erotic and violent rhythms. The gods were reflections of the physical world—sun, moon, stars, earth, fire, water, wind, beast, tree, *and* man. Paganism sometimes was an earth-worshiping cult. The gods of Greece, however, were set on Mount Olympus, touching the sky, looking down on man. But earth-cult and sky-cult were both image-centered religions. Separation of church and state was an entirely foreign concept in ancient civilizations. Paglia is helpful here. Although the controversial professor has been called everything from an anti-feminist to a neo-conservative, she is actually an outspoken and unblushing proponent of pop culture. In her book *Sexual Personae*, she says idolatry is more than the adoration of images; it is best understood as a "fascism of the eye"—"pictorialism plus the will-to-power. It is ritualism, grandiosity, colossalism, sensationalism."[2]

Paglia's definition is not too far removed from the biblical concept of *Babylon*. Geographically, Babylon was the site of the tower of Babel (Genesis 11:1-9) and is believed by some theologians to be the birthplace of polytheism.[3] Henry Morris defines Babylon as "the rebellious system of religious adultery that originated at ancient Babel and has since permeated every nation."[4] It has been suggested that Nimrod (meaning "to rebel") was one of the first kings to establish an empire in the area of Sumeria a short time after the biblical flood. The Bible says the people of Babel built a tower into the heavens to make a name for themselves. Evidently they also developed a religious system consisting of a host of gods corresponding to the planets and stars. God was displeased and confounded their speech. The incident is alluded to in the annals of the later Babylonians. The archaeologist George Smith discovered an inscription in Babylon that reads: "The building of the illustrious tower offended the gods. In a night they threw down what they had built. They scattered them abroad, and made strange their speech."[5] When the people of Babel were dispersed, they took their religion with them. The names of the gods changed, but many of the myths stayed intact. This is consistent with the various overlaps found in the mythologies among the ancient nations. But Babel was the starting point and became the chief refiner of pagan idolatry.

> [The] Babylonians made the pagan religions fashionable. They took the idea of pantheism (that the gods were present in every act or expression of nature and physical matter) and elevated it to an art form. They incorporated art, drama, and music into religion until the pagan ideas were attractively represented as the highest expressions of their culture. Babylon also took the ancient idea of the city-state and expanded it into a system of bureaucracies that established control over the population.[6]

The explanation given here implies that pagan idolatry is a religious system that seeks to steal the glory of an invisible God and give it to the state. Politics and devotion to the gods were all tied together. This is why the Bible calls Babylon "the great whore that sitteth upon many waters: with whom the kings of the earth have committed fornication" (Revelation 17:1-2). Spiritually, Babylon is the relentless competitor of revealed religion and strives to change the truth of God into a lie by idolizing the creature over the Creator (Romans 1:25). The term *mystery Babylon* is allegorical for the political-religious systems of ancient Egypt, Canaan, Assyria, Greece, and Rome—all of which bowed to the image.

The purpose of this chapter is to contrast the locus of pagan spirituality with that of Judaism and Christianity. As Gene Veith says, one is centered upon the *image*, concrete and immediate. The other is centered upon the *word*, abstract and transcendent.[7] One is lurid, and the other is restrained. One champions the personality of the ruler; the other focuses on the holiness of God. One binds the populace with visual arts; the other is dependent on popular literacy. Whenever the two meet, there is bound to be tension, for the *image* always humiliates the *word*,[8] always tries to exalt itself above the other, must have the attention. The Hebrews discovered this when they rubbed shoulders with the Egyptians.

WORD ABSTRACT TRANSCENDENT
IMAGE CONCRETE IMMEDIATE (IMMANENT)

IMAGES IN EGYPT

Sometime within their 430-year stay, the Hebrews were lured into worshiping with their pagan neighbors. They never got over it. The difficulty of the wilderness wanderings was not getting Israel out of Egypt, but Egypt out of Israel. When the people thought Moses was taking too long up on the Mount, they begged Aaron for a quick fix: "Make us some gods!" Aaron's response was just as astonishing. He not only obliged them but directed the whole project, saying, "Okay, here's what we need to do. Give me your jewelry."

It was not easy to forget about Egypt. The empire was an emerald snake in a golden desert, a seven-hundred-mile stretch of river extending from the heart of Africa to the Mediterranean Sea. Each year the Nile would fatten itself, roll over, and bestow gifts to its populated banks. A thousand years before Moses, the Egyptians learned to pattern their lives by the river's flood cycles. It was this pulsation that gave life to Egyptian culture and the visual arts we have come to know them by—the colossal pharaoh-headed lion transfixed in the sand, man-made mountains cutting blue sky, the mascaraed eye. Paglia says, "Egypt invented the magic of *image*."[9] They created an absolutist aesthetic that valued the "incised edge." Egyptian art makes the eye "glide" along crisp, clean, sunlit lines.[10] Daniel Boorstin remarks in his book *The Creators* that the Egyptians left few words for us to sift through, but "their visual images survived with the impassive features of their eternal god and the repetitive contours of their daily lives. . . . We think of the ancient Egyptians as pyramid builders from the unique mark they left on the desert landscape. We should think of them too as image makers, for no other people in Western culture has given so crucial a role to its images, and none has nourished so continuous and homogeneous a style."[11]

The Egyptians made themselves effigies for every creature they came in contact with around the Nile. Their pantheon was a literal zoo of cats and crocodiles, bulls and baboons, hawks and frogs. A visitor walking through one of their temples might have found any of these animals roaming freely like curators in a critter museum. (While most of us have been tempted at one time or another to throw a cat across a room with all our might, legend has it that a visiting foreigner actually acted upon this thought, killing the cat. The Egyptians promptly rose up and slew the poor fellow to teach the lesson that the cat is sacred.) The gods of Egypt appeared in human forms as well. But even when humanized, they retained animal parts—a human body with an animal head or vice versa. Ra was the powerful sun god who stood over Isis, Mother of Earth, fertilizing her with his warm rays. Sometimes the sun god was visualized as a divine calf who would sail daily across the sky in a celestial boat. At other times the sun god was pictured as a flying falcon, panning the land below. The god Osiris symbolized the afterlife and was celebrated with a display of sexual fanfare. He was often symbolized as a goat or a bull, sacred to the Egyptians for representing sexual power. Historian Will Durant says that on special days Egyptian women paraded around in religious processions, carrying phallic images, and mechanically operating them with strings. In other words, eroticism was a running theme in Egyptian art and worship.[12]

Like their public-works pyramids, the social order of Egypt was hierarchical. At the apex stood the pharaoh, wielding sufficient power to harness a hundred thousand slaves into lugging two- and ten-ton blocks of stone six hundred miles across the desert and then raising them up on each other to a height of half-a-thousand feet. This might seem like a formidable task for one person to oversee, but one has to understand that the pharaoh was more than an energetic despot. He was, in fact, seen as a god. At the zenith of Egyptian history, the various provinces along the Nile were unified under one authority and one religion. Descending from the top of the organizational chart was an impressive bureaucracy of regional governors and personal staff. Durant says it took an entourage of twenty just to take care of the pharaoh's toilet. Barbers shaved and cut his hair, hairdressers adjusted his royal cowl, manicurists polished his nails, and perfumers deodorized his body, blackened his eyelids, and reddened his cheeks and lips with rouge.[13]

Not only did Egypt invent the magic of image, observes Paglia, but in doing so they also invented the idea of *vogue*. The meshing of the image with the god-person created the first celebrity cult. "Egypt invented glamour, beauty as power and power as beauty. Egyptian aristocrats were the first Beautiful People. Hierarchy and eroticism fused in Egypt, making a pagan unity the west has never thrown off."[14]

In the twentieth century stars are born on a forty-foot movie screen, but in ancient Egypt pharaoh-gods were enshrined in mammoth images. One particular pharaoh, Ramses II, loved gigantic images. He loved them even more if they were images of himself. So he scattered his personal likeness all over Egypt, placing four sixty-seven-foot-tall statues outside the great temple at Abu Simbel. The grand *image* became to the Egyptians what the *word* would eventually become to the Hebrews. Boorstin tells us that when in Egypt, one had to think *big*:

> What they lacked in naturalism they made up in gigantism. No other people was so obsessed by colossi, or so successful with the colossal image. Shape and form and color were prescribed in an almost alphabetic way. And if they could not make it better, they could make it bigger. Since in their tomb and temple relief the larger figures showed the more powerful people, the largest statues would be the most potent. Like messages in large type, Egyptian colossi were headline-hieroglyphs, and because they were abstractions, Egyptian statues had a boundless capacity for enlargement. A gigantic statue in naturalistic style seems bizarre or ridiculous, but an enlarged Pharaoh in conventional style is all the more impressive. Colossi were hieroglyphs of power.[15]

WRITING: GOD'S CHIEF CHOICE OF COMMUNICATION

It was this seductive, highly visual, state-supported polytheism that the Hebrews left behind. In turn, Jehovah God gave the Hebrews a new culture, a new way of life. He wanted them to be a particular people, distinctive in every way from the surrounding cultures. The Decalogue, and all of its supporting articles, in effect formed a covenant instructing the Israelites how to live with each other. More importantly, it was a document revealing the correct way to perceive an invisible God who was not a part of nature, but above it. The first three commandments, also called the establishing commandments, are concerned with how God would be signified to His people. First, God told Moses that He *alone* would be worshiped because He was the only true and living God: "Thou shalt have no other gods before me" (Exodus 20:3). The second commandment forbade idolatry: "Thou shalt not make unto thee any grave image, or any likeness, or of any thing that is in heaven above, or that is in the earth beneath, or that is in the water under the earth: Thou shalt not bow down thyself to them, nor serve them" (Exodus 20:4-5a). The third commandment prohibited any negligent disregard of Jehovah's name: "Thou shalt not take the name of the LORD in vain" (Exodus 20:7a). It should be noted that two of the three establishing commandments deal directly with how God wanted Himself to be symbolized. God was saying to the Hebrews, "Do not signify Me with a stone likeness; and when you do signify Me, be very careful about it."

When God took the initiative to reach down to mankind, it was not a mistake that He purposefully chose the medium of writing to make Himself known. The Ten Commandments, and the entire Bible for that matter, did not come to us through an oral tradition or through pictures. To the contrary, the message delivered to Moses was *written* with the finger of God. The very notion of *divine revelation*, the communication of truth that cannot otherwise be known, demands a method of documentation and preservation that goes beyond orality, pictorial representation, dance, or smoke signals. If one believes that revelation is "God-breathed" (cf. 2 Timothy 3:16), that each *word* of Scripture originates from the mind of God, then writing is the obvious choice, for no other medium possesses the objectivity and permanency needed to tell the old, old story.

I do not mean to imply that God is opposed to all forms of visual imagery. Indeed, writing itself is dependent on symbols to represent

OBJECTIVE   PERMANENT   TRANSCENDENT
SUBJECTIVE   TEMPORARY   IMMANENT

sounds. Furthermore, there are many examples in the Bible where God utilizes imagery to communicate propositional truths. Prophetic visions, divine dreams, even pantomime (e.g., Ezekiel lying on his side for days on end to symbolize God's judgment against Israel) are some of the more dramatic forms of communication found in Scripture. The worship associated with the Tabernacle and the Temple also employed visual imagery. But the brazen altar, the laver, the table of shewbread, the altar of incense, the golden candlestick, the elaborate multicolored curtains, and the ark of the covenant were in reality only "shadows of heavenly things" (Hebrews 8:5) and "figures of the true" (Hebrews 9:24). The structure, furniture, and decorations of the Tabernacle and Temple were different from the images associated with paganism. Old Testament worship pointed the Israelite to the God of redemption through physical sacrifice. The objects of the sanctuary symbolized the person and future work of Christ to which the New Testament would later give clear testimony. Again, they were propositional in nature, not objects of worship in and of themselves.

Writing is the ideal medium to conceptualize an invisible God, says Neil Postman, because "unlike pictures or the oral tradition, the written word is a symbol system of a symbol, twice removed from reality and perfect for describing a God who is also far removed from reality: a nonphysical, abstract divinity."[16] God is described as an abstract divinity because of the intangible nature of His being. God is an invisible, all-knowing, self-existing, eternal spirit. He is perfectly holy, is everywhere at once, does what He wills, controls every atom in the universe, and yet is deeply concerned with His creation, with which He has a long history of involvement, including identifying sin, judgment of sin, and redemption from it. Blocks and paint are just insufficient to convey these kinds of truths. Only writing suffices.

Walter Ong shows in *Orality and Literacy* how writing can transform human consciousness on several different levels. The act of writing detaches thought from its author and allows it to stand alone to be judged on its own merits. The written word lives beyond the life of its creator and may be resurrected time and time again. Unlike oral speech, what has been inscribed cannot argue back—it does not engage in dialogue. It may be judged as true or false, but it will always say the same thing. Oral speech occurs naturally to humans, but writing is a technology utilized by knowing its rules. This artificialness should not be considered a burden, argues Ong, but a blessing because its many fruits can uplift the human spirit.[17] Of course, oral speech carries a host of read-between-the-lines nonverbal cues (facial expressions, gestures, tone) to accompany its delivery, but most primitive oral cultures are limited to a vocabulary of a few thousand words. Literate societies enjoy at least a million and a half words with rich semantic histories to boot. The disciplines of history, science, and literature are all dependent on the technology of writing. Writing things down allows one to investigate the past, create great systems of classification for living things, and feel a sense of irony from a literary work. Writing, in effect, made way for the schoolhouse, the practice of philosophy, and the declaration of religious doctrine.

Anthropologists have a frequently quoted maxim pertaining to writing: "As language distinguishes man from animal, so writing distinguishes civilized man from the barbarian."[18] Wherever writing appears in ancient civilization, asserts I. J. Gelb in *A Study of Writing*, high forms of culture also appear—developed structures of government, commerce, transportation systems, full agriculture, and the domestication of animals. This is not to say that writing necessarily caused these developments; rather, *advanced civilizations cannot exist without writing*.[19] Ancient cultures often associated writing with special powers. For example, the Egyptians believed that Toth, the god of magic, invented writing. Primitives saw writing as a form of divination, as expressed in a story concerning a messenger who was afraid to carry a letter on a long voyage, thinking it would undoubtedly speak to him. He could not rest until he had silenced the mysterious message; so he ran his lance through it.[20] Jack Goody and Ian Watt note that the true magic of writing is the awareness it brings to a people by enabling them to compare the past with the present, plus the power it gives to a culture to detect its inconsistencies.[21] Thus the

convention of "freezing speech," says Postman, gives birth to "the
grammarian, the logician, the rhetorician, the historian, the scientist—all those who must hold language before them so that they
can see what it means, where it errs, and where it is leading."[22]

There are a few similarities, as well as some important differences, in the role that writing played in Egyptian and Hebrew history. The Hebrews possessed a more developed, more manageable
alphabet that they borrowed from the Canaanites. The earliest
Egyptian writings used as many as two thousand concrete pic-
tographs, says Harold Innis; however, this number diminished
over time to about six hundred syllabic signs.[23] In contrast, the
alphabet used by the Hebrews, say C. H. Kraeling and R. F.
Adams, "could [have been] learned in a day or two by bright students and in a week or two by the dullest."[24] Both societies
employed the medium of stone at one time or another in their
record keeping (e.g., Hebrews began with stone tablets off Sinai).
For the Egyptians, stone-engraved hieroglyphics were eventually
replaced with papyrus sheets. The shift from stone to papyrus
enabled the Egyptians to more efficiently run their elaborate
bureaucracy of priests, scribes, and other civil servants. As Innis
explains, "After 2000 B.C. the central administration employed
an army of scribes, and literacy was valued as a stepping stone to
prosperity and social rank. Scribes became a restricted class and
writing a privileged profession."[25]

In other words, the Egyptians had writing, but the use of it was
limited to an elite class and isolated from the majority. Writing was
stuck at the top of the pyramid. The common Egyptian moved
among images. The fact that the complex form of writing in Egypt
remained a skill of a full-time, government-employed, "privileged
profession" differentiates them from the Hebrews, who would
come to develop a universal educational system. From the very
beginning the Hebrews were a "people of the Book." As Postman
notes, "The God of the Jews was to exist in the Word and through
the Word, an unprecedented conception requiring the highest
order of abstract thinking. Iconography thus became blasphemy so
that a new kind of God could enter a culture."[26]

SOCIAL AND CRAFT LITERACY

As with the case of the Egyptians, a culture may possess literate individuals in their midst, even literate individuals who perform important roles, but this does not mean that the entire population can read or write. In Eric Havelock's *Origin of Western Literacy*, a distinction is made between societies in which most of the people can read and societies in which reading is restricted to a privileged class. Havelock refers to the first condition as "social literacy" and the second as "craft literacy."[27] Although Havelock would have placed early Israel in the category of only possessing craft literacy due to their reliance upon a priesthood, one could make a compelling argument that the Hebrews were actually the *first* people to achieve a high level of social literacy. Carroll Atkinson and Eugene Maleska suggest that "[o]f all the ancient peoples in the western world the Jews were the most literate—they were the only people in antiquity to attempt to teach everyone to read."[28] While it *cannot* be said that social literacy *always* characterized the children of Israel, it *can* be said that once the Hebrews gained freedom from Egypt, they collectively endeavored to make the Scriptures central to their culture by memorizing them, writing them, and reading them.

A concise account of Jewish educational history appears in William Barclay's *Educational Ideals in the Ancient World*. Barclay observes that there were two essential facts in regard to the Jewish idea of education. First, Jewish education was entirely a religious one; and second, the center of Jewish education was in the home.[29] Fathers took the primary responsibility in the training of the children. The Talmud says the threefold duty of the father is "to instruct his son in the Law, to bring him into wedlock, and to teach him a handicraft."[30] The classic passage describing the spiritual vigor to which the Hebrews were to train their children is found in Deuteronomy 6:4-9:

> *Hear, O Israel: The* LORD *our God is one* LORD: *And thou shalt love the* LORD *thy God with all thine heart, and with all thy soul, and with all thy might. And these words, which I com-*

mand thee this day, shall be in thine heart: And thou shalt teach
them diligently unto thy children, and shalt talk of them when
thou sittest in thine house, and when thou walkest by the way,
and when thou liest down, and when thou risest up. And thou
shalt bind them for a sign upon thine hand, and they shall be as
frontlets between thine eyes. And thou shalt write *them upon the*
posts of thy house, and on thy gates. (emphasis mine)

Add to this the charge that not *one* word was to be added or
taken away from God's Law (Deuteronomy 4:2) and one begins
to wonder to what degree the early Hebrews were able to read
and write. It seems that if the Law was to be memorized,
explained, expounded, rehearsed, and placed on doorposts, fence
posts, and foreheads, then it is not unreasonable to suggest that
reading and writing were skills that the early Hebrews *could* have
possessed, or at least *should* have possessed if they were to be
faithful in all these endeavors.

Not only do the Scriptures themselves logically support the
notion of universal reading and writing, but Alan Millard
reports that archaeological evidence indicates that social literacy
among the Hebrews was achieved as early as the period of the
Judges.[31] As far as ancient civilizations are concerned, Millard
claims that only classical Greece rivals the degree of social literacy possessed by the Hebrews.[32] Epigraphic discoveries within
the past several decades, says Millard, point to the conclusion
that "writing was theoretically within the competence of any
ancient Israelite, not the prerogative of an elite professional class
alone . . . [and] was, in fact, quite widely practiced."[33] Most
ancient specimens of Hebrew inscriptions now available were
used for mundane and ephemeral purposes, showing that writing was not just limited to scribal practices.[34] There is an
account in the book of Judges of a "young man" who is evidently not a scribe, but who nevertheless possesses the ability to
write (8:14; "wrote down," NKJV). The notion that common
boys in Israel could actually be functionally literate, says
William Dever, is verified by discoveries such as that of a
"schoolboy's practice text" containing a list of alphabetic letters

on a four-line ostracon.[35] Millard argues that the archaeological evidence leaves no question that writing was widely used in ancient Israel:

> Certainly the ability to write was not limited to a small scribal clan. The variety of ancient Hebrew inscriptions—from monumental texts on buildings, tombs and public works, to letters, seals, lists and names scratched on pots—surely suggests the widespread use of writing, especially when one considers that the vast majority of documents were written on papyrus that has not survived in Israel's damp climate. But especially important to our argument are the casual or occasional texts, names on vessels and notes on potsherds. Here are visible the hands of schoolboys and workmen as well as of the trained scribes.[36]

ISRAEL'S STRUGGLE WITH IDOLATRY

There exists a long-standing and irreconcilable tension between the word and the image. One of the major themes running through the Old Testament is Israel's long struggle with idolatry. God forbade the Hebrews to "make marriages" with their surrounding neighbors because they would eventually seduce them to "serve other gods" (Deuteronomy 7:3-4). If God had left it at that, the Israelites might have appeared only as snobs to the adjacent cities; but He commanded the Israelites to go even further and "destroy their altars, and break down their images, and cut down their groves, and burn their graven images with fire" (Deuteronomy 7:5). And the admonitions did not stop there. The laws concerning warfare prescribed the Hebrews to annihilate the Canaanites. Although the Israelites could take unto themselves any widowed women and their children if they were "very far off" (Deuteronomy 20:14-15), no one in the cities in the Promised Land was to be spared:

> *But of the cities of these people, which the* LORD *thy God doth give thee for an inheritance, thou shalt save alive nothing that breatheth: But thou shalt utterly destroy them; namely, the Hittites, and the Amorites, the Canaanites, and the Perizzites,*

the Hivites, and the Jebusites; as the LORD *thy God hath com-*
manded thee.

DEUTERONOMY 20:16-17

Skeptics have often criticized the "slaughter of the heathen nations" as being below the otherwise ethical norms of the Old Testament or in conflict with the spirit of the New Testament.[37] However, theologians John Davis and John Whitcomb say it should be remembered that the Hebrews were under a *divine command* to do this and thus were used as instruments of divine punishment.[38] Since God knew how seductive idolatry could be, He commissioned Israel to destroy all the influence of foreign cults, calling the graven image a "cursed thing" that His children were to "detest" and "utterly abhor" (Deuteronomy 7:26).

Baal and Ashtoreth were the chief Canaanite deities, and both were gods of fertility. Baal rode upon storm clouds and showered the land with rain. Ashtoreth was worshiped not only as a fertility mother-goddess, but also as a goddess of love and war. Leon Wood describes the mythology behind these deities as violent and sensual.[39] Archeologists have unearthed nude images of Ashtoreth holding lotus blossoms, a symbol of fertility. The temple worship was as violent and sensual as the myth behind it, as evidenced by the Canaanites' sacrifice of their children, and by the open practice of male and female prostitution between the temple columns. The ritual celebrated the reproductive process and the energies of nature in hopes that the earth would be incited to yield her fruit. The entire episode was a romp in debauchery where drums pounded, women wailed for Ashtoreth, priests danced and slashed themselves with knives, and spectators, overcome with emotion, emasculated themselves in pledge of lifelong devotion to the goddess.[40]

One should not think the ancient Hebrews were immune to these types of displays; indeed, if their religious life were to be plotted from exodus to exile on graph paper, it would resemble a roller coaster track with majestic spiritual crests and low idolatrous valleys. The Israelites would have eventually assimilated

into the Canaanite culture or, more likely, would have been exterminated by their enemies if God had not raised up judges and
kings to protect them and set them back on the right path. Unlike
the pagan cultures around them, Israel's kings were kept accountable by bony-fingered prophets who denounced idolatry in the
name of Jehovah. The notion that the king was subject to a higher
moral code than himself was a hallmark development for western society. Israel's compromises with paganism after the reign of
Solomon eventually led to the destruction of the Northern
Kingdom by the Assyrians and the captivity of the Southern
Kingdom by the Babylonians.

Babylon, built with the spoils of war and public taxes, was a
feast to the eye and a spiritual test for the Hebrews. The historian
Herodotus described the city as situated near a plain, circumscribed
by a fifty-six-mile wall, enclosing an area of two hundred square
miles. Inside the thick walls, and moving toward the hub, a captive
Hebrew would have encountered brilliant brick buildings, faced
with blue, yellow, and white enameled tiles. Wide avenues and busy
canals cut a grid across the terrain. Jutting up into the sky rose the
famous *ziggurat*, now under renovation. The lofty structure was
topped with a slab of gold, where each night some woman slept to
await the pleasure of a god. To the south stood the Temple of
Marduk, the perpetually honored national deity that took the form
of a serpent-dragon. The temples were kept busy. Herodotus wrote
that every "native woman is obliged, once in her life, to sit in the
temple of Venus, and have intercourse with some stranger . . . [and]
some are continually coming in, and others are going out" to
absolve themselves from the obligation of the love goddess.[41]
Further south were the renowned Hanging Gardens. The Greeks
would come to include this extraordinary feat of horticulture as one
of the Seven Wonders of the World. The Gardens were admired for
the illusion they cast—one of spilling over from green terraces some
seventy-five feet in the air. Down below, enormous stone lions
guarded the entrance to the central palace, where inside a prideful
king named Nebuchadnezzar turned to his administrators and
declared, "Is not this great Babylon, that I have built for the house

of the kingdom by the might of my power, and for the honour of my majesty?" (Daniel 4:30).

This was the man who raised a ninety-foot effigy of himself on the desert plains outside the city of Babylon. The Bible records that when he had assembled his vast bureaucracy around the image, a royal orchestra cued everyone into prostration. As an added incentive to the king's self-inauguration into godhood, a roaring vat of fire stood to the side for those who entertained second thoughts. All went well until, from the sea of fallen bodies, in the distance three lone Hebrews were found standing—erect, calm, staring straight ahead. Shadrach, Meshach, and Abednego would not bow. The Babylonian captivity was God's intended punishment, but it also was a type of refining fire. For the Hebrews would never again be idolatrous. The seventy-year exile also marked the beginning of the synagogue system, where the Old Testament canon, consisting of the law and the historical, poetical, and prophetical books, would be assembled and studied.

THE ROLE OF THE SYNAGOGUE

The synagogue was much more than a house of worship, William Barclay says; it was the center of public Jewish education where the Scriptures were taught and interpreted by the scribe-sage.[42] Although Josephus claimed that the origin of the synagogue went back to Moses, the synagogue school gained its greatest popularity during the Exile and the subsequent return of the Jews to Jerusalem. Upon returning to Palestine, the Jews were determined to avoid the pitfalls associated with the causes of the captivity. A universal and national education, then, was a way to safeguard the onslaughts of paganism. Jewish education began at an early age and was placed in the life of a child before all other labors. Josephus wrote, "Our ground is good, and we work it to the utmost, but our chief ambition is for the education of our children."[43] In the opening song, "Tradition," from the musical *Fiddler on the Roof*, Tevye sings, "At three I started Hebrew school. At ten I learned a trade." One of the first objectives of the synagogue school was to achieve literacy so the Scriptures and its auxiliaries could immediately be written, memorized, and studied. An addendum to the fifth book of *Sayings of the Jewish Fathers* incorporates education as foundational for the rest of life:

> At five years old, Scripture; at ten years, Mishnah; at thirteen, the Commandments; at fifteen, Talmud; at eighteen, marriage; at twenty, the pursuits of business; at thirty, strength; at forty, discernment; at fifty, counsel; at sixty, age; at seventy, gray old age; at eighty, power; at ninety, decrepitude; at a hundred, as though he were dead, and gone, and had ceased from the world.[44]

The school was the equivalent of Mount Sinai, says Schechter in his *Studies in Judaism*, and the first day of school was undertaken with a special ceremony. The boy was wakened before dawn, bathed, and dressed in a gown with "fringes." The father escorted the boy to the school where he was put at a reading-desk. The passage from the Law of Moses was spread out before him and read aloud: "And God spake all these words, saying, I am the LORD thy God, which have brought thee out of the land of Egypt, out of the house of bondage. Thou shalt have no other gods before me . . ." (Exodus 20:2-3). The child was shown a slate of the Hebrew alphabet in various combinations. More Scripture was read, which the new student repeated before the teacher. Honey was put on the slate, and the child ate it off. Then the child was given sweet cakes to eat, with passages from the Law written on them.[45] This ritual calls to mind the prophet Ezekiel's words after God commanded him to eat the roll: "And it was in my mouth as honey for sweetness" (Ezekiel 3:3). Barclay says, "It can easily be seen that this was a ceremony which would remain printed on the boy's mind for ever. Such then was the place which the school held in the Jewish ideal."[46]

G. H. Box says the synagogue system created an environment where the "sacred writings became a spelling-book, the community a school, religion an affair of teaching and learning. . . . Piety and education became inseparable; whoever could not read was no true Jew."[47] The synagogue served as a house of worship on the Sabbath and as a school during the rest of the week. Sometimes "houses of instruction" were separate from the actual synagogue building. It is said that by the time of Jesus, 480 synagogues existed in Jerusalem; and each of them had a school.[48] The brightest students were allowed to further their studies, perhaps becoming scribes or honored rabbis. On the Sabbath the Scriptures were read and then expounded to the flock. It was not unusual for adult males to be called upon to read the Scriptures and then give a brief lesson. This is where we find Jesus beginning His ministry as He reads from the book of Isaiah (see Luke 4:16-32). The Christian church service, with its pastoral sermon, sprang from the customs of synagogue worship. It was the apostle Paul's pattern to always begin his declaration of the Gospel in a local synagogue. Even when dispersed all over the face of the earth, Jewish communities always held education as an indispensable component of their lives. The emphasis the Jews placed upon the *Word* and on *words* would earn them a special place in the western tradition. Their literature, philosophy, and law are a part of our rich heritage.

GRECO-ROMAN CULTURE

It would be difficult to make the claim that the ancient Greeks surpassed the Hebrews in achieving social literacy since 80 percent of the Athenian population were nonparticipants in public affairs. Greek education was elitist. Our English words for *school* and *scholar* are derived from the Greek term *scholazo*, which means "to have leisure," or specifically, "leisure to learn." Therefore, in ancient Greece only the wealthy or leisure classes received the benefits of education. The Hebrews would have equated leisure with idleness, because in their minds, says Marvin Wilson, the purpose of learning was not to *comprehend* but to *revere* and *obey*.[49] The Jews did not "seek" the truth as did the Greeks, but embraced the truth contained in the Scriptures. Nevertheless, we owe our modern concept of school to the Greeks, who not only emphasized reading and writing but also arithmetic, music, physical training, and civic responsibility. The Greeks also gave us the idea of how to organize our schools, dividing the curriculum into elementary, secondary, and higher education.

Goody and Watt say that the procurement of the Greek alphabet around 700 B.C. marked the beginning of the Hellenic Age and that alphabetic reading and writing was the most important factor in the development of political democracy in Greece.[50] There is a distinct connection between literacy and democracy. The free citizens of fifth-century Greece were able to take an active part in elections and in the legislative process because they could apparently read the laws. Literacy created a unifying cultural heritage via the written word.[51]

Hellenic culture spread with the conquests of Alexander the Great and was later adopted by the Romans. However, no one should put themselves under the delusion that Greece and Rome were always champions of democratic ideals, for both systems had their share of tyrants. Legend has it that Alexander the Great's mother taught him that Achilles was one of his ancestors and that his father descended from Hercules. These types of bedtime stories must have worked wonders for Alexander's self-esteem, so much so that he required those whom he conquered to refer to him as a god. Rulers who deified themselves were resentful of any competition. In 168 B.C. the Seleucid ruler Antiochus IV entered Jerusalem and proceeded to slaughter the Jews who would not forsake circumcision, Sabbath-keeping, and abstaining from unclean meats. The Temple was desecrated when the Greek tyrant erected an idol of Zeus (which was probably made to resemble Antiochus) over the altar and then offered swine upon it. The Romans were hardly a better example since they also deified their rulers. America's Founding Fathers knew full well the kinds of troubles experienced by ancient Greece and Rome. They knew how fragile democracy could be. (A lady once asked Benjamin Franklin after the Constitutional Convention had drawn to a close what he had given the nation. The old man replied, "You have a republic, madame. If you can keep it.") The founders knew that keeping a democracy is often more difficult than starting one.

Jewish thought and Greco-Roman philosophy are both analytical, but the latter is also one of pagan idolatry. Paglia borrows from Nietzsche in explaining how the Greco-Roman tradition was both *Apollonian* and *Dionysian*—the Apollonian component representing the world of rationality, the Dionysian representing the world of violence and sensuality.

Although the Greeks made a remarkable attempt to discover universals in nature, says Gene Veith, without divine revelation they could not come to a complete understanding of the truth. This was a culture that had institutionalized infanticide, slavery, war, oppression, prostitution, and homosexuality.[52] For as much as we like to laud the symposium and the gymnasium as cultural hallmarks of classical Greece, one should not forget the homo-sexual element surrounding both of those institutions. The sym-posium was a private, male-only drinking club with a collection of customs that not only included spouting poetry and philo-sophical discussions, but also erotic entertainments and sexual liaisons with slave boys and fellow members.

In his book *The Creators*, Daniel Boorstin accounts how Greek art reflected an adoration of the human body. The early Greeks modeled their life-size marble statues after the gods they encountered in Egypt. The seventh-century Greek *kouros* (youth), which would later become the prototype of the classic male nude, closely resembled its stilted Egyptian counterpart.[53] The art of statue-making flourished in festival contests as Greek athletes were allowed to erect life-size images of themselves in tribute to their victories. We cannot help but associate the ancient Greeks with the Olympic bronzed athlete. The festive games were held every four years in sacred Olympia in honor of the god Zeus. Of course, Olympic athletes competed without any clothes for over a thousand years. In Sparta, women competed nude with other women before a male audience, and on the island of Chios, girls competed with boys in wrestling matches.[54] It is not my intent to give the impression that ancient Greece was a large nudist colony. Greek culture possessed discreet elements as well. For example, women of Athens were generally not allowed to venture out in public without a male chaperone, which was probably a good idea, considering the level of lasciviousness.

The athletic male nude was the Greek ideal in art, says Boorstin. In the fifth century B.C. the *kouroi* became more refined, more lifelike, as the sculptor pressed closer to naturalism. By this time the Greek repertoire also included female nudes. It was during this period that Phidias (500 B.C.) sculpted three statues of Athena for the Acropolis, directed the frieze over the Parthenon, and fashioned the gigantic ivory-and-gold Zeus at Olympia.[55] While the Greeks attempted to make their athletic nudes as "natural" as possible by striving for ideal proportions, they did not individualize them. It was not until the fourth century B.C. that the Greek sculptors produced individual portrait heads of famous figures like Homer, Herodotus, and Alexander the Great. Rome, on the other hand, came to love portraits. The Romans filled their houses and public places with realistic statues, wrinkles and all, dedicated to deceased family members. Self-promoting politicians strategically placed life-size effigies in various localities visible to the public eye, a precursor to the modern political spot ad. Beginning with Augustus (63 B.C.-A.D. 14) the Romans strove to make their rulers godlike.[56] The emperor Nero once built a 120-foot statue of himself and placed it in his prodigious Golden House. Legend has it that each emperor after Nero replaced Nero's head with his own.[57] Rome eventually had to exchange their realism for idealism when the Caesars became objects of worship.

The gods residing on Mount Olympus were reflections of mortals with mortal passions. Their intriguing and sordid lives were more like the characters found in American soap operas. The deeds of the gods constituted the myths of the classical world, depicted in the Greeks' visual arts and celebrated in their religious festivals. The early Christians thought the pagan gods were as depraved as those who worshiped them. Likewise, the Romans thought the Christians most wretched. Tacitus called Christianity a "deadly superstition" and said Christians were "notoriously depraved." Of course, by "depraved" the Roman historian was referring to the scorn Christians felt toward the gods. Idolatry is implicitly forbidden in the New Testament. The apostle Paul told the Corinthian church that those who sacrificed to idols were in effect sacrificing to demons (see 1 Corinthians 10:19-21). Whenever the Romans persecuted the Christians, it was not because the Empire could not tolerate one more divinity. It was because the Empire could not tolerate a growing sect that claimed there was only *one* true divinity. To the Caesars, this was sedition. There were ten major persecutions, the last one the most pronounced. The persecutions began with Nero (A.D. 54-68), who supposedly set fire to the city of Rome and then blamed the Christians for it, and concluded with Emperor Diocletian (A.D. 284-305), who burned Christian literature, destroyed places of worship, required all to sacrifice to idols, and tortured the unrepentant. Between Nero and Diocletian, thousands of Christians were crucified, set afire, and torn asunder by wild beasts.

For Rome, the Dionysian component prevailed. Spectacle eventually won out. The Roman populace demanded "bread and circuses," and the rulers willingly complied. The intent behind building the amphitheaters was to provide free public entertainment. The famous Colosseum in Rome held forty-five thousand spectators who assembled themselves almost daily to watch gladiator fights, plays, and the occasional slaughter of Christians. The emperor Titus once flooded an entire amphitheater to stage a mock naval battle, a feat that must have been as impressive as his show of five thousand wild animals. Not to be topped, the emperor Trajan held a contest in A.D. 107 consisting of five thousand pairs of gladiators, and in A.D. 90 the emperor Domitian held combats between women and dwarfs. Successful gladiators were praised by the poets and pictured on porcelain vases, not unlike the praise we bestow on NBA basketball players and professional wrestlers. The theater wasn't any less sensational. Unlike early Greek theater, the Roman theater used females to play female roles in dramas with explicit sexual content. Elagabalus (A.D. 204-222), a transvestite emperor, decreed that all sex acts on the stage must be real.[58] The Colosseum and the Roman theater still live today inside the American living room. Accordingly, Paglia says pagan Rome has been reborn in Hollywood:

With the rebirth of the gods in the massive idolatries of popular culture, with the eruption of sex and violence into every corner of the ubiquitous mass media, Judeo-Christianity is facing its most serious challenge since Europe's confrontation with Islam in the Middle Ages. The latent paganism of western culture has burst forth again in all its daemonic vitality.[59]

The pursuit of spectacle continued to accelerate. Francis Schaeffer, who was a student of anthropology before he was a theologian, has noted the breakdown of Roman culture:

As the Empire ground down, the decadent Romans were given to a thirst for violence and a gratification of the senses. This is especially evident in their rampant sexuality. For example, in Pompeii, a century or so after the Republic had become a thing of the past, the phallus cult was strong. Statues and paintings of exaggerated sexuality adorned the houses of the more affluent. Not all the art in Pompeii was like this, but the sexual representations were unabashedly blatant.[60]

The earliest forms of paganism associated God with the rawness of nature and its procreative rhythms. The *image* was a trick to capture the life-giving forces of nature in an object of worship. Behind the idol stood the power of the state, sometimes in animal form, sometimes in human form, sometimes in the personality of a ruler who managed to assert himself as a deity (Ramses II, Nebuchadnezzar, Alexander the Great, Caesar Augustus, etc.). So we see, then, that idolatry is more than just the adoration of images. It is, as Paglia says, "fascism of the eye . . . pictorialism plus the will-to-power . . . ritualism, grandiosity, colossalism, sensationalism."[61] Israel resisted this force for over a thousand years.

The early Christians came to realize there were two components in Hellenic culture—one to be shunned and one to be harnessed. The Apollonian component coincided with the word-based culture that they inherited from the Jews. Christianity was not afraid to embrace some of the elements of pagan literature in order to extend and defend the faith. After all, Aristotle had defined rhetoric as seeing all the available means of persuasion in a given situation. Certainly there was a persuasive aspect of the gospel message. Certainly the faith needed to be defended. Augustine would later write, "If those who are called philosophers, and especially the Platonists, have said anything that is true and in harmony with our faith, we are not only to not shrink from it, but to claim it for our use from those who have no lawful possession of it."[62] Likewise, when the apostle John wrote, "In the beginning was the Word [*logos*], and the Word was with God, and the Word was God" (John 1:1), he used a term already familiar in Greek philosophy. *Logos* is translated to mean "word," "reason," or "plan." John was in effect saying, "The cosmos is not chaotic. God has a divine plan. There is an autograph in heaven that has been handed down to man." This was a continuation of the notion that Christianity, like Judaism, was word-dependent— a concept that out of necessity would have to value literacy to remain robust.

Rome fell, but paganism remained intact. As we shall see, the sex, violence, and person worship embodied in pagan idolatry never really died out. It was only repackaged. As Europe slips into a dismal night and lapses from the written word, the gods quietly return and position themselves over the church altar.

CHAPTER THREE

When Night Fell

*Indeed I do visit idols, I consult inspired men and soothsayers,
but I don't leave the church of God. I am a Catholic.[1]*

A CONGREGANT OF AUGUSTINE

*I had never touched them [the Scriptures], for I feared if
I should read them, I would be misled.[2]*

ANABAPTIST MENNO SIMONS

PAGAN IDOLATRY IS BIBLICISM'S CHIEF COMPETITOR BECAUSE
ONE THRIVES IN THE ABSENCE OF THE WRITTEN WORD AND
THE OTHER CANNOT EXIST WITHOUT IT.

Alaric, the Gothic king, threw open the flap and stepped outside. The imperial envoys approached his tent, now pitched within the shadows of Rome's walls.

One of the envoys cleared his throat, assumed a dignified stance, and spoke on behalf of the senate. "We are now prepared to make peace; but we are not afraid to fight. If we cannot come to fair and honorable terms, then by all means sound your trumpets; for we are many and in great anguish." Upon hearing this well-delivered oration, the barbarian bellowed out a great laugh. He knew the inhabitants on the other side were slowly starving to death because of his stranglehold on the city.

"The thicker the hay, the easier it is mowed," pronounced Alaric.

Alaric then listed his demands: all the city's gold, all the silver, all the precious furniture, and all the slaves with German blood in their veins.

"If such, O king, are your demands," sputtered the other envoy, "what do you intend to leave us?"

"Your lives," said Alaric.[3]

How had Rome reached such a predicament? For over six hundred years no foreign enemy had set foot inside the Empire's capital. A host of historians have offered their reasons for the decline and eventual collapse of the Roman Empire. Most agree that Rome's demise was secured both from within and from without.

By the third and fourth centuries A.D. Rome was suffering from a number of cancerous ailments that came in the form of civil strife, high inflation, heavy taxation, and increasing moral decay. The historian Olympius described the life of a Roman noble as being one of continual luxury and leisure. By the time of Alaric's assault, says Edward Gibbon in *The Decline and Fall of the Roman Empire*, 1,780 noble houses could be found in Rome, many the size of small cities, equipped with markets, hippodromes, temples, fountains, baths, porticos, shady groves, and artificial aviaries.[4] On special days nobles flaunted their wealth by parading around town in souped-up chariots, their silk and purple robes waving in the wind, a train of family and servants in procession behind them.[5] Homes were often tended by personal slaves, whom the nobles frequently and arbitrarily abused. Gibbon notes that when a wealthy citizen called for his needs to be met, "if a slave has been tardy in his obedience, he is instantly chastised with three hundred lashes; but should the same slave commit a willful murder, the master will mildly observe that he is a worthless fellow, but if he repeats the offense he shall not escape punishment."[6]

Rome's external problems were just as threatening as her domestic ones. By the second century A.D. the territory beyond the Swiss Alps was becoming crowded. The Germanic peoples occupying Central Europe were shepherds and hunters who moved about looking for better living space among dense forests and marshlands. War and conquest were the traditional ways to secure the best lands. The Germans detested farming because they believed, as the soldier-historian Tacitus claimed, laziness consisted not in shirking honest labor but in "acquiring by the sweat of your brow that which might be procured by the shedding of blood."[7] The barbaric tribes would have migrated south earlier were it not for the Roman legions sprinkled about along the ten-thousand-mile frontier and had the Goths had sufficient motivation to cross it.

The motivation came in A.D. 376 when the Huns came riding out of Central Asia. The Huns were not as numerous as the Germans, but they were just as fierce. Expert archers and horsemen, these Mongol warriors either routed their conquered foes, enslaved them, or, more likely, exterminated them. The Huns fell upon the Ostrogoths (East Goths) in the Ukraine and then engaged the Visigoths (West Goths) near what is now Romania. The Visigoth army was brutalized, but eighty thousand of them managed to flee across the Danube River where they were granted settlement by an empire unprepared for so many refugees.

What does one do with a hungry, non-agricultural, warlike people with a national unity? Conflict with the Empire was inevitable. A century earlier Rome had begun the practice of using the Germans to help protect the frontier, paying them yearly subsidies. When the Emperor Theodosius I died in A.D. 395, the subsidies stopped. The Visigoths were enraged. A king was chosen—Alaric the Bold—an ambitious man who wasted little time in marching toward the capital. Between A.D. 408 and 410 the Goths made three sieges of the city of Rome. Negotiations were attempted, but all faltered.

On July 24, A.D. 410 forty thousand Goths, allied Huns, and newly freed Roman slaves entered the city. Alaric gave instructions for his followers to respect the "laws of humanity and religion." (The Gothic king adhered to Arianism.) Gibbon comments, "In that hour of savage licence, when every restraint was removed, the precepts of the Gospel seldom influenced the behaviour of the Gothic Christians."[8] A cruel slaughter was made of the Romans. Houses were set ablaze. Palaces were stripped. Statues of gold and silver were melted down. Captives were taken and sold for ransom. Women were raped. Even the feeble and innocent did not escape. The wealthy were especially targeted so that "the private revenge of forty thousand slaves was exercised without pity or remorse; and the ignominious lashes which they had formerly received were washed away in the blood of the guilty or obnoxious families."[9]

This was just the beginning. Fifteen years prior to the sack of Rome by the Visigoths, the Empire had split into east and west halves. Emperors became weaker and weaker. In A.D. 406 the Rhine barrier lay open for all to enter. Despite her majestic appearance, the French medievalist scholar Ferdinand Lot said, the Empire had been reduced to a hollow husk.[10] The German tribes in the north flew down upon a rotting carcass. The Goths, Huns, Franks, Lombards, Angles, Saxons, and others staked out their territories, further splitting and splintering the Empire on into the twelfth century.

In European history the Middle Ages are recognized as that period of time between the barbarian invasions and the Renaissance, roughly A.D. 400 to A.D. 1500. The first half of the era (A.D. 400 to A.D. 1000) has sometimes been referred to as the Dark Ages. Although the second half of the Middle Ages saw advances in literacy (e.g., the invention of the university and the rise of scholasticism), many of the problems of the first half were not easily shaken off. To use the term "Dark Ages" today is to make certain kinds of value judgments. One who manages to keep the term in his vocabulary is easily pegged as adhering to one of two perspectives concerning that time in history. For those who extol the virtues of the Enlightenment, the term symbolizes an era of unprecedented irrationality and superstition. On the other hand, for those who lay claim to their Protestant heritage, the phrase represents an age in which the original gospel message was distorted and the common people were deprived of the Scriptures.

Both camps can find common ground upon which to castigate the Dark Ages, and both would agree that the period illustrates what can happen to a society when it lapses from the written word. Even Charlemagne, said to be the noblest of all medieval rulers, was illiterate.

Few dispute that literacy was spurned during the Dark Ages; however, there is another characteristic of the period that is sometimes overlooked and perhaps disregarded. While Protestants have traditionally held to the idea of a syncretized church to help justify their existence, recent scholarship has demonstrated that the paganism of late antiquity did not die out after the fourth century, but rather attached itself to the church, reshaping it. The aim of this chapter is to examine the reasons behind the church's assimilation of pagan forms and Europe's subsequent plunge into the night. Why did the analytical components once embedded in the Roman culture fade away? What were the consequences of the disappearance of literacy? To answer these questions one must begin with Rome's "first Christian emperor."

COMPROMISES AFTER CONSTANTINE

As to what Constantine actually saw in the afternoon sky, we can only take him at his word. He related to his friend and biographer, Eusebius, Bishop of Caesarea, that it was a bright cross accompanied with the words, "By this sign conquer." The vision could not have appeared at a better time. Constantine's army was outnumbered four to one when it confronted Maxentius, a rival to the imperial throne, and his troops. Spurred on by the sign from heaven and a new cause for which to fight, Constantine and his army prevailed.

The genuineness of Constantine's conversion is suspect. It is difficult to tell where his faith began and his political opportunism ended. He built churches, issued fat salaries to bishops, and took an active role in religious affairs. He ran the Council of Nicaea himself, saying, "You are bishops whose jurisdiction is within the church. . . . But I also am a bishop, ordained by God to oversee those outside the church."[11] He had difficulty following abstract theological arguments and often exploded in frustration at meetings. He was not baptized until the end of his life, probably to allow for all the nasty duties of an emperor's life—such as executing an elder son, a second wife, and a brother-in-law. While Constantine ended the persecution of Christians with his policy of toleration (introduced a year before his conversion), he set in motion the conditions by which pagans and other dissenters would later be persecuted by Christians.

Paganism did not end after Constantine. In his book *Christianity & Paganism in the Fourth to Eighth Centuries*, Ramsay MacMullen demonstrates that the two systems were blending and mixing together "to a much later point in time than anyone would have said until recently."[12] As to when "the Grand Event . . . was over," MacMullen says, "I would say, [it] never ended, at least not if the disappearance of paganism is what's in question."[13]

At the time of Constantine's conversion (A.D. 312), perhaps a tenth of the Empire subscribed to Christianity. But by the beginning of the fifth century, says MacMullen, the number of professing Christians dramatically climbed to include half the population.[14] One might conclude that the cause of the rapid growth lay in the fact that the persecutions had ceased and there was a new missionary zeal that took hold. Not exactly. There were two simple reasons for the great sweep—positive inducements and negative inducements.

MacMullen explains that there were three varieties of positive inducements. After Constantine it not only became popular to be a Christian, it also became economically advantageous. By A.D. 400 the government in both the east and the west was sufficiently infiltrated with Christians,[15] and one could not smoothly climb the social ladder without being associated with the faith. Although the prospect of economic prosperity provided an adequate reason to embrace Christianity for some, it took a miracle for others. It was not unusual for conversions to occur upon witnessing some kind of miracle—an exorcism, a divine healing, a raising from the dead, or perhaps the freezing of an idolater in his steps. These kinds of anecdotal religious experiences, not uncommon in our own day (see Chapter Eight), convinced pagans that the Christians were *right* when mere words were not enough.[16] Christian emperors also had their inducements. For example, while Justinian was smashing pagan temples with one hand, he was offering "many months' wages" to those who would submit to baptism with the other.[17]

Social standing, the witness of miracles, and bribes were some of the positive incentives to accept the faith. However, as time passed, most inducements were of the negative sort. MacMullen says, "These must have seemed all the more necessary because, without them, progress was slow, complete victory apparently impossible; and unlike positive inducements, they had their own drama, their own triumphs which can be traced through dates and headlines."[18] Constantine had already set the example for imperial involvement in church affairs. The two forces, imperial and ecclesiastical, worked together to squelch paganism. Christian emperors eventually made church attendance mandatory for all citizens with the consequences of having property seized and being sent into exile if they disobeyed. After the 420s pagans were banned from all imperial service and forbidden to serve as lawyers and teachers.[19] John Gooch recounts one thinking Christian of Constantine's day who pondered the wisdom of such heavy-handedness and asked the question, "How can there be anything like persuasion when fear of the emperor rules?" An excellent question, but a dangerous one. The one who asked it was sent into exile four times.[20] MacMullen says emperors and bishops worked together on all manner of inducements to secure compliance, using threats, fines, confiscation, exile, imprisonment, flogging, torture, beheading, and crucifixion.[21] In the spirit of Constantine, the Frankish chieftain Clovis commanded three thousand of his soldiers to submit to baptism in a single day (A.D. 498); three centuries later, Charlemagne beheaded 4,500 conquered Saxons for refusing to submit to baptism.

Wholesale conversions, then, came rather easy when conducted under physical threat. But few understood their faith, and hearts were not necessarily changed. There now existed a great diversity of people, most of them unlearned, loosely assembled under the banner of Christianity with lists of demands and greater expectations than previously known before Constantine. A good number of them saw no reason to part with their old gods. The entire progression, says William Manchester, went something like this: "Imperial Rome having yielded to barbarians, and then barbarism to Christianity, Christianity was in turn infiltrated, and to a considerable extent subverted, by the paganism it was supposed to destroy."[22]

There were laws forbidding pagan practices since Constantine, but they were not enforced in any strict manner. MacMullen notes that up until the sixth century there is no account of anyone being put to death for making a pagan blood sacrifice.[23] Remarkably, islands of pure paganism persisted on into the tenth century.[24] And even while public displays of feasting, drinking, dancing, and staying up through the night were not censured by the clergy, these practices still flourished. When the bishops looked around, they found themselves still in Rome. How could they help but do as the Romans do? Compromises were made. The old system was incorporated into the new. MacMullen explains that paganism kept its original character but was placed under new management:

> Christianity became (as a salesman would say today) a "full-service" religion. Converts could find in it, because they brought in to it, a great variety of psychological rewards that had been important to them before, when they had addressed the divine within the pagan tradition.[25]

Many sites of worship did not change because of the custom of building churches directly on the foundations of pagan temples. Sometimes entire temples were just "baptized" into the faith. This no doubt had a psychological effect on worshipers who now tried to offer prayers to Jesus where only a short time before they had been offering prayers to Zeus. The Christian calendar was borrowed from the pagan one, so that Pentecost replaced the Floralia; All Souls' Day replaced a festival for the dead; the Feast of the

Nativity replaced the feast of purification of Isis; and Christmas replaced Saturnalia, the birthday of the sun.[26]

Pagan idols were also rechristened. Of course, images have always been a staple of paganism, shrouded in mystique, rumored for their ability to sweat, smile, cry, crawl, and raise themselves off their bases. Jesus and John the Baptist were the first to appear over the church altar, then Mary (Queen of Heaven and Earth), the saints, and the angels. The pictures and statuettes were all too familiar with the older system. Jesus looked liked Horus, the Egyptian sky god; and Mary bore an uncanny resemblance to Isis, the goddess of royalty.[27] Jean Seznec has shown in *The Survival of the Pagan Gods* how the lush mythological heritage of antiquity was absorbed into medieval culture, protecting it from hostility. The gods never were "restored" to life during the Italian Renaissance, for they never really disappeared. One cannot speak of a "rebirth" of the gods, Seznec explains, "when one has gazed at the great mass of . . . barbaric images, scattered offshoots of the Olympian line— obscure in their descent, no doubt, but still endowed with the divine right of immortality."[28] The unlearned received their ideas about religion from the mosaics, paintings, sculptures, and stained-glass windows adorning the churches. It was here that paganism and Christianity were visually reconciled. Some people saw the blatant idol worship for what it was. In A.D. 726 the Byzantine emperor Leo III issued an edict to remove all icons from the churches. However, his subjects and the lower clergy were enraged. Forty-six years later the policy was abandoned.

How the saints came to be worshiped is a case study in syncretism. Christians who had suffered cruel deaths under Roman emperors were often remembered and honored by the faithful. But soon their names came to be memorialized, prayed to, and mounted over church doors. Eventually bishops and famous holy men enjoyed a similar status. It was said that the bishops themselves had the power to heal, exorcise demons, and fight off dragons; and some, believe it or not, managed to fly through the air. (MacMullen offers one story in circulation at the time concern-

ing Saint Stephen, who flies from his tomb to rescue mariners in
distress and then returns to the shrine dripping water on the
floor.[29]) Christian emperors were also worshiped. Even
Constantine made arrangements before his death to be memorialized on coins as "deified." With so many grabbing a piece of
deity for themselves, it wasn't too long before a pope residing in
the church at Rome declared that the Vatican is now a "sharer in
the divine magistracy, and [is granted], by special privilege, immu-
nity from error."

DARKNESS

Sometime between A.D. 400 and A.D. 1000 the analytical elements
once embedded in the Roman culture faded off the scene. Literacy
faded. Education faded. Civility faded. Superstition seeped in.
Europe was cut up and resettled by tribal chieftains, triumphant
warriors, and a handful of patricians left over from the Empire.
A new hierarchy was established. At the top were kings who ruled
over their territories by divine right but competed with the popes
for political power. Further down the ladder were the dukes, earls,
counts, and barons we now associate with European aristocracy.
The images we have of Medieval Europe—that of Grimm's fairy
tales with deep dark forests, lurking wolves, hags, and roaming
highwaymen—are not too far removed from the reality of the
times.

By the time of Charlemagne's reign (A.D. 768-814), European
society was predominantly rural. The Romans had not built roads
in Central Europe, and it largely remained a vast woodland.
Medieval villages were islands, cut off from other villages, the residents rarely venturing too far from town. G. G. Coulton comments in *The Medieval Village* that these villages averaged fifty to
five hundred souls at the most. "The people are few, and their
ideas and words are few, the average peasant has probably never
known by sight more than two or three hundred men in his whole
life; his vocabulary is almost certainly confined to something even
less than the six hundred words. . . ."[30] So isolated were these
hamlets that a villager, if perchance he wandered into a neigh-

boring village twenty miles away, might not be able to understand the dialect of the other inhabitants. James Burke says the average day's journey was seven miles away—the time it took to go out on foot and return before the sun went down.[31] And you did want to return before the sun went down. One was twice as likely to be murdered than to die by accident, says Barbara Tuchman in *A Distant Mirror*, and your murderer faced only a one in a hundred chance of being brought to justice.[32] Roving gangs, sometimes composed of renegade knights, waited in the woods to fall on the lone traveler.

Of course, a serf could not leave his manor anyway, and the peasants who could, preferred to stay put and endure a life of absolute misery. Ninety percent of the population was tied to the land. Before A.D. 900 there were no horse collars or harnesses, so the earth had to be turned by hand using crude tools. Thankfully, life was short. Half the population died before their thirtieth birthday. Manchester says a woman who reached this age might be called an "Old Gretel" since her life expectancy was only twenty-four. Girls traditionally received a fine piece of cloth from their mothers on their wedding day that could be made into a frock; six or seven years later it could be used as a shroud.[33] If the villain in the forest, daily labor, or childbirth did not kill you, then perhaps a pandemic would.

Harry Gaff says that in the second half of the first millennium the reduction of literate man in the west coincided with the great swellings within the Roman Catholic Church brought on by the conversions of the barbarians.[34] According to Kenneth Clark, for five hundred years the ability to read and write was practically unknown, not only to the average layperson, but also to kings and emperors.[35] This is not to say that *no one* could read or write; rather, these skills were restricted to a privileged class. In other words, medieval Europe possessed only craft literacy. Interestingly, Gaff explains, the word *laity* (*laici*) was synonymous with the word *illiterate* (*illiterati*). Likewise, the word associated with the clergy (*clerici*) was synonymous with the word *literate* (*litterati*).[36] Latin was the traditional language of literacy. (English

clergy - literate
laity / illiterate

and French did not become standardized until well after 1300.)
Although the clergy made up an elite social class, Gaff explains
that they still could not, at least early on, hold a pen to the let-
tered men of ancient antiquity:

> These first clerical *litterati*, whose sparse knowledge had scarcely
> anything in common with the Latin scholars either of ancient
> Rome or of the Twelfth-Century Renaissance, established a priv-
> ileged status for themselves in society by despising non-Latinists
> as an ignorant crowd of *laici*. In reality the *clerici* were unsure of
> their status, as Europe was dominated not by them but by war-
> riors with a non-literate sense of values.[37]

It would almost be enough to say that literacy faded because
the barbarians cared nothing for books. However, Neil Postman
says there were other reasons the lights went out in Europe.[38] For
one thing, the alphabet became disguised as styles multiplied. The
fashion was to make letters elaborate and calligraphic to the point
of also making them unrecognizable. As Eric Havelock says,
"Calligraphic virtuosity of any kind fosters craft literacy and is
fostered by it, but is the enemy of social literacy. The unlucky
careers of both the Greek and Roman versions of the alphabet
during the Dark Ages and the Middle Ages sufficiently demonstrate this fact."[39] Literacy also faded because of the scarcity of
papyrus and parchment. Either there was a lack of resources to
produce these materials or there was a lack of collective will to do
so; in any case, the scarcity of writing surfaces only served to
maintain craft literacy.[40] Beyond an ornate alphabet and a want
of media to write on looms another cause, perhaps greater than
all the others, for the eclipse of literacy. Simply stated, reading and
writing were restricted by the Church. The Vulgate Bible, produced by Jerome in the fifth century, was written in Latin and was
therefore out of reach to the common man. The Roman Catholic
doctrines of the priesthood, transubstantiation, purgatory, and
indulgences were rarely challenged because the people could not
read the Bible for themselves. So then, it is easy to see how craft
literacy was a "means of keeping control over a large and diverse

population; that is to say, of keeping control over the ideas, organization, and loyalties of a large and diverse population."[41]

James Burke has noted how medieval people lived in a world without "facts."[42] Information coming from outside the village walls was scant and could not always be corroborated. As a result, rumor and hearsay prevailed. Since all knowledge was either experienced, observed, or based on word of mouth, the written word was held suspect. Records were rarely kept. Since there were few calendars and clocks, one marked the passage of time with the seasons and events. In an island world such as this, there could not exist a sense of history or geography or science because information could not be cross-referenced or confirmed.[43] Rhyme was the prevalent literature of the day, and memory was the essential tool of conveying cultural knowledge. Writing had a magical quality, and books, when they could be found (there was no library file system), were miraculous objects. A manuscript was a rare thing, and those who could read one did not necessarily possess the ability to write one because reading and writing were separate skills. Reading was always performed aloud—a habit that explains why some texts contained little warnings such as, "Do not read this in the presence of others, as it is a secret." Those who read in silent were thought odd. Augustine once remarked after observing Ambrose that it was quite remarkable that "when he was reading his eye glided over the pages and his heart sensed out the sense, but his voice and tongue were at rest."[44]

When literacy faded, so did education. Institutions of higher learning in the Roman Empire, housed within cities like Athens and Alexandria, were specially targeted by post-Constantine emperors in the fourth and fifth centuries, who cared little about cultivating the mind or preserving the past, so that books and philosophy eventually faded.[45] Because human communication was primarily oral and because there were few books and facts, no general body of knowledge about the past or present state of the world to transmit to others, there was little reason for a formal system of education like we have today. Of course there were schools in the monasteries and some private tutoring, but primary education, where a child develops the skills of reading and writing, was unknown.[46]

This would be a good place to pause and ask an important question: What is so fabulous about reading and writing anyway? This is a question I think will be asked with greater frequency as we continue to ease on down the visual-friendly road. Educators in general, and Christian educators in particular, must begin to gather some answers together because the digit directors who have set themselves to the task of creating a new virtual world on our behalf are going to offer more and more reasons as to why literacy should be "redefined" to accommodate a less articulate society. Let me begin with two very good reasons to keep our culture a literate one. First, Christians surely must realize that if they are going to *be* a "people of the Book," they must first *know* the Book. As stated earlier, God purposefully chose the medium of writing to make Himself known. Only the written word is sufficient for communicating all the theological complexities of an abstract divinity. A second reason literacy should remain valued in our culture, not unrelated to the first reason, is that childhood and all that it entails was an outgrowth of literacy.

As Postman explains in *The Disappearance of Childhood*, childhood did not exist in the Middle Ages. Of course, biological children existed—that is, people smaller in stature than adults, but childhood as a social artifact did not exist. Postman makes the argument that in a literate culture, a child has to be separated from the rest of the community to be taught how to read and write. In an oral society the distinctions between child and adult are almost invisible because both share a communication environment where competence is measured only by the ability to speak—something a child becomes competent at by age seven. In the Middle Ages because children and adults shared the same world, the same games, the same stories, the same activities, there was nothing—absolutely nothing—hidden from a ten-year-old within the home or village. It was not until after the printing press, Postman says, that "children had to *earn* adulthood by achieving literacy, for which people are not biologically programmed."[47] By the sixteenth century, schools became one of the primary instruments to help civilize society. Children were slowly and carefully introduced into an expanding world where adults had decided to keep some information secret and safe from little ears and eyes. The process of providing a child a literate education had to begin at an early age when, as we now better understand, the brain is at the greatest point of neuron growth. Childhood, then, became the transition period to prepare oneself for adult civility.

To say all of this is to also say that Medieval Europe was less civil before the spread of literacy, which is true. Manchester comments that the "level of everyday violence—deaths in alehouse brawls, during bouts with staves, or even playing football or wrestling—was shocking."[48] We like to think of the period as a wonderful time when knights in shining armor wooed lovely princesses with courageous acts of chivalry at jousting tournaments. Actually these tournaments were just as likely to be "occasions for abductions and mayhem." In 1240 sixty knights in shining armor were brutally hacked to death at a tourney near Düsseldorf.[49]

Medieval blood thirst was only rivaled by that of sexual vulgarity. Manchester says the close quarters people lived in did not help matters. The typical peasant house consisted of a single room where in the center lay a "gigantic bedstead, piled high with straw pallets, all seething with vermin. Everyone slept there, regardless of age or gender—grandparents, parents, children, grandchildren, and hens and pigs. . . ."[50] In such conditions intimacy was hard to come by. Strangers would also share in the same sleeping arrangements. If a husband happened to be away, perhaps on a pilgrimage, and returned to find his wife with child, the common way to deal with it was to say that while sleeping she had been impregnated by an incubus—an excuse theologians of the day readily would confirm.[51]

Children and adults lived their lives together, never apart. Historian J. H. Plumb says, "The coarse village festivals depicted by Brueghel, showing men and women besotted with drink, groping for each other with unbridled lust, have children eating and drinking with adults."[52] The practice of adults playing with children's genitals was a widespread tradition, says Philippe Ariès, and "[e]verything was permitted in their presence: coarse language, scabrous actions and situations; they had heard everything and seen everything."[53] The legend of the Pied Piper is actually based upon the acts of a psychotic pederast who sexually abused and butchered dozens of children in the Saxon village of Hammel.[54]

The persistence of paganism, coupled with the decline of literacy and the dreary remoteness of rural life, opened the cracks for superstition to seep in. After darkness swallowed up the Empire sometime after A.D. 400, the analytical elements that once existed before this time were replaced with "popular," more superstitious ones. MacMullen says, "For reasons having nothing to do with [early] Christianity, the habits of mind once characterizing the [educated] elite—the more intellectual, analytical, comparativist, and empiricist elements of ancient thought—lost favor."[55] Where at one time events in the weather were explained in natural terms, now they were explained with supernatural ones. Pagan sorcery and Christianity were forced into a type of common partnership. "Weathermen" (*tempestarii*) were summoned to towns to bestow their enchantments toward the sky. Bishops wore the hat of magic men who not only blessed crops but also cast spells to ward off evil spirits. People saw fairies and goblins in the flickering lights of marsh gas; fireflies were said to be the souls of unbaptized infants; and there was a reliance upon the signs of the zodiac to explain natural disasters. (The University of Paris came to the conclusion that the Black Death was caused by the conjunction of Saturn, Jupiter, and Mars.)[56]

IN DARKNESS, LIGHT

James Burke says that by the fourteenth century there were growing pressures in Europe for literacy.[57] The trader, whose appearance became more frequent in the village, needed an easier method of keeping international banking accounts than cutting notches in sticks. The number of grammar schools and universities increased as students prepared themselves for a growing world of commerce and spreading monarchical bureaucracies. The price of paper dropped as methods of production became more economical. The invention of eyeglasses also fostered literacy by increasing the longevity of the copyist and the reader. The late Middle Ages showed the first great writers of literature since the Greeks, particularly Dante and Chaucer. Both of these writers were laymen and revealed a break from the craft literacy of the clergy. In *Canterbury Tales* Chaucer lampoons the indulgence-selling Paronder:

> *By this fraud have I won me, year by year,*
> *A hundred marks, since I've been pardoner.*
> *I stand up like a scholar in pulpit,*
> *And when the ignorant people all do sit,*
> *I preach, as you have heard me say before,*
> *And tell a hundred false japes, less or more.*

The stirring for literacy created an insufferable itch for religious reform beneath the skin of the Church. There had always been voices of dissent, but now the dissenter had a Bible text in his hand. "If ever a movement was inspired by books . . . ," says medieval historian R. I. More, "it was this one":

They spoke for their age in measuring their belief and conduct against the text, confident that virtue and orthodoxy consisted in stripping away the encrustations and deformations of tradition which literacy alone . . . enabled them to recognize as departure from the historically authenticated canon upon which they took their stand.[58]

Literate individuals and communities sprang up, forming pockets of passive resistance to Catholic orthodoxy. First among these was Waldo of Lyons, who began to contemplate the plight of his soul when one day his friend dropped dead by his side. Because Waldo wanted a copy of the Scriptures for himself, he commissioned a cleric to translate a good portion of the New

Testament from the Latin Bible into his own vernacular. He then sold his possessions and went about preaching in the marketplace, gaining disciples along the way. When the Archbishop of Lyons got wind of this and tried to put a stop to it, Waldo responded with one of his Bible verses: "It is better to obey God than man." The archbishop was not impressed and kicked him out of the city. The setback, however, did not prevent Waldo's disciples from spreading the Word. The Waldensians continued to preach and give out Bible translations and devotional material throughout southern France, Switzerland, and northern Italy. The "poor men of Lyons," as they were known, were so successful in their endeavors that the Church eventually had to restore the Inquisition. For several hundred years the Waldensians were hounded in places like the Swiss Alps, where, whenever discovered, their persecutors inflicted them with such tortures as setting fire to the mouth of a cave where four hundred of them lay hidden or rolling mothers with their babies down the mountainsides.

Another dissenter with a nagging voice and script in hand was John Wycliffe. The Oxford scholar's belief in the supreme authority of the Scriptures flew in the face of Catholic teaching. Wycliffe wrote, "Forasmuch as the Bible contains Christ, that is all that is necessary for salvation, it is necessary for all men, nor for priests alone. It alone is the supreme law that is to rule the Church, State, and Christian life, without human traditions and statutes." His passion to get the Scriptures into the hands of the laity led him to be the first to translate the entire Bible into the English language. Wycliffe developed five principles for interpreting the Bible:

1. Obtain a reliable text.
2. Understand the logic of the Scripture.
3. Compare the parts of Scripture with one another.
4. Maintain an attitude of humble seeking.
5. Receive the instruction of the Spirit.

If it were not for his alliance with the English nobility and his patriotic services to the crown, Wycliffe would have been burned at the stake early in his life. So despised was Wycliffe by the

Church that his bones were dug up forty-four years after his death, burned, and scattered over the River Swift.

John Hus was not as fortunate. Influenced by Wycliffe's writings, the preacher from Prague made it a practice to deliver his uncompromising sermons in the tongue of the people rather than in the traditional Latin. The local archbishop thought this ill-advised and collected his books, threw them in a pile, and set fire to them. A short time later the Church set fire to Hus himself. They scattered *his* ashes over the Rhine.

Such was the fate of those who disagreed with the Church. The Waldensians, Lollards, Hussites, and Anabaptists shared in common a fierce loyalty to the Scriptures that superseded any loyalty to the state or pope. The pre-Reformers were "people of the Book" in the truest sense, and their literacy helped earn them the title *heretic*.

DARKNESS FALLING AGAIN

Pagan idolatry is biblicism's chief competitor because one thrives in the absence of the written word and the other cannot exist without it. The story of the Middle Ages is the story of the relentlessness of the gods. Since the old system just would not go away, the Church made the necessary accommodations. The similarities between ancient antiquity and medieval Christianity cannot be ignored. Both possessed religions backed by the power of the state. Both contained violent and debased components. Both deified their leaders. Both were image-dependent. And both persecuted "the people of the Book." We also cannot ignore the parallels between the Middle Ages and our own times. We have no barbarians at our borders; nevertheless, as with Rome, our own analytical elements are in jeopardy. Night seems to be falling once again. The great irony of our age is that for all our technological prowess, we are remarkably less articulate, less civil, and more irrational than we were one hundred or even two hundred years ago.

As noted earlier, there are distinct differences between oral cultures and literate ones. Oral cultures think concretely and subjectively, have limited vocabularies, rely heavily on memory, and focus primarily on the here and now. Literate cultures think abstractly and objectively, have large vocabularies, process information in a detached and analytical fashion, and are capable of grasping and learning from the past. America seems to be sliding back into what Walter Ong calls a state of "secondary orality."[59] Ong believes electronic communication technologies are having a powerful influence on the mind-set of contemporary cultures. Although still dependent on its literate past to keep society's trains running on time, cultures of secondary orality have an environment "in which a majority of people, particularly the young, spend a great deal more time, and give a great deal more allegiance, to sound and image-based media than to written and printed words."[60] Ong suggests that the ways of thinking and expressing by today's young have more in common with oral cultures of the past than with literate cultures. In this sense, our new communication technologies are pulling us back into the Dark Ages.

The irony sharpens when one considers the fact that in our own culture we require children to spend at least twelve years attending school. It is not my purpose here to point out all the shortcomings of America's educational system, but it is my aim to expose the unintended effects of our new communication technologies. Therefore, I agree with Neil Postman when he calls electronic media the "first curriculum," signifying the tremendous influence that television, videos, CDs, and movies have over the minds of our children. The school, of course, is the second curriculum.[61] The entertaining programs, the magnetic personalities, and the lusty music flowing forth from electronic media have gained *first place* in the hearts of our children. The school, at least the traditional concept of school, with its *word*-based modes of learning, earns a halfhearted *second place* because it cannot hope to compete with the *image*. This is one reason why schools are now focusing on the tangible and the experiential. As Gene Veith points out in his book *Postmodern Times*, "Instead of students learning primarily from language—from books and the mental discipline of reading and writing—the new curriculum relies on *images*—computer screens and VCRs—and on manufacturing elaborate but entertaining experiences, such as interactive games and field trips."[62] Educators have concluded that if they cannot beat the image-makers in Hollywood, they might as well join them.

That we are less civil than we were a century or two ago has been articulated by Stephen Carter in his timely book, *Civility: Manners, Morals, and the Etiquette of Democracy*. Carter argues that civility is declining in America because of a spiritual crisis. In sum, our crudeness and rudeness stem from our obsession to get what we want at all costs. Carter notes that it was Erasmus (the first humanist scholar to fully utilize the printing press) who put forth the notion that *self-discipline* is the true mark of civilization and the main ingredient separating the barbarian from the non-barbarian. Erasmus was extremely popular among a growing literate middle class who were accustomed to a world where people ate with their hands from a common plate, urinated in the street, and chopped each other up over minor disagreements.[63] Erasmus's book *On Civility in Children* (1530) warned Europe that unless humans were willing to control their impulses, there would be nothing to distinguish them from the animals.

There is no doubt that our growing lack of civility is a moral problem, but I would add it is a moral problem acerbated by technological innovations, particularly innovations in electronic media, which have conditioned us to expect immediate gratification. Whether it be fast food, instant entertainment, or immediate sex, the dominant value of all technological innovation from the microwave oven to the birth control pill is *speed*—we cannot wait until next year, nor tomorrow, nor an hour from now—we must have it this very second! It is the barbarian, Erasmus would say, who must satisfy all bodily desires the moment they surface. Are we surprised then when driving down the road we are suddenly cut off by a three-ton sport utility vehicle with an obscene-gesturing, screaming maniac at the wheel? Add to road rage air rage, talk show rage, and after-the-athletic-event-mash-every-thing-in-sight rage and you get a better picture of what kind of people we are becoming—very selfish ones. A pack of men roam Central Park on a Sunday afternoon groping and stripping helpless women while police officers look the other way. Two teenage Goths laden with bombs and guns emerge from their suburban bat cave in Littleton, Colorado, and commence to blow up their school and massacre their fellow students.

Sadly, we now reward individuals for being as nasty as they want to be. A basketball star kicks a photographer and is offered a multimillion-dollar endorsement contract. Major corporations support talk shows with daily themes like "I impregnated thirty girls and I'm proud of it"[64] and recording artists with names like Cannibal Corpse whose lyrics describe overt sexual acts with the severed head of a child.[65] Alan Bloom was right when he said in *The Closing of the American Mind* that "[s]uch polluted sources issue in a muddy stream where only monsters can swim."[66]

One does not have to look too far over the castle walls of modernity to find monsters swimming about in the stinky moat of popular culture. Only now we do not summon the local bishop or the magic man to fetch them out, but instead blow them up with twenty tons of TNT, an exciting new development hatched in fertile imaginations of authors like Stephen King. The demons that once lurked in the dark forests of medieval Europe seem to have migrated to the wardrobe rooms of Hollywood where they have zipped themselves up in exotic new costumes. Screwtape, C. S. Lewis's scheming demon, had hoped this would happen. The evil spirit told his nephew Wormwood that the trick was to:

> . . . emotionalise and mythologise their science to such an extent that what is, in effect, a belief in us, (though not under that name) will creep in while the human mind remains closed to belief in the Enemy. The "Life Force," the worship of sex, and some aspects of Psychoanalysis, may here prove useful. If once we can produce our perfect work—the Materialist Magician, the man, not using, but veritably worshiping, what he vaguely calls "Forces" while denying the existence of "spirits"—then the end of our war will be in sight.[67]

C. S. Lewis, an apologist who aimed his arrows at modernism's secular doctrines, understood there might come a day when demonology would transform itself into a kind of public fascination with devils, but it would be a fascination absent of traditional Christian presuppositions. Our enchantment with aliens is in keeping with such a notion, for our fascination with them has become a regular media bonanza going as far back as Orson Welles's famous radio broadcast "War of the Worlds" (1938). Since that benchmark event, extraterrestrials have been showing themselves as our friends (e.g., *Close Encounters of the Third Kind*), our enemies (e.g., *Alien*), and our personal savior (e.g., *E. T.*). But alien mania is more than a harmless flirtation with the "what's out there?" world; it is a sign, says Robert Bork, that Americans are refusing to apply reasoning to their beliefs, that we are rejecting the very idea of rationality.[68] According to polls, 40 percent of Americans think aliens have visited our planet.[69]

It is no small coincidence that members of the Heaven's Gate cult were avid consumers of *Star Trek*, *Star Wars*, and *X-Files* fare. Like overanxious children awaiting a much anticipated summer vacation, members readily packed their space bags when their wide-eyed leader, Marshall Applewhite, announced that the UFO tailgating the Hale-Bopp comet was ready for boarding. Americans want to hear messages from outer space because Jodie Foster wanted to hear them; we longed to hear them with her, which is why one media outlet was so quick to call the 1999 HD119850 signal a "close encounter with what promises to be the most important scientific discovery of all time."[70] As it turned out, the signal was not the most important scientific discovery of all time, but such proclamations are now typical of the news media, whether they are associated with distant radio static or traces of life on Mars.

New Age mumbo jumbo is big business in the United States. According to Charles Strohmer, calls to psychic hotlines approach one-third of all 900 numbers and constitute a billion-dollar industry.[71] There is even a revival of overt, old-fashioned paganism, as in Wicca, which has a significant following on university campuses. Wicca priestesses now are represented on Campus Ministry boards and are applying for positions as prison chaplains. Of course, there is nothing *new* about New Age religions. Behind all the hype of horoscopes, astrology, and channeling lurks old-fashioned divination, magic, and demon possession, explains Veith: "With the eclipse of Christianity, primitive nature religions come creeping back in all of their superstition and barbarism."[72] What *is* new about all this preoccupation with phantoms is how the same irrational components found in popular culture are now showing up in academia. "It is perhaps unclear whether the universities are instructing the culture at large in the joys of anti-intellectualism or whether the universities have been infected by a culture already lobotomized by television,"[73] says Robert Bork. Nevertheless, the conservative Supreme Court nominee believes universities have abandoned "logocentrism" to make room for the politicization of "new intellectual fields" in the same way that European fascists rejected rationality in the first half of the twentieth century to make way for their new order.[74]

The Middle Ages demonstrate that when a society lapses from the written word, the vultures of incivility and irrationality begin to circle overhead. It was true then, and it is true now. Likewise, New Testament Christianity faded, in part, because the word faded. If the spirit of the apostles were to revive, it would have to revive under a return to the word. And this is precisely what happened. Even as the smoke of the martyrs was ascending upward toward heaven, Europe was on the verge of undergoing what Myron Gilmore calls the most radical transformation of intellectual life in the history of western civilization.[75] Thirty-five years after Hus's ashes were thrown into the Rhine River, another German, several hundred miles downstream, was busy developing metal punches for movable type. They had silenced Hus and others like him, but a new invention was about to shatter Europe's darkness with an all-engulfing firestorm.

CHAPTER FOUR

The Fiery Word

Yes, it is a press . . . from which shall soon flow,
in inexhaustible streams . . . pure truth . . .;
like a new star it shall scatter the darkness of ignorance,
and cause a light heretofore unknown to shine amongst men.

JOHANN GUTENBERG

AMERICA WAS BORN OUT OF A PRINT-ORIENTED CULTURE.

The words of the German goldsmith and gemstone cutter were
prophetic. Gutenberg's contraption was instrumental in
unleashing three significant word-based movements: the
Protestant Reformation, Puritanism, and the American experiment. The printing press harnessed biblicism to a new communication technology that would place the Scriptures directly into the
hands of the people. The result was unprecedented. Gutenberg,
already familiar with the art of making metal punches, developed
engraved steel signatures for each letter of the alphabet. When the
letters were locked in a frame or "chase" and evenly inked, the
type made perfect impressions that could be repeated over and
over again. Borrowing money for the enterprise, Gutenberg published a three-volume Latin version of the Bible (1457-1458). He
did not profit financially from his invention because patents did
not exist. In a very short time others were repeating his methods

and establishing their own print shops. Although the press found its way its way to Rome in 1464, then Venice in 1469, and Paris in 1470, the Catholic Church eventually restricted its use to ward off further heresy. In 1502 all books questioning papal authority were ordered burned. While the Renaissance careened after the *image*, the Reformation became a predominantly *word*-based movement. As Neil Postman observed, the real religious fervor and intellectual power pulled to the north, so that England, Scandinavia, and Germany became the realm of the word, and the south returned to spectacle.[1] We cannot help but associate the Renaissance with great cathedrals and the visual arts that came to embellish southern France, Italy, and Spain.

The period between the fifteenth and seventeenth centuries is one of stark contrasts. As Francis Schaeffer has noted, "The High Renaissance in the south and the Reformation in the north must always be considered side by side. They dealt with the same basic problems [What is man? Who is God?], but they gave completely opposite answers and brought forth completely opposite results."[2] The Renaissance sought to revive pagan Rome. The Reformation sought to rekindle the spirit of the first-century church. Although both movements were aided by literacy, in southern Europe pagan art held as much of the public's attention as did pagan texts.

As the Renaissance gained momentum, an ecstatic mania for the past reached dizzying heights, as when in 1485 the preserved body of a Roman maiden was discovered and placed on public display in the city of Rome.[3] Thousands flocked to adore the beautiful corpse and saw in her a lost and glorious age. Inspiration was taken from Greek and Roman classics. It was not just the *words* of Cicero that inspired them; it was also his *way of life*. Villas were built again in the classical mode. Scholars pored over the old writers. Artists brought to life on canvas and in sculpture the myths of ancient antiquity. Whereas the Middle Ages made an attempt to disguise the gods in Christian garb, the Renaissance stripped off their clothes, figuratively and literally, to expose them in all their vivid colors.

[handwritten notes at top:]
1ˢᵗ CENT. CHURCH ENGLAND, SCANDINAVIA, GERMANY
REFORMATION — WORD
RENAISSANCE —IMAGE — SPECTACLE - FRANCE, ITALY, SPAIN
L PAGAN ROME PAGAN ART, PAGAN TEXTS

Donatello's bronze *David* was the first statue to disrobe (c. 1430-1432). The effeminate giant slayer with stylish hat and braided locks stands over his defeated foe with a cocked hip; his skinny arms look incapable of wielding the sword by his side. As I am not an art historian, my comments on Renaissance art should not be taken as an authoritative critique of technique or form. Without a doubt the period achieved remarkable feats in precision and realism. I do not dispute that. But it is not difficult to detect a sensual cord running through the repertoire that goes beyond the "nakedness before God" justification. What the Florentines did was breathe fresh life into older forms anxiously awaiting a full display. Antiquity's lush mythological heritage comes rushing back in Botticelli's *Primavera* (c. 1482) and *Birth of Venus* (c. 1485-1486), Bellini's *Feast of the Gods* (1514), Fiorentino's *The Daughters of Jethro* (c. 1523-1524), Correggio's *Venus, Satyr, and Cupid* (1524-1525), and Titian's *Diana and Actaeon* (c. 1559). One would be hard pressed to deny the pornographic elements in Bronzino's *Allegory of Venus and Cupid* (c. 1545) or *Woman with a Red Lily* (anonymous, c. 1540). Painters relied on secular works as much as religious ones, says David Freedberg, insomuch that one observer could not help but remark that lewd art "was oftener enquired after the shops than any other."[4]

As southern Europe flowered, the Roman Church adorned herself from the sale of indulgences. The Vatican City was majestic to behold, but inside the pontiff's palace walls the moral laxity was absolutely shocking. About the time Gutenberg released his Bible to the public, Pope Pius II wrote a stinging letter to the future pope, Cardinal Rodrigo Borgia. In his book *The Bad Popes*, E. R. Chamberlin says it was rumored that the cardinal had engaged in "the most licentious dances" with several ladies of Siena and that "none of the allurements of love were lacking." "Our displeasure is beyond all words," complained the pope. "A cardinal should be beyond reproach."[5] The advice had little effect. When Borgia (Pope Alexander VI, 1431-1503) donned the papal hat, he carried his wild parties right into the Vatican. One must remember this was an unprecedented time of pomp and pageantry, plotting and nepotistic politics for the Holy See. The parties were just part of the package. "As guests approached the papal palace," says William Manchester, "they were excited by the spectacle of living statues: naked and gilded young men and women in erotic poses."[6] What took place inside is unspeakable. Alexander's debauchery—the greed, the murders, the orgies, the incest, the unbridled lust that history credits him with—was but an imitation of the life of a Roman emperor. His life is an example of the Renaissance's feverish nostalgia for the pagan past, best summed up in the Augustinian assessment, "No law, no divinity; Gold, force and Venus rule."

The general population took their cue from the Vatican. Extramarital affairs among the nobility were considered obligatory. Morals were lax among the young. Convents were impregnated with scandals. The priesthood was despised. Conditions were so dissolute that one chronicler was made to remark, "Sodomy was frequent . . . prostitution was general, and adultery was almost universal."[7] Girolamo Savonarola could not help but notice the great disparity between this kind of behavior and the moral standards found in the Bible. The Dominican monk who later came to rule Florence attempted to reform the corrupt morals of the city, but the citizens could only endure him for four years. In 1498 he was excommunicated, imprisoned, and then burnt at the stake by Pope Alexander VI.

Since Vatican pomp needed a constant flow of income, everyone within Rome's reach paid papal taxes. However, indulgences were the favorite source of ecclesiastical revenue. In 1479 Pope Sixtus extended indulgences to rescue those in intermediate torment. The peasants were the most vulnerable. Church historian David Schaff remarks that some of the poor starved themselves and their families to get relatives out of purgatory.[8] At least the peasants found some relief in 1517 when Pope Leo, broke after a religious war, put indulgences on sale so he could rebuild St. Peter's basilica. Johann Tetzel, a Dominican friar (and a great salesman), was chosen to promote the grand event.[9] When Tetzel entered a village, church bells rang out and a crowd gathered. As the propagator walked through the center of town, priests, prominent citizens, jugglers, singers, and enthusiasts waving banners, relics, and candles formed a procession behind him. Reaching into a bag he pulled out and held up a receipt. "I have here the passports," he barked, "to lead the human soul to the celestial joys of Paradise." His pitch promised not only to absolve past sins but future ones as well—a kind of "buy one, get one free" deal. The rhetoric got stronger. "Think of your mother, tormented by the flames of purgatory, suffering because you, who might release her with one penny. Ah, woe to your ingratitude!" And, "As soon as the coin rings in the bowl, the soul for whom it is paid will fly out of purgatory and straight to heaven." It was the bargain of the millennium. Because of Frederick the Wise's reluctance to go along with this particular sale, Tetzel was forbidden to cross the boundary of Saxony. He got too close.

THE GREAT STIR

Some of the Saxons crossed over the border and bought indulgences from Tetzel. Several of these purchasers carried their receipts to a devout professor at Wittenberg to judge their authenticity. The professor, Martin Luther (1483-1546), pronounced them as frauds. The tonsured monk then posted his Ninety-five Theses against indulgences on the door of the Castle Church at Wittenberg. Luther's anger had been brewing for some time. His study of the Bible had revealed to him that trust in God alone was sufficient for salvation, and not good works; that "the just shall live by faith." Luther's visit to Rome seven years earlier must have helped him form strong opinions about the Vatican. For example, he could not help but notice that the closer he got to the Holy City, the more unholy things appeared. While at the papal court he was quite astonished to be served supper by "twelve naked girls."[10] This makes one pause and think. Luther later remarked, "If there is a hell, Rome is built over it." He quietly handed over his theses to a local printer. The match had been struck. As Elizabeth Eisenstein notes in *The Printing Revolution in Early Modern Europe*, "Luther had invited a public disputation and nobody had come to dispute. Then by a stroke of magic he found himself addressing the world."[11]

The story of the Protestant Reformation is a story of how printers and booksellers were enlisted to bypass the priests and place the gospel message directly into the hands of the public. The process of reform now transpired at speeds unknown before Gutenberg's invention. Luther's denunciations were said to have been known throughout Germany in a fortnight and throughout Europe in a month.[12] Since copyright laws were unknown, Luther's work was often reprinted by unauthorized presses. This "wildcat printing" helped create a new market for religious literature. Congregants would even scribble down Luther's sermons and sell them to enterprising printers. Luther was surprised when in 1519, after he had preached a sermon on matrimony, copies of it came back to him, not exactly as he had delivered it, from Breslau, a hundred miles away. Luther complained, "I beg all who are down there committing my sermons to paper or memory not to print them until they have my own draft, or until I have myself had them printed here in Wittenberg."[13]

"Luther's books are everywhere and in every language," wrote the Renaissance humanist Erasmus just four years after the theses; "no one would believe how widely he has moved men."[14] Luther had little concern that printers were profiting from the volumes of writing flowing from his pen. The Gospel was being driven forward. Between 1517 and 1520, Luther's thirty publications probably sold well over 300,000 copies.[15] The literature coming out of Germany was printed increasingly in the common language. S. H. Steinberg says in *Five Hundred Years of Printing* that in the year Luther published his theses (1517), Germany put out forty books in the German language; in 1519 that number jumped to 111; in 1521, it climbed to 211; in 1522, 347; in 1525, 498. Of the last year cited, 183 were publications of Luther and 215 by other reformers, leaving only twenty anti-reformation books and about eighty vernacular books on secular subjects. In other words, seven years after Luther's initial protest, book publishing in Germany had dramatically increased; and 80 percent of the vernacular books were pro-reformation in content.[16] While at Wartburg, Luther worked on translating the Bible from the original Greek and Hebrew into German, so that a complete German Bible was ready for the press in 1534. Daniel Defoe, the author who gave us the narrative of a man alone with the Scriptures (*Robinson Crusoe*), would later come to write, "The preaching of sermons is speaking to a few of mankind [but] printing books is talking to the whole world."[17] Both Erasmus and Defoe rejoiced in the new "Apostolate of the pen"— a phrase assigned to the *printed word's* making its presence known in Europe to accomplish the church's mission.

Each reformer had his sphere of influence. Although Erasmus (1466?-1536) cannot be considered a reformer in the strict sense of the word because he remained an orthodox Catholic all of his life, he nevertheless made several significant contributions to the Protestant movement. He was first and foremost a scholar and once declared, "My home is where I have my library." Since Henry VIII wanted Erasmus's home to be in England, the monarch invited him to the royal court to exercise his pen. It was probably a wise move for Erasmus because what he came to write would have no doubt kindled a bonfire in his behalf. His "Colloquies" were forbidden in classrooms by the pope—any teacher found using it was to be executed on the spot. Erasmus found both the will and wit to release many fiery arrows into the Vatican's side. For example, in a dialogue antagonistic toward Pope Julius II he put these words into the mouth of the apostle Peter: "If Satan needed a vicar he could find none fitter than you. . . . Fraud, usury, and cunning made you pope. . . . I brought heathen Rome to acknowledge Christ: and you have made it heathen again." Unlike Luther who received absolutely nothing from his publications, Erasmus actively made agreements with publishers, receiving fees, individual gifts, and annual pensions for his efforts. He edited the first printed copy of the Greek New Testament (1516) and urged that it should be translated in all vernacular languages. This was Erasmus's most important contribution to the Reformation because it became the primary source for translations by Martin Luther and William Tyndale.

What Luther did for Germany, William Tyndale (1492-1536) did for England. Tyndale was the first to translate and publish a mechanically-printed New Testament in the English language. While a student at Oxford and Cambridge, he became disturbed over the theological shallowness of the universities: "In the universities they have ordained that no man shall look on the Scripture until he be noselled in heathen learning eight or nine years, and armed with false principles with which he is clean shut out of the understanding of the Scripture."[18] Echoing Erasmus's preface to the Greek New Testament printed five years earlier, Tyndale vented his frustration on a cleric: "If God spare my life, ere many years pass, I will cause a boy that driveth the plough shall know more of the Scriptures than dost." Providing an English translation of the Bible was no easy matter. Fearing the Lollards, the Catholic Church had established a law in 1408 forbidding vernacular translations. Anyone suspected of being a follower of Wycliffe's teachings faced the death penalty, as in the case of Thomas Norris, who one day asked the wrong questions to his parish priest. *Foxe's Book of Martyrs* tells how the "poor and harmless" man was reported to the bishop, arrested, condemned, and burned alive.[19]

Tyndale was forced to produce his translation in Germany, where it was printed and then smuggled into England. Few copies of Tyndale's early editions survive because the bishops burnt them as soon as they were found. The archbishop of Canterbury tried to buy up as many copies as he could and thereby unknowingly provided the financing of more editions. Betrayed by a fellow Englishman in 1535, Tyndale was confined for a year and a half and then burned at the stake. His dying words were said to have been, "Lord, open the king of England's eyes." Three years later vernacular Bibles sat in every parish church in England. Henry VIII was persuaded to approve the publication of the Coverdale Bible, a translation heavily dependent on Tyndale's. "The tortuous policy of Henry VIII illustrates rather well the half-Catholic, half-Protestant position of the schismatic Tudor king," writes Eisenstein. "But if one wanted to keep English Bibles from lay readers, it was probably unwise to tantalize congregations by letting them hear a chapter per week. Appetites are usually whetted by being told about forbidden fruit."[20] As the flame of protest swept across the island, English translations reached a climax with the publication of the King James Bible. Although a team of fifty scholars worked on the project for seven years, 90 percent of Tyndale's wordings found their way into the authorized text. "In doing this," says a recent Tyndale biographer, "he made a language for England."[21]

The printing press was the mechanical engine that drove the Protestant Reformation. In turn, the Protestant Reformation was the impetus for the spread of literacy and education. The Reformers understood that their movement could not be sustained without widespread literacy. This is why Luther pushed for the establishment of public schools in Germany for both boys and girls as early as 1524. He later extended his arguments for education in a sermon entitled "That Children Should Be Sent to School." The sermon (at least three hours long if preached) emphasized the community's dependence on the learned professions (pastors, preachers, and teachers) to maintain a moral and stable society. "Who rules the land and its people in peacetime?" asked Luther, "Why, I say it is the quill."

There is an old saying that goes, "Erasmus laid the egg of the Reformation, but Luther hatched it." I would only add to this that it was John Calvin (1509-1564) who cooked the egg and served it to Europe and the New World. Calvin profoundly shaped the Reformation, influencing the likes of John Bunyan, George Whitefield, Jonathan Edwards, and Charles Haddon Spurgeon. The Enlightenment philosopher Voltaire called Calvin "the Pope of the Protestants." Like all of the Reformers, Calvin was a scholar whose evangelical faith was deepened by his study of the Bible in the original languages. Calvin was not asked to be the pastor of Geneva because of any outward charisma he possessed (he was really quite a frail individual). Guillaume Farel begged him to take up the pulpit because he saw in him an intense intellect as revealed in his *Institutes of Christian Religion*.

Geneva was a microcosm of what a Christian society could be if the Bible alone was held out as the sole determinant of faith and civil governance. Like Luther, Calvin believed in public education for the young. The Genevan school system was established in 1541 complete with headmasters and secondary and elementary teachers. Unlike Luther, Calvin wanted to keep civil and church authority separate. His belief in church democracy set a pattern for states to later imitate. His notion that tyrants should be resisted under certain circumstances would prove to be revolutionary. These distinctions make Calvin one of the fathers of modern democracy. Thousands of Protestants fleeing persecution throughout Europe made Geneva their refuge. The city became an incubator of learning—a model to emulate. John Knox (1513?-1572) wrote that Geneva was the "most perfect school of Christ that ever was in the earth since the days of the Apostles." Knox took Calvin's theology and political ideas back to Scotland and started a reformation of his own, as did others. In this way Calvin sowed the seeds of both religious and political reform. John Locke (1632-1704) would later build on Calvin's political philosophy by stressing the familiar principles of inalienable rights, government by consent, separation of powers, and the right of revolution.

As Eisenstein has shown, the printing press can be credited with facilitating six major revolutions—fundamentalism, nationalism, democracy, exploration, modern science, and higher scholarship. Putting the Bible in the vernacular promoted literal fundamentalism and nationalism. Printing lowered the cost of books, enabling the literate to read for themselves the very words of God. The emergence of rigid "pulpit rule books" helped to kill off flexible medieval Latin speech, and published sermons continued to live long after the preacher had gone to his grave.[22] Vernacular Bibles gave countries rich vocabularies and a common language to call their own. Both Protestantism and printing promoted antiestablishmentarianism and an incipient pro-democratic attitude. Exploration was enhanced with large-scale data collection and the cross-cultural exchange of maps, charts, and ships' logs. Modern science was born, and the "sorcerer who exploited fear of the unknown eventually became the charlatan who exploited mere ignorance."[23] Printing fostered individualized learning, intense cross-referencing between books, systematized scholarship, increased disciplines, and a general knowledge explosion. All these movements were streams flowing into the swelling river of the modern age—waters that would soon flow into the great Industrial Revolution of the eighteenth and nineteenth centuries. Marshall McLuhan put it this way: "The invention of typography confirmed and extended the new visual stress of applied knowledge, providing the first uniformly repeatable commodity, the first assembly-line, and the first mass production."[24]

THE PURITANS

Black-smocked. Tight-lipped. Condescending. Intolerant. Unhappy. These are the words that come to mind when some hear the word *Puritan*. H. L. Mencken once said, "Puritanism is the haunting fear that someone, somewhere, may be happy." In truth, one person's happiness often can be another person's misery. This must be the reason why the Puritans were banished to freaky land over a century ago. Room had to be made for a more permissive social order to take hold. If one can get beyond the modern stereotype to the actual facts of history, the Puritans look less like the monsters the morally paranoid make them out to be and more like real people. In his book *Worldly Saints*, Leland Ryken says the *real* Puritans were highly educated, joyful, athletic, balanced, vibrant, affectionate, and much of the time colorful dressers.[25] Yes, they led regimented lives, but it was from them that we inherited our work ethic. We cannot afford to hate the Puritans without hating ourselves. If it can be said that American democracy got off on a good foot (and I think it can), we must acknowledge that the foot was a Puritan foot. When America declared her independence in 1776, as much as 75 percent of the revolutionary dissent came from a Puritan heritage.[26] Our leaves, our branches, our trunk go back to Puritan roots established in the New England soil. The American character was to a great extent shaped by Puritan piety and Puritan intelligence.

According to Martyn Lloyd-Jones, it was Tyndale's English translation of the Bible that fired the first shot of Puritanism across the bow of Anglicanism.[27] Tyndale's willingness to circumvent established authority in order to obey a higher authority expressed the Puritan ideal. Truth was placed before civil authority or church tradition. Puritanism was an attempt to "purify" the Church of England of all Catholic elements and return to the simplicity of the New Testament. The Puritan practice of not allowing musical instruments or paintings inside their sanctuaries have led critics to see them as hostile to the arts. However, what they objected to was not music or art per se (organs and portraits could be found in their homes), but the paganism and pomp of Romish worship.

As most of us learned in school, the Reformers who wanted to change the Church of England and still remain a part of it were called Puritans. Those who thought the Church was beyond reform and therefore left it altogether were called Separatists (e.g., the Pilgrims). Efforts to reform the Church of England proved futile, and many Puritans concluded that the only way to carry out their faith was to migrate to America. In 1630 John Winthrop (1588-1649) called the Massachusetts Bay Colony a "city on a hill," the implication being that all of Europe was watching the Puritan experiment.

For the Puritan, "carrying out the faith" meant being literate. "Ignorance," said Cotton Mather, "is the mother of HERESY."[28] And because children were born ignorant and evil, literacy was the means to salvation and the knowledge of God. Today the primary motivation to teach reading and writing in the schools is economic, education equaling job security, but this was not the case with the Puritans, who believed Satan's "chief project" was to keep men from the Scriptures. In 1642 Massachusetts enacted a law requiring masters of families to instruct their children and apprentices how to read. The law attached a penalty of twenty shillings for noncompliance. Five years later the colony required townships with fifty households to financially support one individual to teach children to read and write. Townships with one hundred households were required to set up a grammar school to prepare boys for the university.

Measures like these dramatically drove up literacy rates. From the mid-seventeenth century to the end of the eighteenth century, says James Hart, Massachusetts and Connecticut achieved male literacy rates as high as 95 percent, and the literacy rate for women was perhaps as high as 62 percent in the years between 1681 and 1697.[29] Kenneth Lockridge claims in his book *Literacy in Colonial New England* that the chief motivation for the great leaps in literacy was not economic but religious. Lockridge documents that when a vigorous Protestantism was not connected with compulsory education, as in the case of England and the southern colonies in the seventeenth century, literacy rates rarely climbed above 50 percent. On the other hand, in Protestant countries like Scotland and Sweden, where compulsory education was later implemented, male literacy rates came to match those of late seventeenth-century New England.[30] Lockridge concludes that it was a vibrant Protestantism that drove up literacy rates in New England:

> This [Puritan New England] was essentially a world of the past, in which a form of Protestantism was the sole force sufficient to generate high-level change in literacy . . . prior to the mid-nineteenth century the Protestant religion and its associated schools were the prime forces involved in raising literacy, while the enticements or demands of economic and social change had little impact.[31]

That the chief motivation behind teaching colonists to read was religious rather than economic is amply illustrated in the relations between the Puritans and the New England Indians. Alden Vaughan says the natives were not seen as foes to be rooted out or conquered, but as original occupants to deal with fairly.[32] Vaughan argues that the Puritans never attempted to force their views on the Indians, and when evangelism occurred, it was always done through soft, noncoercive persuasion. The conversion of the Indians was one of the stated justifications for establishing American colonies from the beginning, especially with the Puritans. Unlike the Jesuit missionaries before them, the New England colonists were not content to sprinkle water on heathen heads, raise a flag in the village, and proclaim it Christianized. The Puritans sought nothing less than a full conversion experience and a substantive knowledge of the Bible. One could not be a communicant otherwise. Therefore, literacy was a tool of evangelism. A superficial conversion was worthless, said Roger Williams in a pamphlet entitled, "Christenings make not Christians, A Briefe Discourse concerning that name Heathen, commonly given to the Indians." In the pamphlet, Williams asserted that the Indians were no more heathen than most Europeans.

It should be said that some New Englanders were more zealous at winning the Indians to Christ than others, John Eliot being the most noteworthy because of his translation and subsequent publication of the Bible into the Algonquian language (1663). But no one should accuse the Puritans of being indifferent to the physical, moral, and spiritual well-being of the natives. Because the spreading of the Gospel and education were mutual endeavors, the colonists established schools for the Indians in their own "praying towns," opened the village grammar schools to their youth, and instituted a college for them at Harvard.[33]

While efforts to educate the native Indians should be applauded, the Puritans put a great deal more energy into the education of their own children. It was the parents' duty by law to see that their children learn how to read. This could be done either at an elementary dame school (a woman teaching reading and writing in her own home), at a private school, or at home by the parents. Once a son mastered the *New England Primer* and Bible reading, he could then go on to "writing school." (Little provision was made to educate girls outside the home, but a good number learned how to read under the tutelage of literate parents.) If a family wanted to send their son to the university, then he went on to grammar school at age seven or eight. Here he read the classics, honed his writing skills, became proficient in Latin, and was introduced to Greek. In seven years he was ready for college.

Of America's first college, Cotton Mather (1662-1727) declared, "[It was] the best thing that ever New England thought upon."[34] The Puritans must have been thinking about it for a long time. Six years after they set foot in the New World, the money was appropriated for the building of Harvard. The account is etched in the record:

> After God had carried us safely to New England, and we had built our houses, provided necessaries for our livelihood, reared convenient places for God's worship, and settled the civil government; one of the next things we longed for, and looked after was to advance learning, and perpetuate it to posterity; dreading to leave an illiterate ministry to the churches, when our present ministries shall lie in the dust.

The quote reveals a great deal about the Puritans. First, it demonstrates that education was ranked along with food, shelter, worship, and government in their hierarchy of needs. Second, it suggests that the New England colonists were looking down a long road, that they were building a society for the future. Third, it shows their utter disgust for stupid clergy. The Puritans were sometimes criticized by other Protestants for being too smart for their own good. For example, the antinomians believed preaching was more of a matter of opening the mouth and letting the Spirit fill it. "I had rather hear such a one that speaks from the mere motion of the spirit, without study at all, than any of your learned scholars," complained one antinomian. A Puritan would counter, "I deny not but a man may have much knowledge and want of grace, but on the other side, . . . you cannot have more grace than you have knowledge."[35] Unlike the antinomians, the Puritans did not see faith and reason as antagonists. This is why Harvard's first college laws required students not only to read the Scriptures twice a day, but to be able to resolve them logically. Subjects at Harvard not only included the Bible and the ability to parse it in the original languages, but a student also studied mathematics, astronomy, physics, botany, chemistry, philosophy, poetry, history, and medicine. The desire for a broad education in the liberal arts tradition was an influence from Luther and Calvin. The person fit for everything was a Puritan ideal.

Toward the end of the seventeenth century Puritanism lost its religious vitality. Increase Mather lamented from a Boston pulpit in 1702, "You that are aged and can remember what New England was fifty years ago, that saw these churches in their first glory, is there not a sad decay and diminution of that glory! How is the gold become dim!"[36] The reason this happened can be attributed to three factors. First, distinctions between the converted and the unconverted were blurred. In 1630 only professing believers were allowed to be church members, but by the 1660s baptized infants of second-generation parents grew up and failed to tell of their conversion experience and were therefore denied membership. Then when these non-communicants brought *their* children to the altar for baptism, a compromise was made. The "Half-Way Covenant" in effect made qualifications for church membership as broad as possible, allowing non-professors entrance into the fellowship. The Puritan John Owen credited this practice to the ruination of previous religious vigor: "The letting go this principle, particular churches ought to consist of regenerate persons, brought in the great apostasy of the Christian Church."[37]

But there are two additional reasons for the waning. As New England prospered economically, materialism began to dull the spiritual senses. Iain Murray notes the change of attitude in Northampton during the 1730s: "With the more peaceful years of the eighteenth century, and the corresponding weakening of any danger to their corporate survival, townsmen became more likely to be motivated by individual interests and ambitions."[38] Finally, Enlightenment thinking in Europe began to find its way into places like Harvard. Yale was started because of concerns that America's first college was losing its spiritual vitality.

The baton of the Reformation might have been dropped altogether had it not been for a spiritual shaking that occurred at mid-eighteenth century. The Great Awakening was as much of an attempt to return to the glory days of the early 1600s as it was a flash of lightning out of the blue. As Murray explains, the New-Light preaching was an "earnest re-statement of the older Puritan teaching on the need for men first to be humbled if they are to be soundly converted."[39]

The Awakening cannot be properly understood without some remarks about the man who helped start it. Jonathan Edwards (1703-1758) is commonly associated with his sermon, "Sinners in the Hands of an Angry God." Few remember him as a giant intellect and perhaps America's best philosopher-theologian. Never one to waste his time, while a student and later a tutor at Yale, he entertained himself by compiling notebooks with entries like, "Place of Minds," "Space," "Thought," and "Existence." Edwards was just as comfortable in the domain of natural science as he was in that of moral philosophy, possessing a remarkable ability to relate aspects of nature to spiritual truth. The same man who preached, "The God that holds you over the pit of hell, much as one holds a spider" (actually only a small percentage of Edward's sermons are of this ilk) also wrote, "Pardon me if I thought it might at least give you occasion to make better observations on these wondrous animals . . . from whose glistening webs so much of the wisdom of the Creator shines."[40]

Edwards, says Murray, spent thirteen hours a day in his study. In sermon preparation, careful attention was made to "shadings of diction, choice of metaphors, and allusions."[41] But there is little evidence that he "read" his sermons in the pulpit.[42] During his daily woodland rides, he made it a practice to record his thoughts on little bits of paper, which he pinned to his coat, later to be picked off by his wife, Sarah. Always the spiritual scientist, Edwards not only helped kindle the flames of the Awakening but devoted himself to explaining the source, nature, and effects of the flames in a series of popular publications: *Narrative of Surprising Conversions* (1737), *The Distinguishing Marks of a Work of the Spirit of God* (1741), *Thoughts on the Revival* (1742), and *Religious Affections* (1746).

Of course, Edwards was not alone in spreading the revival; nevertheless, Puritan scholar Harry Stout says he was the primary tone-setter for pulpit discourse during the period.[43] And what was that tone? It was the tone of Luther, the tone of Calvin, the tone of Knox, and the tone of his grandfather, Solomon Stoddard, who said, "We are not sent into the pulpit to show our wit and our eloquence, but to set the consciences of men on fire."[44] Martyn Lloyd-Jones called this the "Logic of fire!"[45] All Puritan preaching was logical and aimed for the head, but Edwards and the New-Lights bent their bow and made ready their arrow at the human heart. The average Puritan sermon was one and a half hours long and required immense demands on the intellect. Fortunately, most of the listeners were literate and therefore fully capable of grasping its content, some even taking notes, says Ryken, for later meditation or for family devotional material.[46]

If members of the audience were incapable of taking notes, it was only because they were under a heavy burden of sin-guilt, which was probably the case most of the time when listening to George Whitefield (1714-1770), whose preaching Ben Franklin said could reach an audience of thirty thousand and be heard at a "great distance." It was not unusual for audience members to shriek or faint during the closing years of the Awakening, giving opportunity for the Old-Lights (ministers who opposed the likes of Edwards and Whitefield) to criticize the movement as mere emotionalism. And this is where Edwards's writings played such an important role.

Edwards's pen was wielded as a two-edged sword in a public word war over the nature of the human condition. One side of the blade sought to legitimize the Holy Spirit's work in the revival while acknowledging the potential for counterfeit emotionalism wrought by the flesh. To use a trite phrase, he saw no need to throw the baby out with the bathwater. In *Religious Affections* Edwards made a distinction between the "affections," which he said stemmed from the mind or the soul but were redirected after conversion, and "passions," which were "sudden actions" whose effects on the body were "more violent." "Holy affections" not only belonged to true religion but were an essential part of it.[47]

Edwards wielded the other side of his sword at Enlightenment thinking by insisting that man's will was bent toward doing evil unless divinely changed from within. This was a reassertion of Puritan theological principles. While Edwards believed humans were highly rational creatures, human reasoning was insufficient without the guidance of revelation. In the long run, the notion that man is "totally depraved" would become instrumental to the Founding Fathers' adoption of a three-branch system of government, so that if one branch became corrupted, the other two branches might be able to check the abuse.

The Great Awakening set the stage for America's entrance into the world as a free nation in several ways.[48] First, it transferred the clerical power of Old- and New-Light alike into the hands of the laity. Stout says:

> In the process the clergy could not fully understand, their legacy of regular preaching had not failed the fourth generation but had succeeded too well in inculcating a popular culture of the Word in which ordinary men and women were able to formulate theological opinions, defend them from Scripture, record them in their own words, and express them publicly in religious meetings.[49]

Second, the revival built up other denominations. When converts left the fields where Whitefield preached, they not only returned to Congregational and Anglican churches, but they also swelled the Presbyterian, Baptist, and Quaker ranks. Third, the revival gave a needed boost to educational and missionary endeavors. At least six new colleges were started as a result of the Awakening: Princeton, Dartmouth, King's College (Columbia University), Queen's College (Rutgers University), William and Mary, and Brown University. Finally, the spiritual renewal helped prepare the colonies for the Revolution and the subsequent founding of a new government. There was a new desire for both religious and political reform. The Great Awakening had reached back to the first Puritans who had reached back to Calvin and Luther before them. It was this Reformation spirit that electrified pulpits with "revolutionary rhetoric," making it an easy matter to accept republican democracy over monarchial tyranny. "In these terms," says Stout, "the Revolutionary generation had more in common with their theocratic and aristocratic Puritan forebears than with the pagan 'republicans' of ancient Greece and Rome."[50] So we have Peter Muhlenburg in 1774 standing before his Virginia congregation after returning from a stirring speech delivered by Patrick Henry. Muhlenburg quotes from the book of Ecclesiastes: "To every thing there is a season, and a time to every purpose under heaven . . . a time of war, and a time of peace." After this, the good pastor casts off his clerical robes to reveal a militia uniform.

THE AMERICAN EXPERIMENT

Compared to the darkness of medieval Europe, the type of society that emerged in America toward the end of the eighteenth century was one of intense religious and political vibrancy. The intensity was not just a matter of nation-building, although that was part of it. But there also existed a "terrain" by which the exchange of ideas were acutely made aware to the public at large for the vital purpose of deliberation—civil deliberation—that uniquely distinguishing feature of democracy that places ideas on the table of public inspection to be analyzed, criticized, refuted, rejected, and endorsed. (The antithesis to deliberation would be a type of blind obedience to an authoritarian government.) The "terrain" I am referring to might also be called the "information environment," as discussed in Neil Postman's book *Teaching as a Conserving Activity*. Just as we all live in a physical environment that determines the air we breathe, the water we drink, and the food we eat, the information environment directs our ideas, social attitudes, definitions of knowledge, and intellectual capacities.[51] The Dark Ages were "dark" because they lacked the necessary information systems conducive to democracy—namely, literacy, a printing press for serious public discourse, a passionate desire to deliberate, and the freedom to exercise all of the above. America was born at the moment she possessed all of these features while at the same time being plugged into an agreed upon directive of biblical moral virtue derived from the Word. It is this information environment that demands our attention, not only because it was the root of our wonderful appearing, but also because the disappearance of such an environment throws the American experiment into great jeopardy.

Two important factors played a role in shaping colonial America—education and the existing media of the day. In the late eighteenth century, the cracks had not yet fully formed between Puritan pietism and Enlightenment philosophy that would later become great fixed gulfs. Before the Revolution all colleges were private and sectarian. How easily one forgets that our system of higher education had its roots in American Protestantism, that 106 of the first 108 colleges were distinctly Christian. It was while the First Amendment was being debated that the Northwest Ordinance was passed, requiring all new states entering the Union to have educational systems in place emphasizing the teaching of both religion and morality.

There were other motivations, in addition to religious ones, to pursue an education. In *American Education: The Colonial Experience (1607-1783)* Lawrence Cremin says that after the Stamp Crisis of the 1760s, "a premium was placed on literacy in segments of the population where illiteracy had long been a stigma. In the process, the pressure for schooling mounted."[52] The pressure would continue to mount right up through the Constitutional debates in 1787 and 1788. Higher education was a means of preparing for the ministry, but schools were also increasingly sought out because of economic and political reasons. Education was the ticket to personal advancement and the door to participation in public affairs. One might choose to be a minister of the Gospel or a minister of the law, and both were considered to be honorable professions. James Madison was pulled between the pulpit and the statehouse in regard to his future profession because he felt, like so many of his contemporaries, that something unique was taking place in the country, something that had never happened before. John Adams wrote to George Wythe in 1776, "You and I, my dear friend, have been sent into life at a time when the greatest lawgivers of antiquity would have wished

to live. How few of the human race have ever enjoyed an opportunity of making an election of government, more than of air, soil,
or climate, for themselves or their children!"[53]

The information environment of early America created an
extraordinary gallery of men whom we refer to as the Founding
Fathers. Space does not permit a discussion of the depth of knowledge most of these individuals possessed (most of them wrote any-
where between five and twenty-five books), so several examples
will have to suffice.[54] John Witherspoon (1723-1794) stands at
the head of the class, not only because he served as the president
of Princeton during the Revolutionary period, but because the
clergyman-educator trained at least eighty-seven of the Founding
Fathers. His portfolio includes one President, one Vice-President,
three Supreme Court justices, ten cabinet members, twelve governors, and thirty-nine congressmen. Witherspoon brought the
principles of Samuel Rutherford's *Lex Rex* to bear on the writing
of the Constitution. The assertion that "Law is King" challenged
Europe's tradition of the divine right of kings by asserting that a
government of law should be submitted to rather than the arbitrary whims of men.

While Witherspoon gave us men who shaped the nation,
Noah Webster's (1758-1843) *Spelling Book* gave us the words
that shaped the language of the nation. His speller sold some
twenty-four million copies between 1783 and 1843.[55] It standardized spelling in the United States and remained the standard
in the schools for a hundred and fifty years. Webster, who was
among the first to call for the Constitutional Convention, saw
Christianity as the bedrock of American democracy. In his *History
of the United States*, Webster wrote, "[O]ur citizens should early
understand that the genuine source of correct republican principles is the Bible, particularly the New Testament, or the Christian
religion."[56]

Helping Webster with his dictionary was John Trumbull
(1710-1785), the only colonial governor to serve from the start to
the finish of the Revolution. Trumbull was a product of the New
England educational system in Connecticut. At the age of four he

had already read through the Bible. At the age of six he won a
Greek contest by beating out a local minister. And at the age of
seven he passed his entrance exam to Yale. (They held him back
until he turned thirteen.) One might think that such educational
achievements were the exception rather than the rule. But then
there was John Quincy Adams (1767-1848), who at the ripe old
age of fourteen received a U.S. Congressional diplomatic appointment overseas to the court of Catherine the Great.

Then one cannot forget about Benjamin Franklin (1706-
1790), who at the age of sixteen fancied himself enough to try his
hand at writing for his brother's newspaper. "[B]eing still a boy,
and suspecting that my brother would object to printing any thing
of mine in his paper if he knew it to be mine," says Franklin in his
autobiography, "I contrived to disguise my hand, and, writing an
anonymous paper, I put it in at night, under the door of the printing house."[57] Franklin's pieces ran for six months and were considered to be more witty and better written than the other
contributors'. Franklin escaped from his jealous brother and
moved to Philadelphia to start his own newspaper. He was so successful at the printing business that he was able to retire at forty-
two to pursue other endeavors. There is a narrative painting
depicting a middle-aged Franklin standing on the steps of his print
shop conversing with a patron over the cost or content of some
books. What is most interesting about the painting is a colonial
lady who is standing behind the patron reading an open book.
The point is clear. Women in the mid-eighteenth century were as
interested in printed material as their male counterparts. The
scene captures the emergence of a new social phenomenon—a
reading public that spent much of its spare time consuming
printed sermons, pamphlets, newspapers, and books. Franklin
was many things (inventor, diplomat, nation-framer), but he
remained a printer at heart. For his own epitaph he wrote, "The
Body of Benjamin Franklin, Printer, (like the cover of an old Book,
its contents worn out, and stript of its lettering and gilding) lies
here, food for worms! Yet the work itself shall not be lost, for it
will, as he believed, appear once more in a new and more beauti-

ful edition, corrected and amended by its Author."[58] That Franklin would compare his life to a worn-out book is an indication that the book was a powerful metaphor in the early American conscience.

America was born out of a print-oriented culture. Newspapers, pamphlets, and books played a major role in our independence and in the ratification of our founding documents. After 1750 the number of existing newspapers in the colonies exploded from twelve to forty-eight in twenty-five years.[59] The Stamp Act had the effect of transforming the newspapers into an extension of the Patriot movement. David Ramsay, one of the earliest historians of the war, wrote, "In establishing American independence, the pen and the press had a merit equal to that of the sword."[60] After the Revolution, newspapers were the major vehicles of public conversation. The partisan press, as it is sometimes called, aligned itself with political parties in much the same way that Rush Limbaugh aligns himself with Republicans. The partisan press served a valuable purpose for the country because it allowed for a diverse spectrum of discourse when we most needed it. And people took the debates seriously. In the same manner, pamphlets provided a necessary forum to express ideological and constitutional positions to justify the rebellion and later the adoption of the U.S. Constitution. A literate, informed, and engaged populace was believed to be a primary safeguard to democracy. In 1787 Thomas Jefferson wrote to a friend, "I should mean that every man should receive those papers [newspapers free from government control], and be capable of *reading* them."[61]

Books also flourished. Benjamin Franklin started the first "circulating library" in 1731, and it served as a model for others to copy. A steep fee was usually required for membership, says Hart; yet the demand for books was so high that poorer folks would pay their fees in grain, butter, and flax.[62] America's great trinity of school books consisted of *The New England Primer*, Webster's *Speller*, and McGuffey's *Readers*. At one time a Boston bookseller stocked nearly five hundred copies of the *Primer*, "all of which were read, dog-eared, and shredded out of existence by successive students, so that fewer than 1,500 copies remain of the six to eight million."[63] The eighteenth century also witnessed the popularization of the novel. Although fiction was considered by some to soften the intellect, novels like Samuel Richardson's *Pamela* and Hannah Webster Foster's *Coquette* were favorites among women.

The information environment existing at the brink of the nation's birth continued to strengthen in the nineteenth century. Early Americans possessed what Postman calls a "typographic mind," that is, a mind shaped by the habit of reading. Having submitted to the "sovereignty of the printing press," the typographic mind had "a sophisticated ability to think conceptually, deductively and sequentially; a high valuation of reason and order; an abhorrence of contradiction; a large capacity for detachment and objectivity; and a tolerance for delayed response."[64] One might argue that Americans today have more books and newspapers than in 1776, which is absolutely true. However, there is a difference between having books or newspapers and actually wanting to read them. Early Americans did not have "competing" media (radio, movies, television, the Internet). Most of what they saw were black words on a white page. Therefore, the mind grew accustomed to exercising linear logic to process information. The product—the fruit—of all this was a sharpened ability to reflect on what was read, detect error, and perceive the consistency of an argument. In turn, the level of public discourse became highly sophisticated. The *Federalist Papers* were written for the common upstate New York farmer of 1787, says David Barton, but today some law students cannot even fathom these essays because they are too "complex."[65]

The U.S. Constitution is the grand culmination of three hundred years of Reformation thought refined through the emergence of a print-oriented culture. What the Founding Fathers gave us was a constitutional republic as opposed to a direct democracy. The framers wanted a rule of *law*, not a rule of *passion* by the majority. They fully understood that national perpetuity and stability were dependent on unchanging, transcendent laws derived from the Scriptures. "So, to the extent to which the biblical teaching is practiced," says Schaeffer, "one can control the despotism of the majority vote or the despotism of one person or group."[66] In their wisdom, the Founders left room to amend the Constitution as needed. But they also assumed that citizens would and *could* pay attention—pay attention to public debate, pay attention to logical versus emotional appeals, pay attention to *words*. Despite their wisdom, they did not foresee an age in which moving pictures would come to subvert the written word.

The Big
Shift

VICTORIAN
1830 - 1910

CHAPTER FIVE

Something in the Air

What hath God wrought?

SAMUEL MORSE ON THE OPENING OF THE NATION'S
FIRST TELEGRAPHIC LINE (1844)

Something was in the air. Something was happening,
about to happen.[1]

FLOYD DELL OF *THE MASSES* AT THE BEGINNING OF THE
NINETEENTH CENTURY

AS THE INDUSTRIAL REVOLUTION TRANSFORMED AGRICUL-
TURAL SOCIETIES INTO URBAN ONES, OLD SOCIAL NORMS,
HABITS, AND CUSTOMS, WHICH TRADITIONALLY HELD SWAY
SINCE THE BEGINNING OF CIVILIZATION, GAVE WAY TO THE
RHYTHMS OF THE CONCRETE CITY.

One of the more interesting attempts to discover the proper-
ties of electricity occurred at the grand convent of the
Carthusians in Paris in 1746. Two hundred monks stood in a
mile-long, snaking line, each holding a twenty-five-foot wire in
each hand, all connected together. Then, without warning, French
scientist and abbé Jean-Antoine Nollet attached one of the ends
to a primitive battery. A new Gregorian chant was heard that day,
affirming that electricity could indeed travel by wire, even by

monks if need be—*instantly*.[2] That Samuel Morse would attribute the invention of the telegraph to God gives us some indication as to where Americans have traditionally assigned technological progress. As with the printing press, the telegraph was initially observed by some to be a divine gift, a tool to extend God's kingdom on earth. The *American Telegraph Magazine* spoke of a "'manifest destiny' leading the 'lightning' abroad over this capacious continent of ours."[3] One preacher of that era, Gardner Spring, declared that America was on the verge of a "spiritual harvest because thought now travels by steam and magnetic wires."[4] In the same breath Spring associated the railroad with the telegraph—two blazing infrastructures crossing the western plain.

In a technical sense, the telegraph "split" transportation (movement of people and goods) from communication (transmission of information and thought). Although the telegraph obliterated time and space, our mental association between transportation and communication still remains. The association is difficult to shake off because it extends beyond the laying of the first railroad track and even beyond the first transatlantic sea voyage. As communications scholar James Carey points out, "From the time upper and lower Egypt were unified under the First Dynasty down through the invention of the telegraph, transportation and communication were inseparably linked."[5] History tells us that efficient communication systems were the stuff out of which empires were built. Even today our common perceptions of communication still carry an empire-building component. Communication, for most practical purposes, is typically viewed as "the transmission of signals or messages over distance for the purpose of control."[6]

It should not surprise us, then, that evangelists eyed the television once it dawned upon them that the invention could be utilized to reach large audiences. In the same way that Protestants harnessed the printing press, modern preachers have harnessed electronic media to spread the Word. One might even say that evangelicals have *excelled* in their utilization of electronic media in procuring converts. However, the Christian community has not always fully comprehended how electronic media can also *shape* the culture. If the printing press was capable of propelling Europe out of the Middle Ages and into a modern one, why should we think it strange that a new communication medium is not also capable of changing the information environment and our way of seeing the world? Perhaps, without our realizing it, electronic media are converting *us* in some strange ways. Of course, the thesis of this book is that electronic media *have* changed us and *will continue* to do so.

This chapter describes that period of time known as Victorianism. It was an age not only of significant technological upheaval, but also of cultural upheaval. The Americans who came out on the other side of the nineteenth century were not the same people who went into it. By culture I mean our *values* (what we believe), our *practices* (what we do), and our *artifacts* (the physical things that we make).[7] All three components of culture—values, practices, and artifacts—are remarkably interrelated. For example, what we do is often predicated by what we believe. Likewise, what we make (our technologies) can dramatically influence both our values and our practices.

VICTORIAN VALUES

President Calvin Coolidge once remarked, "America was born in a revival of religion." Over a century ago one could assert with a large degree of confidence that America was a "Christian nation." This is not to say that everyone was a Christian, only that Christian values and practices pervaded the culture. So, what happened? Or as James Lincoln Collier asked in his book *The Rise of Selfishness in America*, "How did America turn from a social code in which self-restraint was a cardinal virtue to one in which self-gratification was the norm?"[8]

"Europe and America are united by telegraph. Glory to God in the highest. On earth peace and good-will toward man." These were the words exchanged by Queen Victoria and President Buchanan in a Morse code message in 1858. Historian Daniel Howe says the message typifies Victorian culture with its sense of

Atlantic community, its excitement in technology, its biblical rhetoric, and even its premature self-congratulation.[9] American Victorianism was not wholly a derivation of British Victorianism. Howe explains that "by the end of the Victorian era influence had flowed in both directions."[10] In other words, Dwight Moody, Henry Longfellow, and Samuel Morse influenced British values as much as Charles Spurgeon, Charles Dickens, and Her Majesty the Queen influenced American ones.

Modern-day definitions of Victorianism tend to associate the period with moral prudishness. However, Collier appropriately defines the era as a conscious ideal of order and decency felt in England and America between 1830 and 1910 that manifested itself in a new gentility, religious fervor, civic activism against vice, and an effort to control sexual impulses.[11]

Why Victorianism became a tour de force in American culture can be attributed to several factors.[12] After the Revolution, Americans began to see themselves as a people favored by God. The revolt against the British was accomplished against insurmountable odds. Americans were aware that Providence had given birth to a new and different kind of nation. A fresh attempt was made to forge an alternative to European aristocracy juxtaposed with Europe's hungry masses. The humility of the hour was perhaps best symbolized by President-elect George Washington, who stood in his dark brown American-made suit before a hushed crowd on the first Inauguration Day. Here was a man who could have been crowned Emperor but instead appeared on that day to possess a rather grave countenance. As one observer noted, the General's aspect was "almost to sadness; his modesty, actually shaking; his voice deep, a little tremulous."[13] Washington's schoolboy demeanor embodied the nation's own determination to break away from Old World pomp and monarchical systems of governance.

In addition to our desire to have a fresh start at the great endeavor of nation-building, Victorianism can also be seen as a reaction to the disorderly conduct of the eighteenth century. As Americans began to move westward, they had a tendency to leave

their civility behind them. A certain amount of crudeness characterized wilderness life more than we would like to think. Although
the fire of the Great Awakening did not completely go out, the
flame did diminish. For one thing, alcohol consumption was a real
problem. As Collier remarks, "The drunken farmer staggering
home from the tavern by moonlight was a regular part of the noc-
turnal landscape."[14]

Furthermore, the bloody excesses of the French Revolution
had repulsed many Americans. We even had our own smaller version of mob rule in Shays's Rebellion (1786-1787). If the
American experiment was to work at all, it would have to have a
new moral ethos—a conscious ideal—to guide the steps of the
nation and prevent it from flying apart.

The guidance America needed was provided for in the Second
Great Awakening. Religiosity was the most significant factor con-
tributing to the rise of the Victorian ideal of order and decency.
In the truest sense, Victorianism can be thought of as an outgrowth of Protestantism. Howe says, "The era was ushered in
during the 1830s by what was probably the greatest evangelical
revival in American history."[15] The first half of the nineteenth century saw the introduction of the camp meeting, the circuit-riding
preacher, the American Sunday School Union, the rise of the popular religious press, and the phenomenal growth of groups like the
Methodists and Baptists. It was also a period in which many
African-Americans embraced Christianity. In 1775 Christian ministers numbered eighteen hundred. By 1845 that number had
jumped to forty thousand.[16] Methodist membership was at a
quarter of a million in 1820. Ten years later, twice that many
could be found on the Methodist church rolls.[17] Historian Nathan
Hatch says, "The wave of popular religious movements that
broke upon the United States in the half century after independence did more to Christianize American society than anything
before or since."[18]

Victorianism, Collier explains, was built on the twin pillars of
order and decency with self-control as its central tenet. The notion
of what it meant to be a gentleman changed. One was no longer

born a gentleman (a European idea) but *became* one through cul-
tivation of proper habits. The goal of the gentleman was to conquer pride and passion. "They wanted to make the age-old
concept of gentility an achieved, rather than an ascribed, status,"
says Howe; "they hoped to accomplish this through a massive
educational and propaganda effort."[19] The cultural ideals of order
and decency were not just confined to the northern states, for the
southern planter and the northern Yankee essentially shared the
same British-American Protestant heritage. Both of these groups,
says Howe, "liked to think they were benefiting their workers,
civilizing them."[20]

This self-conscious effort to shape the culture best characterizes
Victorianism. An array of values whispered to the nineteenth-century conscience: work hard, improve yourself, resist temptation,
stay sober. The Victorians attempted to live out their religious
beliefs in a larger social context. Collier says that Victorianism was
a "revolution in thought, attitude, and manner which touched virtually every aspect of ordinary life."[21] Homes and streets became
cleaner. Table manners improved. Smoking and chewing in public
became taboo, and a lady did not smoke at all. Dress standards
changed. The neckline moved up, and the hemline moved down.
Premarital pregnancy rates dropped sharply. Obscenity laws were
passed. Alcohol consumption rates dropped to half of what of
what they were in the eighteenth century.[22]

Victorianism also brought new meaning to the word *family*.
As work became less and less a family endeavor because of growing urbanization, the Victorians saw the need to make everything
else outside of work more family-centered. Our mental pictures
of parents, progeny, parlor, and piano really do accurately depict
the era. The nineteenth century spawned a number of family rituals still observed today: the family vacation, the birthday party,
Thanksgiving and Christmas holidays. While the world outside
the home could be harsh, competitive, even brutal, inside the
home one expected to find warmth and nurturing. The primary
leader standing behind this "cult of domesticity" was the ever-

handwritten annotations at top

ELITE — PARTISAN PRESS SUBSCRIPTION

POPULAR   Penny press — ADVERTISING

present mother who extended her influence over the children as an "agent of cultural transmission."[23]

The dominant communication medium of the Victorian Age was print. Newspapers, magazines, and novels blossomed. The invention of the steam-powered printing press in 1811 and the manufacturing of paper using cheaper wood pulp rather than rags allowed the newspaper business to sell papers for as little as a penny. The "penny press" sought to capture a mass audience and reflected a much broader spectrum of social life than the subscription-based partisan press. Penny papers contained stories appealing to a growing middle class as well as to the urban worker. The penny press downplayed political associations and supported itself with advertising dollars rather than subscriptions only.

The American magazine industry achieved remarkable growth in the nineteenth century. In 1800 only a dozen magazines were being published in America. In 1820 that number increased to over one hundred. By 1860 the number of magazines published in America had climbed to six hundred.[24] The content of these magazines was diverse, ranging from popular literature, serially running novels, religious affairs, scientific and agricultural matters, and social concerns. (In 1852 *Uncle Tom's Cabin* ran as a serial in the *National Era*.) Although diverse, magazine content was of a serious nature and reflected the Victorian ideal of order and decency. Historian Agnes Repplier characterized nineteenth-century magazines as "propriety-bound patronization-editors seeming to say to their readers: 'We will help you. We will uplift you and improve you.'"[25]

Both magazines and novels kept the content on a high plane. Literature was consciously decent and was meant to be socially redeeming. For the Victorian novelist sex was highly obscure, almost nonexistent. This is not to say that men and women in the nineteenth century suddenly stopped having sex; rather, such matters were not part of the public conversation. As Collier comments, "Writers like Twain, Dickens, and the rest of the classical novelists of the Victorian Age had to avoid the subject. People got married and had babies, but a reader could spend years wading through this vast heap of novels and never suspect that babies were not brought from the stork or found in the cabbage patch."[26]

Reading and the betterment of oneself through learning were not only private values but also public ones. Nineteenth-century Americans eagerly requested public schooling. As a result high schools were created. The college curriculum stretched to meet the growing demands of industrialization. Higher education became open to women, who in turn chose the classroom as their place of vocation, which in turn helped meet the needs of an expanding educational system. Of course, the overall effect of an astute reading public and a schooled citizenry was high literacy rates. For all white, native-born men and women over nine years of age the literacy rate in 1880 was 91.3 percent.[27]

Victorianism, then, was a conscious ideal of order and decency initiated by three rousings: a reaction to the disorderly eighteenth century, a desire to act in a responsible manner in the face of building a new nation, and an attempt to live out religious experience in a collective context. But by the time Victorianism had become an established social system, the seeds of its undoing were already sprouting. Three significant cultural events pressed their way up through the social sod and onto the American landscape. These events were vines that choked the Victorian ideal. Although the building of the modern industrial city was primarily a Victorian endeavor, its rise had the ironic effect of strangling family and community life. Then, in the midst of this domestic restructuring, new ideas about God and man began to penetrate American intellectual life, producing a crisis of faith. Finally, as will be shown in Chapter Six, the business of show business sprang out all over, revolutionizing older leisure behaviors.

SEDUCTION IN THE BIG CITY

Colonial America was distinctly rural with a smattering of small towns and isolated farms dotting the Atlantic seaboard. A typical pre-Revolutionary New England town consisted of a central church building, a town hall, a school, and a village green—all of which lay in the center of town. Radiating out from these central items were the homes of the townspeople. On the perimeter of the town were farms and pastures. Hallmarks of these small communities included a high level of political participation and interdependence. About 90 percent of the early colonists made their living at farming. After independence, westward expansion kept the land to people ratio thin. Even by the early nineteenth century only 5 to 6 percent of the American population lived in towns of 2,500 or more.[28] Naturally, rural life had consequences upon the family. Family members were tightly bound by the demands of the farm and therefore worked together, learned together, and played together. The level of social accountability for proper moral behavior was extremely high for both the family and the community.

Technological inventiveness gave rise to the industrial city. The production of the cotton gin, the steam engine, the sewing machine, the telephone, the electric stove, and the automobile were some of the important inventions that helped moved the country from a barter market to a market economy based on cash. Farmers began setting aside a portion of their land for "cash crop," which allowed them to purchase items that would normally be made or produced on the farm. These purchased commodities eliminated labor around the home and freed sons and daughters to go work in the city factories. It was a self-feeding system that began to slowly erode rural life.

America in the early nineteenth century consisted of two main socioeconomic classes—a wealthy elite, constituting about 10 percent of the population, and an agricultural work force (farmers and tradesmen), constituting about 90 percent of the rest of the population. But industrialization introduced a new class system made up of two distinct groups—a working class to run the assembly lines and a middle class to furnish managerial positions. Workers for the industrial machine were supplied by immigrants who settled in larger cities like New York and Chicago. (Between 1865 and 1918 the urban population in the United States increased sevenfold due to two major immigration surges.[29]) The majority of the working class were immigrants who often found themselves in extremely poor living conditions within the cities.

It was not uncommon for a typical family of five or ten to live in one room with no running water, no heat, and no indoor toilet.

One must remember that the Victorian consciousness was primarily an American and British phenomenon. The ideals of order, decency, and self-restraint were not always adhered to or appreciated by immigrant communities within large cities. While seventeenth- and eighteenth-century English immigrants brought Reformation and Puritan values to the colonies, nineteenth-century immigrants from southern and eastern Europe transported customs that were somewhat more lax—looser drinking habits, public dancing, more liberal attitudes toward sex, and a certain downgrading of the Protestant work ethic. Collier notes how the newcomers viewed life in a different way:

> Indifferent to Victorian notions of success, which they believed to be unobtainable in any case, they wanted to enjoy their lives as much as possible through the warmth of associations with family and friends; by means of public entertainment as they could afford; and through drinking and dancing in saloons, concert gardens, and taverns they created for themselves in their own neighborhoods. The work ethic meant little to them: they had come out of cultures where work got you nothing but calluses and a sore back.[30]

Large industries not only needed laborers to stand behind assembly lines, but also workers who could use their heads more than their hands—record-keepers, salesmen, accountants, planners, managers, and clerks. These workers needed to be educated, speak English, and possess a certain measure of manners. The new middle class naturally filled this vacuum. This was the same generation that had moved to the city from small towns and farms. They were primarily Anglo-Americans whose parents a generation earlier had adopted the Victorian ideal. "[I]t was obvious that the bulk of this new middle class would have to be drawn from the old stock," says Collier; "the immigrants . . . were simply out of the race. Few of them could speak standard English, many of them were illiterate even in their own languages, most of them did not understand the folkways and customs that they would be required to follow in corporate offices."[31]

As the Industrial Revolution transformed agricultural societies into urban ones, old social norms, habits, and customs, which traditionally held sway since the beginning of civilization, gave way to the rhythms of the concrete city. The transplantation from the meadowland to the metropolis had the effect of jolting the rural psyche. Adjusting to the shock of the new environment necessitated a redefining of the self. A host of historians and sociologists have addressed this modern disruption of the social order. For example, German sociologist Ferdinand Tönnies distinguished between *Gemeinschaft* (folk society) and *Gesellschaft* (modern industrial society). By *Gemeinschaft* Tönnies meant those communities held together by a web of mutual interdependence due to strong family ties and religious tradition. New *Gesellschaft* societies lacked such interdependence and therefore were less morally obligated to each other. David Riesman in *The Lonely Crowd* argues that urbanization contributed to the decline of the rugged individual (the inner-directed person) and the subsequent emergence of the peer-dependent individual (the other-directed person), one who gets his cues for living from the peer group and the anonymous voices of the mass media.[32] Collier claims that the industrial city gave birth to a new ethic in which the first loyalty was not to the community or the family but to the self. "And it followed ineluctably that if the self was the significant social unit," says Collier, "people had a right, even an obligation, to gratify themselves."[33]

Of course, farm life did not allow for a great deal of self-gratification. Leisurely activities were fairly limited to the reading of a book by candlelight, listening to Uncle George's fish story on the front porch, and the social interaction at a church picnic. By contrast, rising wages and shorter work hours put more change in the pockets of city-dwellers who, having more leisure time to spend their money, looked for whatever amusements the cities had to offer. (In 1890 the average work week was sixty hours; in 1920 that figure fell to fifty-one; then in 1930 it dropped to forty-two.[34])

1850→

In the second half of the nineteenth century there came into existence in every major city in America segregated vice districts. New York city had its Tenderloin, Chicago its Levee, San Francisco its Barbary Coast, Philadelphia its Hell Town, and New Orleans its Swamp. These were areas given over to a variety of vices, including alcohol, dance halls, gambling, drug dens, burlesque theaters, and brothels. Venereal disease was rampant. Much of what went on in the vice districts was illegal, but corrupt city officials simply levied fines upon the peddlers of vice that came to be seen as "operating fees."

One authority has noted how the burlesque show had a "scattering" effect on "boys, sons, brothers, husbands and lovers," whose curiosities were awakened by the advertisements outside theaters featuring scantly dressed girls: "The flare of the poster with girls in tights, the engaging title, the open promise of iniquity, drew the lad from high school as well as the commercial drummer [traveling salesman], the unfaithful husband and the hardened round-the-towner."[35] Truant youngsters found their way into the dark galleries, while older boys sometimes met showgirls at the stage door. "When we were kids," recounts one Michigan frequenter, "we used to keep the money mother gave us for Sunday school and buy tickets. . . . Then we'd meet the more timid kids . . . hit them on the head; take their Sunday school cards away from them, and show them to mother at home as proof of our attendance."[36]

The prostitutes in the vice districts were unusually young, the majority teenagers of below average intelligence who came from poor immigrant families. "To these girls," says Collier, "who spent their days in wretched, filthy sweatshops and their evenings in crowded and grimy tenements, even the seediest sort of saloon, theater, or dance hall seemed glamorous."[37] Brothels varied in scale from the ornate to the ordinary. Some houses of prostitution were furnished with expensive tapestries; others contained beds overlaid with only a dirty oil cloth. It was not unusual for a saloon to double as a brothel. In most cases, however, a hotel was conveniently located nearby. Saloon shows offered coarse entertainments ranging from naked women performing various kinds of dances to lesbian shows to even women copulating with animals.[38]

The vice district was a subculture within the industrial city that allured the middle-class male. Author and poet Carl Sandburg captured the seduction of the big city upon young men in his 1916 poem "Chicago" when he penned, "They tell me you are wicked and I believe them, for I have seen your painted women under the gas lamps luring the farm boys." According to Collier, what middle-class men found in the vice district was not just prostitution—it was a lifestyle, a new and different culture that justified itself and institutionalized anti-Victorian attitudes and behaviors. The red-light district provided a school for the American middle class in a way of thinking, feeling, and behaving that their fathers and grandfathers had not known.[39]

The vice district sharply clashed with the values of the Victorian established order. Increasingly, the tone of city life was set by a burgeoning working class that managed to push its way into the political system. Old-guard Victorians, shocked by what they saw, responded by launching a series of crusades and reforms. From the Progressive Party to Prohibition, they set out to put down demon liquor, immorality, filth, and political corruption using legislative means. But these legal restrictions were merely *external* constraints to vice, whereas the original Victorian ideal had actually been one of *self*-restraint. As it turned out, the reforms were like sticking one's finger in a crack of a dam that was about to give way.

NEW IDEAS

The Victorians probably would have extended their cultural influence deep into the twentieth century had it not been for other eroding forces running parallel to the institutionalization of vice in the big cities. As middle-class males were being exposed to a more promiscuous way of life, they were also finding a rational justification for casting off traditional constraints. The latter half of the nineteenth century and the first half of the twentieth century brought sweeping changes in American intellectual life, dramatically altering the Victorian state of mind.

If one assumes that the educated classes are primary custodians of culture, then it stands to reason that Victorianism could survive only as long as institutions of higher learning supported its tenets. As discussed in Chapter Four, the American university was a product of the Great Awakening, a movement carried out in the spirit of the Protestant Reformation. In the beginning, American higher education was sectarian and evangelical. The Ivy League schools were established primarily to train ministers so they could evangelize the Atlantic seaboard. One wonders, then, how a system with such a religious heritage could evolve to a place where traditional Christianity is now either routinely marginalized or, more likely, totally disdained.

George Marsden contends in *The Soul of the American University* that early compromises made by Protestant educators eventually subverted the overall Christian mission of higher education. To begin with, early educators assumed that classical learning could be made subservient to Christian doctrine. Nothing new here; as stated earlier, both the church fathers and the Reformers saw nothing wrong with using what was true and good in pagan literature. Besides, it was one of the best ways to come in contact with Greek and Latin grammar, as well as mathematics. Protestants justified the teaching of the classics by appealing to the principle of "common grace." (Today Christian educators sometimes prefer the phrase, "All truth is God's truth.") Theology, "the queen of the sciences," was somewhat compartmentalized from the rest of the curriculum as a specialized discipline. In colonial America, science and religion were not competitive. Natural science was viewed as a part of God's whole truth. Nonetheless, one of the first compromises Protestants made was a shift of focus from Aristotelian philosophy, which left room for the supernatural, to the new Newtonian philosophy, which viewed the universe as a machine. Marsden says examining the universal mechanics of the creation offered a new rock-solid foundation of authority amidst sectarianism, which tended to be

NATURALISM

theologically fragmented. Whereas theology had not provided an integrating feature for growing colleges, the new moral science would. The tendency was to argue that Christianity was compatible with the latest cultural and scientific trends in much the same way that the classics were justified under common grace. This compromise was the first crack in the old Puritan heritage that eventually led to a great gulf.

The early history of American higher education shows that Protestantism and Enlightenment thinking were made to coexist. Throughout the nineteenth century particular Christian doctrines, especially Calvinism, were watered down and replaced with a civic-minded Christianity stressing virtue and character building. Protestants developed what historians refer to as a "Whig conscience," seeing personal liberty as derived from a "higher moral law" and free inquiry as necessary for modern science. Whig educational ideals found root in the "common school" that synthesized evangelical Christianity, Enlightenment thinking, modern science, republican principles, and morality.

But how long could such a partnership last? Francis Schaeffer has noted that the utopian dream of the Enlightenment can be summed up in five words: reason, nature, happiness, progress, and liberty.[40] On the surface these seem like desirable values, and to some degree they are. These values are infused into the American dream, but are also tempered by Reformation piety. However, as Schaeffer points out, the European Enlightenment, like the Renaissance, had no biblical foundation: "They [French Enlightenment philosophers] looked across the Channel to a Reformation England, tried to build without the Christian base, and ended with a massacre and Napoleon as authoritarian ruler."[41] The Enlightenment looked back to the Renaissance, which looked back to pre-Christian times. (Perhaps the most well-known of the Enlightenment philosophers, Voltaire, had a painting of the goddess Diana hanging over his bed—the first thing he saw every day.[42]) The Enlightenment made human reasoning the primary vehicle for discerning truth. With the birth of modern sci-

(pre-christian)(christian) Renaissance) Enlightenment)

DEISM

ence, the rationalists perceived the universe as a giant clock; and God, the clock maker, had gone off on a long vacation.

But not all Victorians felt comfortable with a cold and distant God. The romantics, for example, did not see nature as a machine, but as an organism. Making its first appearance in England at the dawn of the eighteenth century, romanticism spread to Europe before making its presence known in America in the first half of the nineteenth century. Romanticism was not monolithic but came in a variety of forms. Second-Awakening revivalism had romantic elements to it, as did the transcendental movement that tended to deify man and devalue sin. The basic tenets of romanticism included a nostalgic longing for a more natural environment absent of society's corrupting influences, rugged individualism, and a certain emotional intensity or what some have called "moral enthusiasm." Concerning this last tenet, Jacques Barzun says that in romantic literature, enthusiasm "turns from being a dangerous form of folly [the Puritan view] to the prerequisite of all great deeds. As Goethe's Faust says at the start of his adventure, 'In the beginning was not the Word, but the Act.'"[43] There is a definite visual aspect to romanticism that is found in its subjectivism and pathos directed toward a world beheld with the roving eye. As Barzun says, "The imagination emerges as a leading faculty [in romanticism] because it conceives things in the round, as they *look* and *feel*, not simply as they are conceived in *words*."[44] The visual element of romanticism is highly significant because it would later find its way into the great eye machines of the twentieth century—cinema and television. It would also lay the foundation for existentialism, the forerunner of postmodernism.

Marsden says that the evangelicals who dominated higher education at the middle of the nineteenth century assumed that modern science and Christian scholarship would help usher in the coming of Christ's kingdom. It was increasingly argued that the classical curriculum was not practical because it catered to those training for the ministry, law, or medicine. Since America did not possess developed graduate schools, men often at this time pursued advanced degrees in Germany. Enlightenment thinking was much more advanced in Europe than it was in America. In the German university, theology was considered a historical development and the Bible a subject for criticism. In essence, higher criticism put the Scriptures on the same level as any other historical document rather than viewing it as a living, breathing revelation. Germany was also making strides in advocating the idea that educational reform should come from the state. Americans receiving advanced degrees in Germany would return to America and make the pronouncement that sectarianism held back a more enlarged, public-oriented university education.

Andrew White, who helped in the founding of Cornell University, serves as an example of these trends. He insisted that Cornell would be Christian, nonsectarian, dedicated to high moral values, but free for scientific inquiry. It was not long, however, before White insisted that the old theory of direct creation be dropped, that humanity was not fallen, and that there was no such thing as supernatural explanations for the Bible's miracles. White made these claims in the name of "divine revelation of science."[45]

The Victorians faced a crisis of faith. Their optimism told them that modern science would yield good fruits for society, but they also knew they were leaving something of great significance behind. In his 1855 poem "Grande Chartreuse," Matthew Arnold voiced the Victorian perplexity by saying they were "between two worlds, one dead, the other powerless to be born." In trying to reach a new synthesis, historian D. H. Meyer says the Victorians of the late nineteenth century tried to replace their faith and reason with a combination of sentimentalism and intellectualism, "producing a statement of belief which was tenuously established, floridly expressed, elaborately vague. Such faith could perhaps reassure those who articulated it, but it would attract few converts."[46]

Because of the disruption of the Civil War, Charles Darwin's *On the Origin of Species by Means of Natural Selection* was not fully digested by American intellectuals until the second half of the nineteenth century. Most Protestant leaders in higher education took a theistic evolutionary stance, a position perfectly consistent with the type of fusion Victorians were becoming accustomed to when confronted with issues that threatened the Christian faith. Darwinism did not get a full public hearing until the first quarter of the twentieth century, climaxing with the antievolution campaigns carried out by individuals like William Jennings Bryan, who introduced state legislation forbidding the teaching of evolution. The evolution debates—for example, the Scopes Trial of 1925—raised a number of questions. Bryan had asked publicly, "If Christianity was no longer going to be the established religion, either officially or unofficially, in the tax-supported schools, then what philosophy would be established?"[47] Walter Lippmann keenly observed at the time that the division between the proponents of evolution and the fundamentalists reflected two different underlying assumptions about the nature of education. One group wanted to hand down the wisdom of the elders, while the other owed its allegiance to the scientific method.[48]

Spiritually, psychologically, and academically, biological determinism wreaked havoc on the Victorian mind. Darwinism posed a direct challenge not only to the Genesis account of Creation and the subsequent fall of man, but also to the notion that God's design was reflected in nature. Howe says, "The greatest scientific discovery of disorder to occur during the nineteenth century, Darwin's theory of evolution, proved profoundly subversive. Despite all efforts to reconcile it with optimism and harmony, it ultimately played an important role in the destruction of the Victorian world view."[49] Darwinism created a gaping hole where once Scripture had provided an overarching intellectual unity in regard to the human condition. New ideas about the nature of man and his social environment rushed in to fill the vacuum. Karl Marx rushed in with atheistic materialism and declared, "The world's greatest problem is class struggle; therefore, workers of the world unite!" Sigmund Freud rushed in with psychoanalysis and proclaimed, "Don't repress your emotions, especially the sex drive, for it is the prime mover of life itself." John Dewey rushed in with his permissive philosophy toward the child and said, "Education should be an opportunity for *self*-discovery." I oversimplify the influences of these individuals, as did the magazine editors who wanted to give their readers something provocative to talk about; nevertheless, Marx, Freud, and Dewey represent how intellectuals grappled with the social implications of the theory of evolution. One common factor behind these ideas was that it called for a new spontaneity and an open expression of feeling rather than self-control. As Collier aptly puts it, "They were demanding that the visceral rawness of life be exposed, a cry exactly contrary to the Victorian idea of modesty and concealment of the rough underside."[50]

The 1920s were a turning point—a watershed period. Victorianism was on its deathbed, and a new age was being born. Floyd Dell, one of the editors of *The Masses* in New York's Greenwich Village, recounted, "Something was in the air. Something was happening, about to happen."[51] Statistical surveys in 1916 reveal that 40 to 45 percent of students attending the more prestigious colleges abandoned their core Christian beliefs.[52] Skepticism toward traditional Christianity turned to smug indifference. Despite Prohibition, drinking was popular among young people. Women were smoking in public largely due to a remarkable publicity stunt initiated by Edward Bernays on behalf of Lucky Strike cigarettes in which he suggested that young women "light up" in an Easter Sunday parade in New York City. Almost overnight Bernays's plot broke an age-old taboo by linking smoking with women's liberation under the slogan that cigarettes were actually "torches of freedom."

Jazz, the new music, had taken off, and public dancing became a favorite leisure-time activity. The automobile allowed couples to pair off. The "petting party" was institutionalized. (According to the *Middletown* study, in Muncie, Indiana, 88 percent of high school boys and 78 percent of high school girls had attended such parties.[53]) Dress standards for women changed. In 1920 skirts were seen at the ankle, but by the end of the decade the hemline was well above the knee. Cosmetic sales shot through the roof. Females, says Collier, were no longer expected to appear modest and virginal, but rather experienced and worldly-wise: "The double standard vanished: not only were women to drink, smoke, and have sex, like men; they were to look like men, and indeed think like men as well."[54]

Ideas always have consequences. Doubts raised about the authority of the Bible seemed to provide a sufficient excuse for a number of middle-class males to visit a girlie show or step into a brothel. As the implications of Darwin, Freud, and others trickled down from academia and into the minds of the mainstream, the Victorian values of order, decency, and self-restraint were compromised. Not only were middle-class males now breaking taboos, but so were women. The looser moral habits common among nineteenth-century immigrants were now shared by the sons and daughters of seventeenth- and eighteenth-century English immigrants.

It was at this juncture that another significant social phenomenon occurred. The entertainment industry was born. The entertainment explosion began around the turn of the twentieth century and was carried out by a series of technological innovations spawned from the Industrial Revolution—the telegraph, the photograph, the moving picture, radio, and television. (The computer is also rapidly becoming an instrument of show business.) The business of show business is one of America's largest exports in today's global economy. The rise of the entertainment industry has dramatically altered our leisure-time habits, so that Americans now spend more time entertaining themselves than they do working or sleeping. The story of how we became one of the most amused peoples on the face of the earth is one of further compromise with our "rough underside."

CHAPTER SIX

The Machines of Show Business

*We may divide the whole struggle of the human race into
two chapters: first the fight to get leisure; and then
the second fight of civilization—what shall we do
with our leisure when we get it?*

JAMES A. GARFIELD (1880)

*An information bomb is exploding in our midst, showering
us with a shrapnel of images and drastically changing
the way each of us perceives and acts upon our private world.
In shifting from a Second Wave to a Third Wave
info-sphere, we are transforming our own psyches.*[1]

ALVIN TOFFLER, *THE THIRD WAVE*

WHILE MIDDLE-CLASS AMERICA HARDLY EVER VENTURES
INTO THE SEEDY SECTION OF THE BIG CITY ANYMORE, THE
RED-LIGHT DISTRICT HAS NOW BEEN CONVENIENTLY PIPED
DIRECTLY INTO THE LIVING ROOM.

꩜

Philosopher Bertrand Russell once observed how the effect of
the Industrial Revolution had been one of making instruments
to make other instruments to make still other instruments. In
regard to the entertainment industry, Russell's observation is especially true. The machines of show business were built upon each

other, one providing a venue for the next. It is entirely interesting that while each new communication technology was heralded as a servant of democracy (or the industrial complex), they all, one by one, fell into the hands of showmen.

This chapter recounts the rise of modern media, from the telegraph to the computer, with a special focus on the leisure habits of Americans during the twentieth century. While the telegraph connected cities and broke barriers of time and space, it also introduced Americans, along with the photograph, to a new peekaboo world. Edison had hoped moving pictures would be used as a sophisticated teaching device, but Hollywood producers quickly grew the motion picture industry into a giant god factory, manufacturing screen personalities for soul-starved urbanites. Later, cinema would evolve into a grand theater of sex and violence. Radio helped get the Depression off people's minds, but radio's golden years mark a period of time in which people began to see entertainment as a *major* component of their lives, a trend that continues to this day. Television, the ultimate peekaboo machine, has within the last several decades yielded to the lowest moral denominator to attract audiences. Serious television is somewhat of a misnomer because it is by design a medium of amusement. Originally an instrument for militarists and scientists, the computer is now being carnalized as well. The great irony of the information age is that the personal computer, despite all the wonders of the Web, is turning out to be a primary instrument of the porn industry.

American-style show business, however, did not begin in the inventor's laboratory, but on the vaudeville stage.

THE BEGINNING OF MODERN SHOW BUSINESS

Entertainment during the nineteenth century usually came to town in the form of traveling circuses, showboats, or opera troupes. The minstrel show also proved to be popular—blackface acts representing Negro life on the old plantation. The minstrel show largely consisted of a combination of songs, dances, jokes, and lengthy skits. In the city the variety show emerged; European in origin and lacking a unifying theme like the minstrel show, it catered to the male subculture by entertaining saloon drinkers with crude jokes, bawdy comedy sketches, and scantily clad singers.[2] Variety eventually moved its entertainment away from the saloon and into the theater house. Then an idea occurred to some of the theater owners who wanted to attract a broader audience and net a larger profit. Since life upon the "wicked stage" was generally avoided by the most devout middle-class women and children, a compromise seemed to be in order. Beginning around 1880 the vice factor was eliminated from the variety show to accommodate families and couples who would have not have otherwise frequented theaters.[3] Obscenity and profanity were curbed. The matinee was created to oblige those who did not venture out at night in some of the rougher districts. Cheap seats in the balcony or gallery could be purchased. Almost every barrier was removed that kept the faithful from entering "Vanity Fair." If Christian on his journey to the Celestial City "would only suspend his assumption that the Christian life required a renunciation of pleasure, that a few hours in a palace devoted to mere amusement could destroy his character, then the palace would willingly meet all other objections."[4] This Christian was willing to do, and variety, rechristened vaudeville, took hold.

Vaudeville arched its way out of the 1880s and into the 1920s, linking together two centuries and creating the first organized system of mass entertainment. Many vaudeville acts became famous and later found their way into other media. Most of us are still familiar with the Marx brothers, Al Jolson, Burns and Allen, Abbott and Costello, W. C. Fields, Jack Benny, etc. The more successful entertainers got heavier billing. Eventually vaudeville came to be dominated by a handful of showmen who owned huge chains of theaters and ran them like a big business. Vaudeville, then, was the beginning of modern show business and consisted of elements still found in show business today: It attracted wide audiences (a mix of all social classes); it was a business whose primary goal was to make big money; those who entertained audiences became "famous" or what we would call celebrities.[5]

A NEW PEEKABOO WORLD

The *mechanics* of the new entertainment industry were provided by vaudeville, but the actual *machines* of show business were powered by electricity. "We are one!" recounted the poem "The Victory," giving tribute to the telegraph's inventor, Samuel Morse. Morse's machine annihilated time and space by allowing information to be transmitted in seconds. Anticipating how the technology could produce a new "global village," Morse wrote, ". . . the whole surface of this country would be channeled for those *nerves* which are to diffuse, with great speed and thought, a knowledge of all that is occurring throughout the whole land; making, in fact, one neighborhood of the whole country."[6] Up until this time few people actually wanted or even needed to know *all* that was occurring in the land. Nevertheless, the telegraph invited a new type of public conversation that provided information with little or no context. Granted, while the telegraph allowed citizens to quickly be exposed to events that sometimes affected their lives in the political and economic sphere (for example, the events leading up to a possible "civil war" were highly important matters, a threat that surely promised to tear Morse's hope for national unity to shreds), most happenings coming off the new wire services and into the newspapers bore, and would bear in the future, little relevance to the daily routines of most Americans. In 1854 Henry David Thoreau wrote in *Walden*, "We are in a great haste to construct a magnetic telegraph from Maine to Texas . . . but Maine and Texas, it may be, have nothing to communicate." "For the first time," Neil Postman says, "we were sent information which answered no question we had asked, and which, in any case, did not permit the right of reply."[7] This was a new way of perceiving the world—taking it all in whole. Of course, one cannot take in the *whole* world at one time. Therefore, newspaper prose was shortened to allow for the sheer volume of information that could now be "transported, measured, reduced, and timed."[8] Information, then, became a commodity, a package of fragments and discontinuities of far-off worlds, made to be sold every single day as "news."

In 1844, the same year that Samuel Morse had asked the "What hath God wrought?" question, the first book of photographic images was published. Entitled *The Pencil of Nature*, the author and co-inventor of the photographic process, Henry Fox Talbot, explained how "the new art of photogenic drawing" was achieved "without any aid whatsoever from the artist's pencil." The camera, he said, will "make a picture of what ever it sees."[9] The invention of photography was quite suitable for the Victorian age, for it combined the Protestant concept of the "divine hand of nature" with the emerging miracles of modern science.

Oliver Wendell Holmes called the photograph a "mirror with a memory."[10] Writing in *The Atlantic Monthly* in 1859 he foresaw the proliferation and the commodification of pictures in much the same way that Thoreau saw the trivialization of information with the telegraph. Holmes said the ability to separate the form from the reality it came from marked the beginning of a new era where the "image would become more important than the object itself, and would in fact make the object disposable."[11] The photographer would become a kind of hunter of animal hides competing with other hunters to divest every animal in the forest of its skin: "Every conceivable object of Nature and Art will soon scale off its surface for us. Men will hunt all curious, beautiful, grand objects, as they hunt cattle in South America, for their skins and leave the carcasses as of little worth."[12]

Taken together, the photograph and the telegraph formed a dynamic duo in the history of communication technology. As Postman explains, like the fragmented and non-contextualized information coming off the wire, the photograph also was a slice of the world, its content possessing no propositions about anything, its subject lacking a past and a future.[13] Newspaper editors surely must have noticed something else about the photograph. When text and image appear side by side on the same page, it is the image that screams the loudest for attention, pushing the exposition into the background. Only a catchy headline comes close to standing up to it. The telegraph and the photograph laid the technological groundwork for the other machines of show business. As America entered the twentieth century, a new peek-aboo world opened up, as Postman calls it; a world that would wage war on the typographical mind; a world without much coherence or sense; a world, like the game of peekaboo, entirely self-contained and endlessly entertaining.[14]

THE MOTION PICTURE

Although Thomas Edison has been credited with the invention of motion pictures, he actually coordinated the ideas of several other inventors in developing both the motion picture camera and the motion picture projector. In fact, if one wanted to get technical about it, it was the Greek astronomer Ptolemy who first realized that the human eye retains an image on the retina for a split second after the image disappears. Those who first tinkered with the idea of a moving picture device correctly theorized that a series of still pictures could appear to be moving in a natural fashion if slight changes were made in each frame and if the pictures were flashed quickly before the eye.

The first moving pictures were novelties. In the 1890s one could enter a phonograph parlor, billiard room, or penny arcade, put a nickel in a four-foot-high box called a kinetoscope, and through a peephole watch a variety of human activities: a man sneezing, a husband stealing a kiss from his secretary, a strong man flexing his muscles, a robbery, a scantily dressed woman jumping rope, cootch dancers, ladies trying to hold their dresses down on a windy day. (Without question, even in the early days, movies had a propensity toward sex and violence.) On April 23, 1896, Edison and other co-inventors introduced to an American audience the first projection system. The debut of the "vitascope" was made in a theater used for vaudeville acts. The *New York Times* covered the event and reported that after watching several short films—breaking surf, a burlesque boxing match, and a "skirt dance by a tall blonde"—a "vociferous cheering" went up. Calls were made for Edison to appear on stage, but he made no response.[15] Edison originally envisioned movies as a type of teaching device, but when he saw in his latter years the dawning of

Hollywood's fantasy world he confessed, "I had some glowing dreams about what the cinema could be made to do. . . . When the industry began to specialize as a big amusement proposition I quit the game as an active producer."[16]

The movie industry exploded at the turn of the century. In 1900, more than six hundred nickelodeons could be found in New York City alone with a daily attendance averaging over three hundred thousand.[17] Attending movies became one of America's most popular leisure-time activities in a relatively short period of time. In 1907 there were twenty-five hundred movie theaters in America. Within seven years the number of theaters grew to seven million, a remarkable 2,800 percent increase.[18] "Why has the love of spontaneous play," asked Reverend Richard H. Edwards one and a half decades into the twentieth century, "given way so largely to the love of merely being amused?"[19] The reverend had asked an excellent question because the rise of the movie industry introduced a fundamental shift in the way people played. Whereas in ages past people amused themselves through active participation—*reading* or *telling* a story—now they were watching someone else perform a story on a giant screen. There was something deeply satisfying about seeing Charlie Chaplin or Mary Pickford charm their way out of a pickle.

To address the reverend's question one must remember that in the city a person was on his own, lost in a crowd, and prone to all manner of anxieties. As noted earlier, there was an erosion of individual identity that had previously been nurtured by the family, church, and community. Media historian Jib Fowles believes that the star system arrived just at the time when these ancient institutions were receding.[20] Victorian literature had typically counseled the anxious to overcome their hardships by strengthening their character. But by the turn of the century, self-help manuals and behavior guides were emphasizing the need to develop one's personal attractiveness to cope with the onslaughts of city life. The virtue of rugged individualism was supplanted with the trait of social desirability. To establish the *self* meant establishing one's *personality*. In short, what the sons and daughters from the little house on the prairie needed in the big city were role models. The desire for attractive role models could only be partially satisfied with vaudeville personalities or the professionalized sportsman swinging a bat on a baseball diamond. Cinema did something the stage and the playing field could never do by providing the close-up shot. D. W. Griffith was perhaps the first moviemaker to grasp the power of the close-up. By employing highly photogenic men and women and by utilizing the correct lighting, makeup, and camera angles, Griffith broke the distance between audience and actor so that the viewer could look upon every feature, every line, every subtle expression of the eyes and mouth. By the late 1920s a voice was added to the face, making the picture complete.

The 1920s was a period when two divergent lines crossed each other. From one direction there were the purity crusades, putting down the vice district, the brothel, and alcohol. From another direction there was an earth-moving, technological dynamo, with its leisure-enhancing household devices, automobile, image-advertising, and new cinema. While the purity crusades were capable of sweeping dirt off the city streets, making the broom reach all the way into the movie houses or into the minds and hearts of a new youth culture absorbed in the images staring back at them from slick magazines was another matter. The "New Morality" associated with the "Roaring 20s" was spurred as much by the *glamorization* of the loose life provided by the new image-making machines as it was by the *justification* of the loose life provided by Darwin and Freud. Unregulated in the beginning, the motion picture industry brought the new morality directly to the screen. Films in the 1920s showed men and women smoking, dancing, and drinking in public. This was all shocking to an older generation still trying to hold on to Victorian values. The display of moral laxity and the much publicized scandals of the private lives of movie stars led the old guard to dub Hollywood the new "Babylon."

Deciding it was best to regulate themselves, the Motion Picture Producers and Distributors Association (MPPDA) hired ex-

Postmaster General and former Republican Party Chairman Will Hays to give in-house oversight to the industry. In 1930 the association established a code of ethics; however, the Code had no enforcement power and was ignored by many producers. During the early 1930s Hollywood "was free to roam far and wide, or at least to venture farther out on the frontiers of free expression," says Thomas Doherty in *Pre-Code Hollywood: Sex, Immorality, and Insurrection in American Cinema, 1930-1934*.[21] But this freedom was soon curbed.

In 1934 representatives from the Hays Office sat in a screening room watching MGM's second Tarzan movie, *Tarzan and His Mate*. In the film former Olympic swimming champion Johnny Weismuller grabs the heroine and throws her into a jungle lagoon. The scene shows a nude Jane swimming in the water. The overseers of the Code knew something had to be done. Complete nudity was forbidden by the Code, and the sequence was cut. Despite the Code's edict, says Doherty, "trailers containing the nude scene and a few uncensored prints continued to circulate, with MGM's defiant complicity."[22] The first two Tarzan films were aimed at the female audience; MGM's ad copy was "both biologically urgent and gender-specific":

> Girls! Would you live like Eve if you found the right Adam?
> Modern marriages could learn plenty from this drama of primitive jungle mating!
> If all marriages were based on the primitive mating instinct, it would be a better world.[23]

Shortly after the release of *Tarzan and His Mate* the MPPDA announced a $25,000 fine for any movie distributed without a stamp of approval from the Hays Office. From 1934 to the mid-1950s Hollywood attempted to stay within the well-defined bounds of the Hays Office.

To satisfy the public's newfound habit of moviegoing and to bring financial stability to an expensive art form, moviemakers developed the studio system. Like vaudeville, the movie industry came to rest on three legs: wide audience appeal, big business methods, and the creation of celebrities. Hollywood cranked out celebrities in much the same manner as Ford cranked out cars. Actors were put under contract, fashioned by the studio, and paraded across the screen: Gary Cooper, Bette Davis, James Cagney, Spencer Tracy, Katharine Hepburn, Fred Astaire, Ginger Rogers, Humphrey Bogart, Judy Garland, and on and on. "If identity was in question," says Fowles, "here were personalities to try on."[24]

Although the Depression and the introduction of radio hampered movie ticket sales, Americans did not stop going to the movies or loving their stars. In 1934, at the height of the Depression, 60 percent of the American public were still attending movies.[25] In the same year there were 535 recognized fan clubs, seventy of which belonged to Clark Gable.[26] Celebrities were also having an impact on consumption habits outside of ticket sales. Shirley Temple generated a whole line of books, dolls, and clothing. Platinum blonde stars like Jean Harlow, Carole Lombard, and Mae West prompted an increase in peroxide sales. And when Clark Gable took off his shirt to reveal his bare chest in *It Happened One Night,* the undershirt industry reeled.[27] This was an entirely new development in the psyche of the nation. No longer would the average American look out and see an empty wilderness to shape by his own design, says social critic Christopher Lasch in *The Culture of Narcissism*; our membership in the "cult of celebrity" made us look out and see the world as a mirror. Loneliness and anxiety were conquered by gazing upon a "grandiose self" as reflected in those who radiated "celebrity, power, and charisma."[28]

When television came along, it posed a serious threat to movie ticket sales as a visual competitor. Drastic measures were in order. Piggy-backing on the burgeoning youth rebellion of the 1950s and 1960s, Hollywood began to explore sexual themes then absent in television. Still conscious of the standards set by the Hays Office, the movie industry devised a rating system in the late 1960s that served to transfer the burden of censorship to the moviegoer. The shift did not stimulate the production of more family-friendly films; to the contrary, the rating system was a green light for producers to move forward with more sexually explicit material. (Why Americans ever thought a ratings system would help solve television's problem of sex and violence in content is beyond me.) One can easily note the change in content when the system was adopted. Even stars who had earlier established themselves in the business were to be found under movie titles carrying an X rating. In 1969 Dustin Hoffman starred in a movie that earned an X rating dealing with homosexual themes. *Midnight Cowboy* went on to win an Academy Award as best picture of the year. In 1973 Marlon Brando starred in *Last Tango in Paris*, a film also earning an X rating. While these two movies were downgraded to R to reach a larger audience, producers felt less restrained to hold back on the element of sensuality, and in fact often pushed their films to the edge of an X rating in the name of artistic expression.

When the movie industry first began rating films, 24 percent received a G rating, and 43 percent earned an M rating (mature audience), later changed to "PG" (parental guidance).[29] But within a decade the industry discovered that violent and sexually explicit films were drawing larger audiences. By 1979 PG movies were carrying the same content of earlier R-rated movies; and today themes that once were reserved for R- and X-rated movies (now NC-17) are frequently found in movies rated PG.[30] The majority of movies in the last decade have earned an R rating.

All cultures have and need stories. Stories are communicated to a culture's youth for the purpose of amusement, inspiration, and instruction. The Greeks looked to the *Iliad* and the *Odyssey*. Jews and Christians embrace the story of David and Goliath. Within all stories are universal narrative forms—heroes and villains, heroines and villainesses. The basic goals of the characters are also universal. Heroes try to overcome the villain or a villainous force in order to accomplish some particular task. Villains typically try to kill the hero or at least prevent him from accomplishing his task. These basic goals never change. What can change, however, are the personal values of the hero or what might be called the "ethics of the hero's action." King David and Odysseus are both hero figures, but their personal moralities are very different. While both are capable of feeling guilt over a wrong action, what is deemed wrong can vary based upon the hero's cultural mores.

In our own culture the cinema has become a dominant storyteller. Whether placed on the western plain, the jungles of Cambodia, or a distant planet, the protagonist is always telling the audience about the consequences of proper or improper behavior by pure example. (Educators call this the Social Learning Theory out of a need to give a common-sense principle a technical name.) Sex and violence are not new elements to drama, but are rather common to it because drama tries to imitate life. However, we find in drama today, and for my purpose specifically in film, two significant changes that were somewhat rare in our culture fifty years ago. First, the ethics of the hero's action is now morally relativistic. And second, spectacle, or what Aristotle called "scenic effects," has upstaged all other dramatic elements.

As to the first change, it really is a question of the hero allowing the villain to live after he has been defeated. It is also a matter of whether the hero will sleep with the heroine after he has rescued her. I do not think it would be far-fetched to say that in many cases the hero shows no mercy, allowing the villain to "make his day." I would also say that the hero almost *always* goes to bed with the heroine in movies today.

In a *National Review* article entitled "Violent Fantasy," Jonah Goldberg says that every Oscar in 1999 for almost every major winning category played upon a theme showing how "external moral authority is illegitimate, or that personally designed morality is superior."[31] In *American Beauty*, a film about a man in midlife crisis who pursues his daughter's best friend (a film that won the Oscar for best picture of the year), the message was evident: "The pursuit of personal liberation, especially sexual liberation, is the only legitimately heroic endeavor in American life."[32] Likewise, in the film *Boys Don't Cry* Hollywood elevated to heroic status the notion that external moral authority is a cruelty and that holding as taboo a transsexual woman masquerading as a boy in order to seduce teenage girls is a type of oppression.

Taken to its ultimate end, moral relativism in cinema allows for anything, including a hero figure who takes personal pleasure in eating the brains of people he does not admire while they are still alive, as with the case of Hannibal Lector, a cannibal with whom audiences are somehow supposed to sympathize.

In his *Poetics* Aristotle wrote that spectacle is a type of attraction in itself, but that it is also the least artistic and the least connected with the art of poetry. By "poetry" Aristotle had in mind Greek tragedy performed on the stage, and he felt that the scenic effects were more a matter of concern for the prop man than for the playwright. That Aristotle put elaborate sets and stage props at the bottom of the list in drama means that he thought good theater could occur without them. The opposite philosophy prevails today in the movies. Computer-generated special effects are trademarks of Steven Spielberg and George Lucas. Every summer digitally-enhanced action films dominate the box office. Homer has taken to the silver screen in a big way. In essence, cinema *is* theater—BIG THEATER. The movie camera amplifies stage action and allows for dazzling backgrounds—the ripping tornado, the hot-breathing dinosaur, the landing spaceship, the exploding White House, even glimpses of heaven and hell. The movie theater is a transport to another world—a glorious, visual escape of a hundred and twenty minutes. Contemporary theater cannot hope to compete with such spectacle. Consequently, opera is much more eye-sensitive than it used to be, and professional performances of Shakespeare are often so bawdy that one can no longer assume that it is safe to take the family to see *Hamlet*.

When *Apocalypse Now* reached the movie theaters back in 1979, the film was noted for its high level of visual exhibition. In 2001 *Apocalypse Now* was restored and re-released. When *Los Angeles Times* film critic Kenneth Turan saw it the second time around, he remarked how tame it seemed in comparison with other movies made twenty-two years later:

> *Apocalypse Now* might have seemed excessive to some in 1979,
> but now that so many actors and directors have raised the bar

for what self indulgence on the screen means, the film plays like poetry. That's either a comment of how far we have evolved as an audience or how far the medium has devolved to what it has made us accept.[33]

The high value that producers and directors place on the element of spectacle tends to glorify violence for violence's sake. The aesthetic scale has tipped in the direction of carnal vividness so that the monsters must be more hideous, the blood must spurt farther, the explosions must be more brilliant, and the body counts must be higher.

RADIO AND THE RECORDING INDUSTRY

Radio owes its existence to several other technological capabilities that merged together in the second decade of the twentieth century. As previously noted, in 1844 Morse demonstrated that coded sound waves could be transmitted over long distances through a wire. In 1876 Alexander Graham Bell introduced the first telephone system, consisting of a microphone, which could convert sound into electrical energy, and a receiver, which could reverse the process. Then in 1897 Guglielmo Marconi perfected the "wireless," so that coded messages could be transmitted through the air. The wireless was soon utilized to send coded messages ship to ship and ship to shore. Finally, in 1906, when Lee DeForest improved the vacuum tube, allowing receivers to pick up voice and music, radio became a reality. A young executive in the American Marconi Company named David Sarnoff was the first to see the commercial use of the new radio technology. In 1916 he sent a memo to Marconi saying, "I have in mind a plan of development that would make radio a 'household utility' in the same sense as the piano or phonograph. The idea is to bring music into the house wireless . . . in the form of a simple 'Radio Music Box.'"[34]

Before the invention of radio, music publishers realized that the way to get a new song widely known was to have it performed over and over. Vaudeville became a vehicle to showcase new songs coming out of Tin Pan Alley, a section off Broadway in New York

City where music publishers had set up shop. By the turn of the century Americans were already listening to music recordings on another invention perfected by Edison—the phonograph. Edison originally saw the phonograph as a tool for businessmen who could use it for dictation, recording phone conversations, or educational purposes.[35] The phonograph extended Tin Pan Alley's "hit mentality" right into the radio age.

The "Golden Age" of radio paralleled the Great Depression. Attending movies and professionalized sporting events became more of a luxury activity in the 1930s. With radio, folks could stay home and be entertained for free. Vaudeville, in effect, leaped off the stage and into the music box. The content of early radio shows consisted of music, drama, variety shows, and general talk formats. The mass entertainment provided by radio helped get the Depression off people's minds as family members huddled around the talking box each night after dinner. Taken together with the movies, Americans were now losing themselves in a fantasy world on a regular, now daily basis. For the first time in the nation's history, people began to see entertainment as a *major* part of their lives, a trend that continued throughout the twentieth century.

Marshall McLuhan has said that the introduction of radio contracted the world to "village size," working a kind of "tribal magic" on its listeners. President Franklin Roosevelt owed part of his popularity to his ability to communicate directly to the American people through his "Fireside Chats." Unlike the book, McLuhan has noted, radio engulfs the listener emotionally. "I live right inside the radio when I listen," commented one early listener. "I more easily lose myself in radio than in a book."[36] At one point, Halloween Eve, 1938, to be precise, some Americans became so engrossed in CBS's *Mercury Theater on the Air* that they temporarily lost their ability to discern fact from fiction. When Orson Welles aired a rendition of H. G. Wells's *War of the Worlds* as an interruption of regular music, some listeners who had tuned in late thought the world as they knew it was coming to an end. So convincing was the broadcast that bulletins reporting that a meteor had blown up fifteen hundred people in New Jersey

prompted two Princeton geology professors to go on a wild
search. When the announcer said it was not a meteor, but an invasion of Martians with a death ray, a national panic ensued—
phone lines jammed, traffic in some areas jammed, the military
went on alert, families fled their homes, and some even attempted
suicide. Out of an estimated six million who heard the broadcast,
one million actually believed Martians invaded the planet.[37]
However, gullibility was not just something Americans were
prone to, for the tribal drum could work its magic in Germany
too, in a different sort of way, so that "the old web of kinship
began to resonate once more with the note of fascism."[38] Unlike
Welles, whose broadcast only pretended to take over the world,
Hitler actually wanted to do it. Hitler used the medium of radio,
as well as film, to seduce the German people to follow him all the
way to the brink.

Radio's ability to tribalize was altered and refocused when
confronted with the new medium of television. As McLuhan has
said, "Now, to the teenager, radio gives privacy, and at the same
time it provides the tight tribal bond of the world of the common
market, of song, and of resonance."[39] Radio was fragmented, as
it remains to this day, serving in part, along with the music industry, as a type of bonding agent for the youth culture. As with the
movie industry, the music industry cultivated its own star system,
sometimes alone, but most of the time in sync with other media
in keeping the hit mentality vibrant. Before World War II, the
singer had always been subordinate to the orchestra in the score
and in the billing. But when Columbia Records released Frank
Sinatra's "All or Nothing at All" during the dark days of
Christmas 1943, this subordination flipped.[40] The blue-eyed boy
from New Jersey, who drew tens of thousands of screaming
bobby-soxers to New York's Paramount Theater, was the first
singer in a line of many to attract a cult-like following.

A little over a decade later, Sam Phillips, a Memphis record
promoter, went searching for "a white boy who could sing col-
ored." What he found was a country-western singer named Elvis
Presley whom he quickly fashioned into the "king" of an upbeat

rhythm-and-blues style dubbed rock and roll.[41] In 1956 Elvis was scandalous, but the original "loose cannon" of rock and roll, according to record producer Don Dickson, was Jerry Lee Lewis. Here was a performer who presented a new kind of "danger" to audiences with such gyrating hits as "A Whole Lot of Shaking Going On" and "Great Balls of Fire." "Elvis had drawn a musical line between the generations a year earlier with his boyish looks and a million dollar grin," said Dickson in a National Public Radio interview highlighting the one hundred most influential songs of the twentieth century; "but Jerry Lee looked like a used Bible salesman with a leer that would make Jack the Ripper smile. Jerry Lee gave us unashamed angst and unparalleled passion. It was the Church of the Holy Roller brought straight to the altar of sex."[42]

Seemingly tame at first, the Beatles sheepishly arrived in America in 1964 on a plane from Liverpool. When they departed in 1970 in a hallucinogenic yellow submarine, they were touting lines about how they were more famous than Jesus Christ. From the disco to the headphone to the concert to the rapping *pow wow* on the wheels of woofer and chant, the tribal beat blares away and continues to attract youth to its flame. Only now the medicine men are not singing, "I want to hold your hand," but songs about suicide and incest, homosexuality and bisexuality, cop killing and the snuffing out of family members. Rock and roll has persisted now for half a century. One would think the dance would have petered out by now. No; the drums are much louder than they used to be, and the natives are still restless.

Because of MTV and the popularity of music videos, the recording industry is more visually oriented than it ever has been. In fact, one cannot separate MTV from the recording industry. The music video channel is a vital venue for selling artists who must now be able to capture the camera's attention as well as hold a tune. When MTV debuted in 1981 its menu was, in the words of columnist John Podhoretz, "a blasé comic nihilism punctuated by tiny explosions of social conscience in the form of save-the-suffering fundraising drives."[43] Now that the twenty-something

crowd has fled, the channel has given way to "a giggly and sopho-
moric tone devoted almost entirely to sex and titillation."[44]
Although Madonna is still popular, MTV now targets a preteen
audience. This is why MTV took a former Disney Mouseketeer
named Britney Spears and exalted her to Bubblegum Queen on
High, a person who, says Podhoretz, combines the face of virginal
innocence with the gyrating moves of an aging stripper.[45] The construction of Britney Spears is not haphazard. While in interviews
she touted the mother-pleasing line, "I'm still saving myself," on
the studio floor her sculptors made use of Gregory Dark, a director of porn films.[46]

Although not everyone chooses to listen to (or now watch) the
harsher forms of popular music in our culture, we nevertheless do
listen to music, *whether we want to or not*. One can hardly escape
background music. For it floats in our stores, in our restaurants,
and in our political commercials. Music has become the "mist that
plays above our culture," says J. Bottum. It is an "all-encircling
noise."[47] Our audio technologies have put music not only in our
private spaces but in our public places as well, so that wherever
we go, someone is putting a mood on us to either buy a product
we might not need or to accept an idea we otherwise would not
have believed. C. S. Lewis said that senseless *noise* was the music
of hell: "Noise, the grand dynamism, the audible expression of all
that is exultant, ruthless, and virile."[48] "We will make the whole
universe a noise in the end," says Toadpipe in *The Screwtape
Letters*. "The melodies and silences of Heaven will be shouted
down in the end."[49]

TELEVISION

The word *television*—from the Greek "far off" and the Latin "to
see"—was first used in a 1907 issue of *Scientific American* magazine.[50] Just as the movie industry was taking off, scientists were
experimenting with the concept that not only could the human
voice be transmitted using wireless technology, but so could images.
A major breakthrough occurred in 1923 when Russian-born
Vladimir Zworykin devised a way for an image to be transformed

into an electronic signal. The "iconoscope" allowed the signal to be transmitted through the air to a receiver where it was made back into an image again. In 1927 Philo Farnsworth patented an electronic scanning system that then sharpened the image. Throughout the 1930s RCA and others honed these technologies until the television image reached a quality fit for commercialization.

The custodians of the old print culture immediately cast a skeptical eye at the new invention. In 1938 children's author and essayist E. B. White remarked, "I believe television is going to be the test of the modern world and in this new opportunity to see beyond the range of our vision we shall discover either a new and unbearable disturbance of the general public or a saving radiance in the sky. We shall stand or fall by television—of that I am quite sure."[51] Carl Sandburg added, "The impact of television on our culture is just indescribable. There's a certain sense in which it is nearly as important as the invention of printing."[52] T. S. Eliot quipped, "It is a medium of entertainment which permits millions of people to listen to the same joke at the same time, and yet remain lonesome."[53]

Now jokes were something television could do well. Comedy became one of television's main entrees. Vaudeville, ever so agile, managed to jump again, this time from the "music box" to what some would later call the "idiot box." Variety, drama, game shows, sports, and news filled in the rest of the menu. Edward R. Murrow's radio show *Hear It Now* became television's *See It Now*. "The instrument can teach, it can illuminate; yes, it can even inspire," explained Murrow, who would go on to bury Senator Joe McCarthy with the instrument. "But it can do these things only to the extent that humans are determined to use it to those ends. Otherwise, it is merely lights and wires in a box."[54] Lofty thoughts. But one should understand that teaching, illuminating, and inspiring are secondary values of television. The "humans" who have their hands on television—producers, programmers, corporate owners—are, as a rule, motivated to do *one* thing, and this one thing is to *make money*. (This truth really should be a child's first lesson in kindergarten, even before they

RADIO - MUSIC BOX
T.V.   IDIOT BOX

learn their ABCs.) As a continuation of vaudeville, television seeks to parade big people before big audiences to make big money. And yet television is much more than vaudeville because it is our most dominant communication medium. It is the medium whereby we conduct a large portion of our public conversations, make our political choices, and form our perceptions about the world.

It did not take long for television to become the most important piece of furniture in the home. The speed at which television took hold outpaced all other household inventions of the last one hundred years. While the telephone took sixty-seven years to reach 75 percent of American households (the vacuum cleaner took forty-eight years and the radio fourteen years), the television took only seven years to reach this many homes.[55] In 1950 Americans on the average were watching four hours and thirty-five minutes of television each day.[56] By 1998 the average daily per household usage had climbed to seven hours and fifteen minutes.[57] Over the last half century TV viewing time has roughly doubled. By 1995 the average American child was watching about five thousand hours of television before entering the first grade and about nineteen thousand hours by high school graduation.[58] Studies bear out that television viewing has addictive powers in the same way that alcohol and drug usage are addictive. Television can act as a sedative, even though it does not bring satisfaction. Like the alcoholic who will down rubbing alcohol for a quick fix, television addicts lack selectivity in viewing. Those who watch it sometimes feel a loss of control, feel angry with themselves for watching too much, cannot bring themselves to quit watching it, and feel miserable when kept from watching it.[59] Children who watch television manifest behaviors of intimacy normally reserved for close friends, siblings, and parents. Upon entering a room where a set is on, their attention is drawn to it; they settle down and scoot in with a warm smile. They cozy up to it with a blanket, pillow, doll, or pet. It brings a sense of security. It is trusted and loved.[60]

Television is the ultimate peekaboo machine because it is *designed* to be amusing. Its fast-moving images seek to grab our attention and keep it for as long as possible before we click to another channel. Postman argues that there is no such thing as "serious television" because all of its content, whether it be the evening news or a nature show, must conform to the entertainment paradigm—a song and dance routine. This is why Tom Brokaw must have a multicolored disc orbiting his head while he anchors the evening broadcast. And this is why the "Alligator Hunter" must find an even more poisonous snake to wiggle in front of his face. ("Watch me put my head in this crocodile's mouth!") Television is vaudeville because the camera abhors a talking head. I do not mean to imply there are no people in the world who could sit through a program of talking heads, only that such shows do poorly in the ratings. News programs that *do* feature talking heads must do so briefly or show the heads yelling at each other or making as many snide remarks as possible. When Bill Buckley, Jr., who in my opinion had the best talking head show, *Firing Line*, appeared on the *Today Show* several years ago for an interview, his spot was given about three minutes. When the host closed by saying, "Well, I wish we could take more time . . . ," Buckley rolled his tongue and brilliantly interrupted, "Well then, why don't you?" There was an off-camera laugh and an awkward pause. Then it was commercial time. Buckley knew why the host could not take more time. Television is not designed to take more time. It must go on to the next visually stimulating picture, the next peekaboo.

Television outlets must compete for advertising dollars with other programs airing at the same time, programs that could number in the hundreds due to satellite and cable. Television also competes with outside media (newspapers, magazines, and the Internet). Television producers have increasingly sought to raise their ratings by appealing to our lowest natures. The so-called "family hour" no longer exists. A study conducted by the Parents Television Council (PTC) assessing television programming between 1989 and 1999 reported that on the whole sexual and violent content, including coarse language, tripled during the 1990s. On a per-hour basis sexual content more than tripled. The overall subcategories of references to explicit sex increased sev-enfold with the most dramatic increase being references to homo-sexuality, which were twenty-four times more common.[61] The Kaiser Family Foundation reported in a 2001 study that movies were the most likely to contain sexual content (89 percent), fol-lowed by sitcoms (84 percent) and soap operas (80 percent). The Kaiser report went on to say the sex act was depicted or strongly implied in 10 percent of all television shows and that almost a quarter of the couples in such scenes appeared to be young adults from eighteen to twenty-four years of age, with 9 percent appear-ing to be under 18.[62] A UCLA study concluded its research by say-ing, "Sex is generally now depicted as a competition, and an exciting amusement for people of all ages."[63]

Frequently at the top of the list for racking up raunchy points in these types of studies are pro wrestling programs, watched by children and adults alike. "World Wrestling Federation Smackdown!" has sued PTC for exaggerating the show's antics, ranging from obscene language to blatant sexual exhibitionism, which is one way to keep concerned citizens off your back. In a study by Indiana University, which looked at fifty episodes of the show *Raw Is War*, researchers found 1,658 instances of sexually explicit grabbing or pointing, 157 instances of the middle-finger gesture, 128 episodes of simulated sexual activity, and twenty-one references to urination.[64] The claim that viewing such material does not affect one's behavior is ridiculous. While not everyone who watches pro wrestling will go out and flip their friends around so as to kill them, as did a North Carolina boy in the sum-mer of 2001, who incidentally weighed a hundred and sixty pounds more than his victim, a review of almost one thousand violence studies, presented to the American College of Forensic Psychiatry in 1998, found that in 98 percent of the reports there was indeed a connection between screen violence and real vio-lence.[65] Furthermore, the American Psychological Association concluded that after forty years of studying the question the truth about violence research is still being ignored and that it was time to admit that the "scientific" debate was over.[66]

Sex and violence not only command non-reality television, but reality programming as well. Some of the most explicit material on television can be found on daytime talk shows. Commentator John Leo of *U. S. News & World Report* calls them "stupid TV freak shows." Leo has criticized major corporations for supporting daily themes like, "I impregnated thirty girls and I'm proud of it." Often these shows pit people against each other—setting up for cameras an inevitable confrontation. For example, one show featured members of the KKK proudly dressed in neo-Nazi uniforms and mouthing anti-Semitic and racist slurs. Another show featured young strippers and their unknowing parents. The highlight of the show occurred when the parents were allowed to watch their children disrobe in front of a mass audience.[67] But these are the kind of spectacles that occur almost every day on the shows of Jerry Springer and Jenny Jones. When Jenny Jones took the witness stand after one of her guests killed a man for sharing his secret homosexual fantasy during a taping, an estimated 334,000 viewers tuned in for live coverage on *Court TV*. Art Bell, the executive vice president of strategic planning for the program, was so delighted after a 350 percent ratings increase that he remarked, "For our viewers, this has all the elements of a terrific trial—it's got sex, it's got murder and it's got a big star."[68] Sex, violence, and celebrity—the magic combination of modern show business.

On June 11, 2000, dozens of young men in New York's Central Park went on a "wilding" rampage during the National Puerto Rican Day Parade. Forty-seven women were reported to have been either robbed, fondled, or stripped during the incident. Critics said police tended to look the other way out of fear of confronting minority groups.[69] Some of the "bystanders" took out their home video cameras and starting shooting. Some of the footage wound up at *New York One*, Time Warner's twenty-four-hour cable news channel. Despite its policy not to identify crime victims, *New York One* put the footage on the air without blurring the women's faces or their uncovered body parts. "It was a grievous error," said News Director Peter Landis a week later to National Public Radio's Linda Wertheimer, who questioned him on the ethics of the decision. Landis admitted that the faces of the victims should have been blurred the first time it was aired. He did not, however, regret airing the naked body parts. Of course, *New York One* could have opted not to show the pictures at all. But Landis said not showing the graphic footage was *never* a consideration of the station.[70] In this case, the news media apologized for exploiting the identity of the crime victims, but not for exploiting their nudity. Here is the point: Even when American television tries to be a serious medium, it so often falls back into its favorite forte—sex and violence.

THE COMPUTER

"What are you thinking about?" one of the members of the Analytical Society at Cambridge asked its founder, Charles Babbage. The English mathematician was musing over a table of logarithms, fixed on finding a way to reduce the number of shipwrecks in behalf of the British Navy by correcting the apparent errors in the Nautical Almanacs. "I am thinking that all these Tables might be calculated by machinery," replied Babbage, envisioning a steam-powered "difference engine" that could be programmed by punch cards to spit out results automatically.[71] After a decade Babbage gave up on the invention, but his idea of putting data on two sets of punch cards, one set for instructions and the other set for data to be processed, managed to materialize a century later in electronic form. The zero-one system, the core of digital technology, had been earlier theorized by the seventeenth-century German mathematician Gottfried Leibniz. Morse code was in fact a type of binary system with its dots and dashes replacing the alphabet. A big jump in computer technology occurred during World War II as "electrical filing devices" were harnessed by the U.S. Military to detect the trajectory of missiles in flight. By the 1950s the word *computer* had entered the public vocabulary as a machine capable of performing complex calculations in a rapid fashion. However, the earliest electrical computers filled an entire room, weighed as much as thirty tons, and required a staff of engineers to reconfigure six thousand cables every time a different function was performed. Computers got much smaller after the invention of the transistor; then, with the introduction of the microprocessor in the 1970s, an entire central processing unit could be housed in a single chip. Today personal computers are so commonplace in our homes and at work that most of us can hardly imagine life without them.

As with the computer, the Internet was originally intended to serve the military establishment. ARPANET utilized "packet switching" technology to link computer terminals around the country with each other to share military information. Soon military contractors, laboratory consultants, and universities were using the network. By the 1990s PCs were being equipped with modems so that anyone else with the same equipment could communicate over telephone lines. User-friendly software programs allowed users to search the growing World Wide Web as well as to receive clear graphical content in addition to text.

Our new computer-enhanced world is highly excited over itself. Technology promises to bestow wonderful gifts upon the inhabitants of the earth. When *Time* magazine peered around the corner and into the year 2025, its editors delighted themselves by asking a series of questions: "Will our cars drive us?" "Will I still be hooked to video games?" "Will my PC be smarter than I am?" "Will we plug chips into our brains?" "Will robots demand equal rights?"[72] The answer that *Time* gave to most of these kinds of questions? Yes, yes, and yes again! "So will computers be smarter than humans? It depends on what you consider to be human," explained techno-enthusiast Ray Kurzweil. "By the second half of the 21st century, there will be no clear distinction between the two."[73] Those like Kurzweil who devote themselves to digital dominion often see the world as they want it to be; they say it is inevitable that the future will be this way; and then they tell us we had better learn to live with it.

It is the same sort of self-congratulatory rhetoric that Bill Gates engaged himself in when he wrote *The Road Ahead* back in 1995. Anticipating a "revolution in communication," Gates claimed he wanted to make "his contribution to the debate." (All proceeds from the book went to put computers into classrooms, which no doubt also helped shape the debate.) In "Bill's World" the information highway will deliver phone service, the Internet, TV programming, and movies directly into the home. (The technology is here now, but not at full capacity.) Computers are spoken to, shopping is conducted in cyberspace, and every room has an electronic screen. One goes about the house, watching a movie or television program downloaded from the night before, talking to the appliances.

"You may wash the dishes now."

"I think I want to watch the 1957 version of *The Bridge on the River Kwai* now."

"Is there a burglar at the door now?"

"What is the weather in Sydney, Australia, now?"

I want to be cautious here and confine my criticisms of digital technology to the Internet, or rather what the Internet is becoming. I have no misgivings about the usefulness of cell phones or personal computers or talking dishwashers. Indeed, the personal computer is a wonderful tool to which I am deeply grateful, the manuscript of this book having been typed on one. Some have asserted that the Internet is the supreme democratic medium because it fosters individualism, liberty, and community, that it is a great social leveler that removes gatekeepers and allows everyone to say what is on their minds. It has also been suggested that we can no longer speak in terms of "mass media" because of the multiplications of personal choice with cable and the Web.

While there is some truth in all of this, I find the "demassification will save democracy as we know it" argument a bit too optimistic. The notion of a demassified media is somewhat of a myth for several reasons. When the television and the PC finally merge into one technology, as the Gates dream dictates, I have no doubt that a sizable segment of the population will use the medium to read news headlines, check the stock market, and do some shopping, much in the same way the Web is used now. But I also cannot help but believe that a much larger segment of the population will use the Internet to further extend its well-developed entertainment habits, behaviors that are by now deeply fixated within our genes. Furthermore, the entertainment spilling out of the new medium (we will call it the TVnet for lack of a better word) will not be significantly different from what is now on cable or in adult video stores. In other words, the TVnet will carry with it the values of Hollywood, the industry that has for the last eight decades set all aesthetic standards. Even if every citizen were a producer and every backyard in America a movie studio, what we will have, more than likely, will be more avenues to view sex and violence. I realize my prediction represents a more pessimistic view, but it is based solidly upon the progressively degenerating tastes of our culture within the last century.

Even today there is growing evidence that people are using digital technology for the purpose of satisfying their sexual appetites rather than for enhancing democracy. In the first comprehensive survey of sexual habits on the Internet, researchers concluded that "erotic pursuits" were among the most frequent uses of the Web and that *sex* was the most searched for word online.[74] In the summer months before the 2000 presidential election Jim Reese, who works for Google, an Internet search engine that likes to monitor what is on the public's mind, wrote in *The New Yorker* that the day after the Grammys he noticed a flood of searches using the words "Jennifer Lopez" and "dress" and "naked." (Ms. Lopez had appeared at the Grammys in an extremely revealing dress.) What was *not* on the people's minds, Reese noted, was the election. In the heat of the presidential contest there were virtually no searches using the words "Gore" or "Bush" or "campaign."[75] It was estimated in 2001 that Internet porn was a one billion dollar industry annually.[76] Sales of pornographic material on the Internet surpass the cumulative sales of all other products sold online.[77] According to a Zogby poll sponsored by Focus on the Family, 20 percent of Americans have logged on to pornographic websites, a statistic holding true for both Christians and non-Christians.[78] Twenty-five percent of teenagers have visited porn sites on the Internet.[79]

Web portals like America Online and Yahoo! are perhaps the largest beneficiaries of the growing Internet porn industry, and they know it. Not only must customers access the web through these services, but portals like CompuServe tease their clients almost daily by posting provocative images of models and movie stars. The television and movie industries, in an attempt to compete for market share, are compelled to cater to what people are already exposed to on the Internet. Holman Jenkins writes in *Policy Review* that the cable industry's resistance to pornography has now "completely crumbled," especially in cities like New York.[80] Jenkins says the film industry went from making one thousand porn flicks in 1992 to ten thousand in 2000. If it is not already there, porn is soon coming to a cable station near you.

Who would have thought a hundred and fifty years ago that Americans would come to this? The Victorians certainly could not have imagined it. By 1910 the purity crusades had all but shut down the vice districts, and it looked as if some moral progress was being made on the street and in the saloon. While the communication technologies of the nineteenth and twentieth centuries were originally designed with practical intentions for business, education, or government, they all one by one fell into the hands of showmen. After World War II most of the American middle class moved out of the city and into the newly created suburbs. Today suburban neighborhoods are nearly identical to each other. Every sprawl has a McDonalds on the corner featuring a monthly movie on a Coke cup. In the Wal-Mart across the street customers are greeted by blaring video monitors promoting yet another movie, the one that was on the McDonalds cup six months ago. Down the road are houses sitting on quarter-acre lots, the lawns neatly cut and weed-free, with a double garage for his and her cars. The neighborhood is eerily empty. People do not venture outside much or sit on their front porches like they used to. At night blue screens flicker. While middle-class America hardly ever ventures into the seedy section of the big city anymore, the red-light district has now been conveniently piped directly into the living room.

Irrationality and
Spectacle

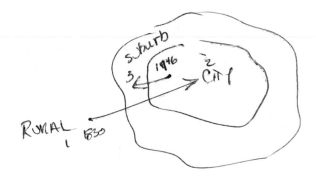

The Image

The twentieth century is not the Age of Anxiety but the Age of Hollywood. The pagan cult of personality has reawakened and dominates all art, all thought. It is morally empty but ritually profound. . . . Movie screen and television screen are its sacred precincts.[1]

CAMILLE PAGLIA

So idolatry has triumphed. I think Luther would join Moses in saying that the cult of the word is defenseless in the face of the image.[2]

NEIL POSTMAN

THE DOMINATING COMPONENTS OF TODAY'S MEDIA CONTENT—SEX, VIOLENCE, AND CELEBRITY—CONFORM TO A PAGAN IDEAL.

ॐ

The old system just keeps coming back. Not that long after the Flood's waters had receded, Nimrod stretched forth his hands to receive the astrological charts from atop Babel's tower. The sands of Egypt were still between the toes of Moses when he proceeded down the mountain of thunderings and lightnings, tables in hand, only to find the Hebrews dancing around a golden calf. The people of God multiplied under the Roman knife, but then the pantheon strangely reappeared over the church altar. The fire of the Reformation pushed the gods back until the icon-making machines of the twentieth century ushered them back again in living color.

Thus far I have attempted to establish that technology is not neutral, that it has the potential to change our beliefs and behaviors; and nowhere is this more evident than in America's shift from a print-oriented culture to an image-oriented one. Out of absolute theological necessity Judaism and Christianity are word-dependent, in contrast to paganism, which is image-dependent. The Hebrews were the *only* people in antiquity to attempt to teach *everyone* how to read. While the early Christians inherited their word-based culture from the Jews, they were not afraid to embrace the analytical components of Hellenic culture in order to defend the faith. Major compromises were made when Constantine sought to wed Christianity to the state. After the barbarian invasions, Christianity became a type of "full-service" faith. Babylon never really died out; rather, it was put into the whole mix. Christianity was subverted by the paganism it sought to extinguish. The Dark Ages were "dark" because as the ability to read faded off the scene, so did literacy's auxiliaries—education, civility, and rationality. Although the second half of the Middle Ages did have education (the universities), some civility (the apotheosis of "courtesy"), and rationality (scholasticism), these were not enough. By the time Luther nailed his Ninety-five Theses to the church door at Wittenberg, there was only a slight moral differentiation between the Holy See and the pagan Roman emperor who had sat on the same throne twelve hundred years earlier.

The invention of the printing press harnessed Protestant doctrines to a new communication technology that placed the Scriptures directly into the hands of the people. The Bibles coming off the press gave Europe a reason to read. Not only did Gutenburg's machine fuel the Reformation, but it also opened the floodgates to liberty, freedom, discovery, and democracy. To a large extent American democracy emerged out of a highly sophisticated communication environment dominated by print. And although our nation-building might at times have been a bloody business (the Civil War was in part a test of the notion of equality—a transcendent value stated in foundational documents like the Declaration of Independence), it was nevertheless a serious business in which the citizenry at large had the intellectual capacity to rationally pay attention and take part. The Victorian Age, that period of time that tried to reconcile the vigorous remnants of the Reformation with the cultural upheavals of industrialization, could not cope with the new ideas hatched by Darwinism, nor could it prevent the raw red-light district from slipping through its fingers and into the great machines of modern show business.

The purpose of this chapter is to show how image-based media have brought forth a revitalization of the pagan gods in popular culture. The dominating components of today's media content—sex, violence, and celebrity—conform to a pagan ideal. A biblical definition of paganism is called for here, as well as a close examination of our narcissistic culture. The chapter concludes with a discussion of "pagan beauty."

WHAT IT MEANS TO BE A PAGAN

> *Pagan.* 1. one of a people or community professing a polytheistic religion, as with the ancient Romans, Greeks, etc. 2. a person who is not a Christian, Jew, or Muslim. 3. an irreligious or hedonistic person.[3]

Paul's epistle to the Christians at Rome is perhaps the most perceptive critique of human nature ever written. It goes beyond the dictionary definition above to tell us how one actually becomes a pagan. In the epistle's opening discourse the apostle exposes the crux of humanity's turning away from God, what we may call the deliberate refashioning of the Creator into the creature. From chapter 1 of Romans one can extrapolate a biblical definition of what it means to be a pagan.

> *For the wrath of God is revealed from heaven against all ungodliness and unrighteousness of men, who suppress the truth in unrighteousness, because what may be known of God is mani-*

fest in them, for God has shown it to them. For since the creation of the world His invisible attributes are clearly seen, being understood by the things that are made, even His eternal power and Godhead, so that they are without excuse, because, although they knew God, they did not glorify Him as God, nor were thankful, but became futile in their thoughts, and their foolish hearts were darkened. Professing to be wise, they became fools, and changed the glory of the incorruptible God into an image made like corruptible man—and birds and four-footed animals and creeping things. Therefore God also gave them up to uncleanness, in the lusts of their hearts, to dishonor their bodies among themselves, who exchanged the truth of God for the lie, and worshiped and served the creature rather than the Creator, who is blessed forever. Amen. For this reason God gave them up to vile passions. For even their women exchanged the natural use for what is against nature. Likewise also the men, leaving the natural use of the woman, burned in their lust for one another, men with men committing what is shameful, and receiving in themselves the penalty of their error which was due. And even as they did not like to retain God in their knowledge, God gave them over to a debased mind, to do those things which are not fitting; being filled with all unrighteousness, sexual immorality, wickedness, covetousness, maliciousness; full of envy, murder, strife, deceit, evil-mindedness; they are whisperers, backbiters, haters of God, violent, proud, boasters, inventors of evil things, disobedient to parents, undiscerning, untrustworthy, unloving, unforgiving, unmerciful; who, knowing the righteous judgment of God, that those who practice such things are worthy of death, not only do the same but also approve of those who practice them.

—ROMANS 1:18-32, NKJV

In the most general sense, the apostle is addressing why all of humanity is without excuse before God and under His wrath. In a more particular sense the apostle is speaking to the non-Jew or the "Greek" (see 1:16). Toward the middle of the epistle Paul makes a strong case that the religious Jew is also under God's wrath, but for now he has in mind the totality of pagan society.

The wrath spoken of here is not necessarily a sudden outburst of anger—Zeus' bolt of lighting; rather, it is an abiding hatred for every thought and every act that violates God's holiness. God's wrath is "revealed from heaven"; that is to say, it is not hidden; it is made plain to everyone who will acknowledge it. However, instead of acknowledging it, humanity *suppresses* it. God's witness of Himself is both *internal* and *external*: "[B]ecause what may be known of God is manifest in them, for God has shown it to them. For since the creation of the world His invisible attributes are clearly seen, being understood by the things that are made, even His eternal power and Godhead, so that they are without excuse" (vv. 19-20, NKJV). Theologians sometimes call this type of testimony "general revelation" in contrast to His "special revelation" (the Scriptures). General revelation does not give one a complete knowledge of God, but it does give an *awareness* of God. Although Helen Keller went blind and deaf before the age of two, she wrote in her biography that she had a sense of God even before she was introduced to the divine concept by her teacher. It is this awareness that sufficiently makes a person guilty. The savage living on a remote island has a knowledge of God and is under the same condemnation as a person living in the Bible Belt because he willfully sins against his own sense of right and wrong.

Internally, all humanity has an awareness of God because we were created in His image. We share with Him the natural attributes of intellect, emotion, volition, dominionship, creativity, and communicableness—in short, those things that animate our personalities. We are *people* because God is a *person*. We also share with God moral attributes, those sensibilities that reflect God's holiness, although not perfectly, because we are marred by sin. Moral attributes include an innate sense of justice, an understanding of kindness, a desire for wisdom, and a desire for truth. Externally, God's *eternal power* and *divinity* (Godhead) are seen in the Creation. Human beings see design in the universe and assume there must be a Designer or a First Cause. God has put a sense of eternity not only in our hearts but also in the heavens. Psalm 19:1 says, "The heavens declare the glory of God; and the firmament showeth his handiwork." As C. S. Lewis once said, "What sort of universe do we demand? If it were small enough to be cozy, it would not be sublime. If it is large enough for us to stretch our spiritual limbs in, it must be large enough to baffle us. Cramped or terrified, we must, in any conceivable world, be one or the other. I prefer terror." The immense size of the universe shows the infiniteness of God.

People take what knowledge they have of God, however limited, and fail to honor Him in the way He has been revealed. The supreme example of this failure is an unthankful heart. What is really meant by thankfulness in Romans 1 is a willingness to live in the light that one is given, to do right when it is apparent that such and such is the right thing to do. Instead people turn and shoot off in another direction—*their* direction. The Bible calls this *unrighteousness*. Furthermore, people create entire religious systems to walk in unrighteousness. As James Montgomery Boice says, "[T]he religions that man creates are actually attempts to escape having to face the true God. We invent religion—not because we are seeking God, but because we are running away from him."[4] Popular religious theory teaches that the earliest religions were animistic and that animism evolved to polytheism, which eventually evolved to monotheism. According to the biblical model, just the opposite occurred. Even anthropological research bears out that primitive polytheistic or animistic cultures that exist today have actually fallen away from a higher standard.[5] Robert Brow has argued in *Religion: Origins and Ideas* that animal sacrifices were first associated with offending a supreme holy being, but when polytheism entered in, guilt was diminished because the humanlike gods and goddesses were frequently unholy and were therefore less to be feared.[6]

This point is crucial in understanding the entire paganizing process. Humanity turns to *futile thoughts* (v. 21), or as the Authorized Version renders it, "vain imaginations," for the simple reason that they do not like the God who has been revealed to them, whether by general revelation or by the Bible itself. The term "imaginations" is the Greek word *dialogismos*, from which we get our word *dialogue*. In other words, a person's rejection of God involves a kind of mental debate, a negotiation of guilt, a rationalization to justify self. Having left the God as revealed in nature and conscience, one is left with his own imagination to *recast* God as he pleases. People worship the God of their own mind. The rejecter moves away from light and into darkness. At this stage a person is not searching for God, groping for Him as it were, but rather is creating a worldview in which to live so that the weight of guilt does not have to be felt. This type of moral folly can occur on an individual level within the lifespan of one person, or it can occur on a collective level and cover the entire history of a people.

The passage goes on to say that pagan societies "changed the glory of the incorruptible God into an image made like corruptible man—and birds and four-footed animals and creeping things. Therefore God also gave them up to uncleanness, in the lusts of their hearts, to dishonor their bodies among themselves, who exchanged the truth of God for the lie, and worshiped and served the creature rather than the Creator, who is blessed forever" (vv. 23-25, NKJV). The key word here is "exchanged" (v. 25). Paul is saying that what is wrong with pagan systems, whether pantheism or polytheism, is that both substitute a lie for the truth. The *image* represents a *transference* of the honorable devotion due to the Creator to an image made with human hands. Of course, the image is merely a representation of whatever religious system a society has imagined for itself. Behind the image are *myths* or narratives to make sense of the human condition, and these serve to establish belief and direct behavior: Where did I come from? How did the world come into existence? What is behind the changing of the seasons? How can I honor the gods and find favor with man? What is permissible? Within the system that is created, room is often given to fulfill the desires of the flesh. The essence of sin is selfishness; therefore, all false religions to some degree or another allow for behavior outside of God's holiness; and the behavior is always regressive. Cultures, as well as individuals, typically move in a downward spiral in regard to moral permissiveness unless God intervenes with His mercy and grace.

When an individual or entire society walks away from the light that has been given to them and continues to walk toward darkness, the parameters of moral permissiveness widen: "For this reason God gave them up to vile passions. For even their women exchanged the natural use for what is against nature. Likewise also the men, leaving the natural use of the woman, burned in their lust for one another, men with men committing what is shameful, and receiving in themselves the penalty of their error which was due" (vv. 26-27, NKJV). Darkness only produces more darkness if the light is ignored. God in effect gives them up or allows them to follow their own base desires, which, like the physical laws that govern gravity, bring about the natural consequences that such behaviors evoke. The *penalty* can come in different forms: disease, psychological confusion, or the breeding of a malevolent culture. Paul deliberately focuses on sexuality because male and female relations tangibly reflect God's design in the created order of things. The term "natural" signifies biological function, and perhaps Paul even has in mind the stability of the family unit (see vv. 30-31). The decline has the potential to move from fornication to adultery to homosexuality to pederasty to bestiality—every perversion one can imagine.

The downward progression leads to a collection of rebellious attitudes and behaviors that have historically been characteristic of civilizations that have forgotten the God of conscience and the Bible: "And even as they did not like to retain God in their knowledge, God gave them over to a debased mind, to do those things which are not fitting; being filled with all unrighteousness, sexual immorality, wickedness, covetousness, maliciousness; full of envy, murder, strife, deceit, evil-mindedness; they are whisperers, backbiters, haters of God, violent, proud, boasters, inventors of evil things, disobedient to parents, undiscerning, untrustworthy, unloving, unforgiving, unmerciful; who, knowing the righteous judgment of God, that those who practice such things are worthy of death, not only do the same but also approve of those who practice them" (vv. 28-32, NKJV). This seems like a long list, but it indicates the type of attitudes and behaviors that can become evident when a people (1) suppress the truth about God given to them; (2) refuse to glorify Him as God by acting unthankful, living a life of sinning against their own conscience; and (3) exchange the majesty of a holy and immortal God for unholy and mortal creatures. The sins mentioned here carry a definite hostility toward God and a certain cruelty toward other people. Is it any wonder that the Romans were often ruthless in the treatment of other human beings? F. Godet writes in his commentary on Romans:

> It calls up before the mind the entire population of the great cities flocking to the circus to behold the fights of gladiators, frantically applauding the effusion of human blood, and gloating over the dying agonies of the vanquished combatant. Such is an example of the unspeakable hardness of heart to which the whole society of the Gentile world descended.[7]

A pagan, then, is someone who has engaged in a substitution process for the purpose of *suppressing* the true God. As a religious creature, one must have a worldview that somewhat *rings true* and provides a framework for being. Therefore, people create religious systems that allow for the pursuit of their own selfish desires. Ignoring God as revealed in nature's design and inward conscience, they turn to experiential or bodily awareness, that which is found in the *self*. Meaning is then transferred to real or created objects in the world. Pagan happiness is found in honoring earthly objects through ritual.

When I said in Chapter One that visual media have the potential to paganize us, I simply meant that in a culture where it is difficult to escape the pervasiveness of images, the devotion that we put into the ritual of watching television, going to movies, attending rock concerts, or devouring the latest *People* magazine approaches the same level of devotion that the Egyptians, Babylonians, Greeks, and Romans had for their deities. It meets the same need, and quite remarkably, the images are all too familiar. The cult of celebrity fills a religious hole dug by modernism. William Blake once said that all deities reside in the human breast (all but one, of course). So it was for the Greeks, and so it is for us. The machines of show business brought the gods back to life.

The ancient Greeks and Romans practiced their devotion to the gods within their particular cults. Cults were local in nature; the gods were woven into a pagan's sense of place, work, or ancestry. Pagan piety has never been the same type of piety one expects or sees in Christian orthodoxy. *The Oxford History of the Classical World* tells us that pagan piety was not a matter of inward reflection or intense private communion with God. For example, no Greek would have ever written in a spiritual journal. The relationship between man and his gods was a casual one:

> It discouraged individualism, a preoccupation with inner states and the belief that intentions matter more than actions. . . . Man was not for Greeks a sinful being in need of redemption; piety was not a matter of perpetual moral endeavor under the watchful eye of conscience. The gods excelled in strength and skill more often than in the quieter virtues. Indeed their behavior in myth was often scandalous: There might you see the gods in sundry shapes/ Committing heady riots, incest, rapes.[8]

The dominant tone of ritual was one of festivity rather than somber sanctimony. The gods delighted in seeing humans enjoying themselves. Therefore, singing, dancing, athletics, crude jokes, obscene gestures, and the occasional orgy accompanied the blood sacrifice. This spirit of festivity is captured in the New Testament when the apostle Paul describes the idolatry of the children of Israel during the wilderness wanderings: "Neither be ye idolaters, as were some of them; as it is written, 'The people sat down to eat and drink, and rose up to play'" (1 Corinthians 10:7). The enormous amount of time, energy, and devotion that swirls around electronically-produced images constitutes a kind of ritual in itself. Images are pervasive, emotionally captivating, and . . . dare I say it? *Sacred.* They are not sacred because we associate the true and living God with them. Just the opposite. We associate *our-*

selves with them. This is what it means to be a pagan. Our images are sacred because we pour meaning into them and receive meaning back. We follow the sordid lives of celebrities both on and off the screen, bestow more honor on them than we do actual historical figures, develop "personal relationships" with them (even though we have never met them in person), buy their products as if they were relics, and make pilgrimages to their shrines (e.g., Elvis, Princess Di).[9] To have the fortune to actually *become* a celebrity, says Neal Gabler in *Life: The Movie, How Entertainment Conquered Reality*, "is widely regarded as the most exalted state of human existence."[10] It is dying and going to heaven—that lucky someone's inauguration to the modern version of Mount Olympus. To beat the insurmountable odds by becoming a "star" is to be cast into orbit with the other gods floating around in the celestial celebrity universe. Our association with electronic images helps us sustain a certain way of life and a certain way of looking at the world while we run away from God. We enjoy looking at ourselves. Our polytheism is not directed at stone idols or marble statues. Our polytheism resides in a house of mirrors.

HOUSE OF MIRRORS

Although the house of mirrors is one of the older staples of the amusement park, it is nevertheless a proper metaphor for our image-saturated culture. In a house of mirrors one may hardly find room to turn around without bumping into a reflection of self. At every angle one finds a multiplicity of images. I can remember as a boy getting lost in such a place, and the panic that came over me before I finally found an exit. But in our own societal house of mirrors there seems to be no escape. As Christopher Lasch has written, we have become a narcissistic culture that worships at the altar of *self*. In Greek mythology Narcissus fell in love with his own reflection in a pool of water and was turned into a flower that now bears his name. Lasch believes that a fundamental change has taken place in the structure of our personalities derived from our therapeutic ideologies, the rationalization of our inner lives, our cult of consumption, and the proliferation of images around us. Concerning the latter Lasch says:

> We live in a swirl of images and echoes that arrest experience and play it back in slow motion. Cameras and recording machines not only transcribe experience but alter its quality, giving to much of modern life the character of an enormous echo chamber, a hall of mirrors. Life presents itself as a succession of images . . . recorded and reproduced by means of photography, motion pictures, television, and sophisticated recording devices.[11]

We are not too different from the Greeks or the Romans or the suffering masses living in the Dark Ages who idolized their gods— mere images of mortal men with mortal passions. But I would go even further and say that the number of images that might have been found in ancient antiquity does not compare with the number of images that dominate our own landscape. The average American adult sees approximately five hundred advertisements each day; by the time a person reaches twenty-one years of age he or she will be exposed to between one and two million ad messages.[12] Children on average see up to twenty thousand television commercials a year, or almost three hours' worth a week.[13] Advertisers have now flocked to the World Wide Web. In the late 1990s one and a half million Internet users signed on to a Victoria's Secret fashion show.[14]

Advertising is not new. As early as 1200 B.C. the Phoenicians painted messages on stones along pathways for travelers to see. Six hundred years before the birth of Christ, ships anchored at port would send criers into the town with signboards to announce their arrival.[15] Initially the word *advertise* simply meant to take note of something: "We have soap. Want some?" But modern advertising has a persuasive component. Furthermore, most advertising today has a "disconnect" between the claim of its message and the actual product: "Want to attract attention at work? Buy this soap." Images make this disconnect less obvious since visual appeals intentionally strike an array of so-called psychological needs: safety, acceptance, escape, success, power, sex, etc.

Highly paid researchers have learned how to push our buttons at the subconscious level, the art being the same as in fishing—to show the worm but not the hook.

Will Rogers was not too far from the truth when he said that advertising is that which makes you spend money you don't have for something you don't want. In this sense Rogers was saying that modern advertising is somewhat of an irrational business. In a consumer culture like ours, marketers spend billions of dollars each year to "create needs" in our minds to make us want to buy products. Since there are so many products on the market, many of them essentially identical, advertisers have to create not only a need but also a "perceived difference" in the consumer's mind. Coke and Pepsi, no matter what one says, really do taste about the same. Therefore, in an effort to reach a younger market, "the Pepsi Generation" was created in a brainstorming session somewhere on the umpteenth-floor of a Madison Avenue building in New York City. Most of us are fully aware of this duplicity by the time we reach the age of forty. We have learned to enjoy the magic of a smart commercial. Of course, by "smart" I do not mean the ability a commercial has to inform me about the features of a product, but rather the ability to make me laugh or identify somehow with the image.

When Adam Smith first published *The Wealth of Nations* in 1776, he assumed the relationship between the buyer and the seller to be a rational one. In theory, the buyer could "beware" because he had the intellectual wherewithal to rationally discriminate. Smith did not anticipate fast-moving images or depth psychology. He did not foresee that advertising would evolve from the actual character of products to the character of the consumer of the products, tapping into our deepest fears, dreams, and fantasies. The president of the National Sales Executives understood the significance of this transformation when he proclaimed back in the 1950s, "Capitalism is dead—consumerism is king!"[16] By this statement he meant that since American producers had achieved an incredible output of goods, more than the consumer would actually ever *need*, the key to keeping the economic wheels turning was to persuade Americans to buy more and more. When television came along, Madison Avenue realized that here was a new technology that could make the wheels turn even faster.

Today consumption habits are directly linked to popular entertainment. Loyalty to company brand is established through "identification" or the building of an "image" to which a particular market can readily associate. The identification can take any number of forms: the building of a personality type that serves as a mirror reflection of the target audience; a product endorsement by a celebrity; or perhaps the display of a certain attitude, already prevalent in the culture, accomplished through a spectacular mini-narrative. A crucial question, however, is, With what do people identify these days? The age in which the stay-at-home mother readily associated with the "purity" of Ivory soap through images of the angelic housewife is quickly fading. When the U.S. Women's Soccer Team won the World Cup in 1999 and Brandi Chastain took off her shirt in front of millions of television viewers to reveal her sports bra, the Board of Directors at Nike probably clapped with glee. It stands to reason that if the tastes, needs, and passions of consumers become degraded, so will the appeals that advertisers use to gain the attention of the consumers. The relation between the entertainment industry and our consumer culture is a self-feeding one, a massive type of idolatry where Hollywood and others flood the public mind with debased images polluting our values. Madison Avenue then taps into these same values, feeds the images to us again, to sell us products. All of this is accomplished through constant repetition, a brilliant assortment of aesthetic styles, and the ubiquitous placement of reflections so that one cannot turn around without seeing their most base desires in iconic form.[17]

One still might be able to sleep well at night knowing that modern advertising is an irrational business. After all, what harm can be done if one chooses Pepsi over Coke? But what happens when the magic of modern advertising is brought into the political arena? Or as one ad person put it: "I think of a man in a voting booth who hesitates between the two levers as if he were pausing between competing tubes of tooth paste in a drugstore.

The brand that has made the highest penetration in his brain will win his choice."[18] According to Kathleen Hall Jamieson, who is perhaps the leading authority on American presidential campaign advertising, the 1992 presidential race between George Bush and Bill Clinton marked the demise of the public political speech and the escalation of a new form of political exposition. It was in this year that candidates were more likely to have been seen answering questions on talk shows or on MTV than giving a formal televised address.[19] Perhaps more significant than this change, the political ad has also supplanted the political speech. "Political advertising is now the major means by which candidates for the presidency communicate their message to the voters," says Jamieson. "By 1980 the half-hour broadcast speech—the norm in 1952—had been replaced by the 60-second spot."[20]

In order for me to describe the severity of this current social phenomenon, I must pause here for a brief lesson in classical rhetoric. In classical rhetorical theory, the enemy of democracy has always been the demagogue whose mode of operation is to appeal to the audience's emotions or what Isocrates called "the rhetoric of pleasure and gain." The formal study of rhetoric emerged in fifth-century B.C. Greece for two reasons. First, rhetoric was studied because philosophers were interested in the nature of reality, knowledge, and the power of language to persuade. Second, rhetoric was studied because the ability to persuade was connected with democracy, political discourse, and the judicial system. Since there were no lawyers in ancient Greece, one had to learn to defend himself in court. If one were to succeed as a statesman, the ability to speak was essential.

Three systems of thought emerged in this period that still linger today. The Sophistic tradition basically held that rhetoric could be used to get what one wanted, an entirely success-driven proposition by which a person could hire a "skilled or trained man" to teach him the art of persuasion. The first speech teachers were called sophists. Plato, who embodied the second tradition, hated the sophists because he said they were dishonest. "Truth is more important than rhetoric," was Plato's motto because he believed that the ability to persuade could not produce knowledge but only belief. Aristotle, Plato's former student, did not completely agree. The Aristotelian tradition falls somewhere between the two other traditions and espouses that rhetoric is indeed useful for instruction and as a means for self-defense. For Aristotle, the study of rhetoric can help a person learn how to use all the available means of persuasion in any given situation. Despite their differences, both Plato and Aristotle agreed that rhetoric is put to bad use when it helps bring about bad ends.

Aristotle, the first to develop a unified system of rhetoric, believed there are three types of persuasive appeals at a speaker's disposal—logical appeals (*logos*), emotional appeals (*pathos*), and appeals derived from one's own character (*ethos*). In rhetorical theory *logos* refers to rational arguments consisting of claim (what one proposes to be true but is not always clearly seen) and proof (facts or evidence readily agreed upon by the audience). Emotional appeals are perfectly legitimate in persuasion but must not be used to blind the eyes of the intellect. (The problem with images is that they naturally evoke emotional appeals in the persuasive process.) Emotional appeals are most useful in establishing that the claims of the speaker are consistent with the audience's own beliefs, but ethical speakers should not substitute *pathos* for proof. This was precisely the fear connected with the demagogue—that he relied primarily on emotional appeals to secure his power. *Ethos* is the believability of the speaker and is established through the speaker's perceived intelligence, knowledge of the subject, competence, trustworthiness, and moral character.

Jamieson warns that morselized ads and news bites are merely claims without proof and that a person who watches a political spot ad is forced to judge a claim based solely on the *ethos* of the speaker or on the *pathos* enveloping the claim.[21] In other words, commercials substituting pictures for proof is in itself a type of sophistry. One cannot argue with a picture, and we know full well that pictures have a manipulative quality. Political spot ads can work their magic, and have worked their magic in the past, by juxtaposing highly evocative images that invite the audience to impute causality. For example, when in 1964 the Johnson campaign aired a commercial showing a little girl sitting in a field plucking the petals off a flower and then juxtaposing this warm scene with the explosion of a nuclear warhead, a certain kind of sophistry was taking place. Speaking over the mushroom cloud the audience heard Johnson say, "These are the stakes. To make the world in which all of God's children can live, or go into the dark. We must either love each other or we must die." Of course, the obvious message of the commercial was that Barry Goldwater was a hate-monger and could not be trusted with his finger on the red button. This type of discourse is irrational, says Jamieson: "It solicits a visceral, not an intellectual response."[22]

If there is anything more perplexing than living in a house of mirrors, it is living in a house of smoke and mirrors. We have a term in our dictionaries for what our public discourse has disintegrated to—*spectacle*. This is a word we usually assign to a public performance or a display, as discussed in the last chapter with the evolution of cinema. But the term also carries with it the idea of a marvel or curiosity. One might say, for example, that P. T. Barnum stooped to spectacle when he decided to feature a stuffed mermaid in his New York museum, an oddity later discovered to be a dead fish with a monkey's head attached. Barnum was the master of hype and the originator of the "pseudo-event." In 1835 Barnum showcased Joice Heth, whom he advertised as the 161-year-old Negro nurse of George Washington. This spectacle earned him fifteen hundred dollars a week. When the nurse story became stale, Barnum claimed the woman was really a "curiously constructed automation of whalebone, india-rubber, and numerous springs," all operated by a ventriloquist.[23] An autopsy later revealed that Joice Heth was actually an eighty-year-old woman. The crowds that flocked to the New York museum knew they were being fooled, and Barnum knew that they knew. Upon his death in 1891 the London *Times* characterized the showman's relationship with his patrons as a "comedy of the harmless deceiver and the willingly deceived."[24] The harmless deceiver was laid to rest, but his methods of creating pseudo-events lives on in the vast world of modern public relations.

I cannot help but believe that Edward Bernays, who did more than anyone to shape the profession of public relations, was a secret admirer of P. T. Barnum, for Bernays pioneered the notion that public relations is "the science of creating circumstances"— the mounting of events that are geared to make news and yet do not *appear* to be staged. Bernays cut his teeth on cranking out American propaganda for the Committee of Public Information during World War I. Bernays did not like to use the term *propaganda* and once told PBS's Bill Moyers that he preferred to call it *proper*ganda because the war effort was, after all, a worthy cause. It is no secret that our government used the magic of the image to rally Americans behind the war to end all wars. There was Howard Chandler's playful, curly-topped girl Christy in sailor blues beckoning men to look at her in the recruiting poster with the slogan, "Gee! I wish I were a man—I'd join the Navy." How could any blue-blooded American boy not join the military after seeing that? After the war Bernays and others like him lent their talents to corporate America. Often quoted for saying, "Everything depends on the consent of the public," Bernays employed the tools of social science and the principles of Freudian psychology (he was Freud's nephew) to master public opinion.

One of Bernays's better-known pseudo-events involved his efforts to improve Calvin Coolidge's image, a man whose demeanor had been described as that of one "weaned on a pickle." Bernays arranged a breakfast between the President and a number of celebrities, including Al Jolson and the Dolly Sisters. The event was a great success and incurred a tremendous amount of publicity. Bernays's stunt was not at all different than what happened when, say, Bill Clinton routinely flanked himself with people like Barbra Streisand and Tom Cruise or when George W. Bush told Oprah Winfrey that his favorite food was a peanut butter sandwich. Two of Bernays's books, *Crystallizing Public Opinion* (1923) and *The Engineering of Consent* (1955), are benchmarks in the field of public relations.

In addition to despising the word *propaganda*, Bernays also resented the word *image* to describe his new art of reputation-building. But others have thought *image-making* to be precisely the correct term for what Bernays pioneered. In his book *The Image: A Guide to Pseudo-Events in America*, Daniel Boorstin described how "we have used our wealth, our literacy, our technology, and our progress, to create a *thicket of unreality which stands between us and the facts of life.*"[25] His term "pseudo-event" found its way into our vocabulary as "an event staged to call attention to itself." The pseudo-event (sometimes called a "media-event") is a favorite tool of business and politics and is used to sell products and to secure favorable public opinion. This is even more true today than when *The Image* was first published in 1961, for now we have corporate monstrosities that are nothing more than mega-factories of cultural symbols (e.g., Time-Warner and Disney). Boorstin's concern was that Americans not only confused the *copy* with the *original*, but that we actually *preferred* the copy to the original. News was no longer *gathered*, it was *made*. Gone are the days of the *traveler*, a word derived from *travail*. Instead, we use the word *tourist*, a mere pleasure-seeker in a sea of fabricated attractions. We no longer have *heroes*, people known for their achievements. Instead, we have *celebrities*, persons known for their well-knownness.

The phenomenon of celebrity, which gathered extraordinary strength in the twentieth century, is the great human pseudo-event of our times. Boorstin said that the celebrity had "been fabricated on the purpose to satisfy our exaggerated expectations of human greatness."[26] Anyone has the potential to become a celebrity as long as he or she can wiggle his or her way under the spotlight out of sheer persistence and force of personality. People from the entertainment industry and the sports world seem to be the preferred choice for the pedestal. The celebrity is a type of tautology—an echo—a "needless repetition of the same in different words and images."[27] Celebrities' claim to fame is fame itself; they are people notorious for their notoriety; they are known for being well-known. And if they are successful enough, said Boorstin, media stars may actually overshadow the real figures they portray.[28] That is to say, the image of Charlton Heston may actually overshadow the figure of Moses; the image of Nick Nolte may actually overshadow the image of Thomas Jefferson.

Celebrities freely mingle today on the biography bookstore shelf among real historical characters whose heroic deeds run pale against those sparkling mass-produced personalities sitting next to them. James Madison is humiliated by Marilyn Monroe. On television, biography has become a popular genre. But the repertoire of "the world's most notable personalities, past and present" are more likely to be movie and TV stars than the historically significant. In the month I was writing this chapter (August 2001) I looked to see what notable personalities were appearing on A&E's *Biography*. Here was the lineup: Kris Kristofferson, Helena Bonham Carter, Roddy McDowall, Raquel Welch, Ben Stein, Andre the Giant, Richard Simmons, Don Knotts, Lee Marvin, Nicolas Cage, Shirley Jones, Mary Hart, Mary Kay Letourneau, Mary Magdalene, Mary Tyler Moore, Mary Queen of Scots, Jennifer Jones, John F. Kennedy, Jr., Caligula, Leona Helmsley, Ivana Trump, James Garner, Jean Simmons, "Hitmakers: Teens Who Stole Pop Music," Dionne Warwick, Bobby Darin, Jerry Leiber and Mike Stoller, and Burt Bacharach. Out of twenty-eight shows, only six can actually be categorized as featuring non-celebrities. Three of the non-celebrities appeared during "Mary Week" (Mary Kay Letourneau, Mary Magdalene, and Mary Queen of Scots). One, Caligula, was a Roman emperor known for his legendary lunacy and sexual perversity. And two shows featured pop song writers. One might argue that John F. Kennedy, Jr. and Leona Helmsley should be classified as non-celebrities, but both were media personalities with little actual historical significance other than the images they created.

One of the characteristics of a celebrity culture is that we sometimes cannot distinguish between the legitimately notorious and the person who is only notorious for his notoriety. We therefore naturally tend to make political leaders out of our Hollywood stars and Hollywood stars out of our political leaders. Advocacy groups, using the same advertising methods associated with product endorsements, use celebrities to rally every cause under the sun. Politicians stoop to spectacle. Richard Nixon appears on *Laugh-In* barking, "Sock it to me! Sock it to me! Sock it to me!" (They did.) A B-movie actor and spokesman for General Electric is voted President of the United States in a landslide election. Jane Fonda and Sissy Spacek plead before a U.S. Senate Committee about the plight of the American farmer, their only credentials being that they both portrayed farm women in films. President Clinton plays himself in a made-for-TV movie. Sonny Bono is elected to the U.S. House of Representatives. A professional wrestler is catapulted into the highest political office in Minnesota. I do not mean to imply that actors or comedians or recording artists are not capable of serving as elected officials. In my opinion Ronald Reagan was one of our best Presidents, but it seems that celebrities have now earned the right to speak for us based solely on the depth of their image penetration, their potential political power being the equivalent thereof. Likewise, any national candidate automatically *becomes* a celebrity of sorts upon entering the political arena and must conform to the principles of spectatorship if he is to be elected. In the process democracy becomes a matter of *style* over substance, and *image-making* becomes our public discourse.

While a Rembrandt will lose its splendor if copied over and over for a mass market, just the opposite happens when the individual life of a celebrity is mass-produced, says Stuart Ewen in his book *All Consuming Images*: "In their ability to magnify, and create near universal recognition, the mass media are able to invest the everyday lives of formerly everyday people with a magical sense of value, a secularized imprint of the *sacred*."[29] Although celebrities shine above us, says Ewen, many of them are like us. We *identify* with them. Or as Dolly Parton once said, "I think people see themselves in me. People don't come to see me be me, they come to see me be them."[30] The whole story of the celebrity's success is that he or she comes from "the mass." Ewen explains:

Celebrity forms a symbolic pathway, connecting each aspiring individual to a universal image of fulfillment: to be someone, when "being no one" is the norm. Whereas the beginnings of celebrity often begin with a local, word-of-mouth following, invariably, becoming "someone" is a gift bestowed upon people by the image machine. The myriad stories of chance meetings and lucky breaks fuel the belief, for many, that it "may happen." Each success feeds the hopes of millions who will never make it. . . . In celebrities, people find not only a piece of themselves, but also a piece of what they strive for.[31]

The phenomenon of celebrity has not diminished since the Hollywood studio system of the 1930s; rather, Ewen says, "It has been transcended by somewhat less centralized image machinery that is far more vast, more diverse in its applications. Through it all, the commodity status of celebrity remains. To be known is to be sold."[32] What the machines of show business do best, of course, are to make *icons*. I do not use the term here to mean "the most famous of the famous," but in the same sense that the theatrical world uses the term *physical types*. Walter Lippmann called them *images in our heads*. Nietzsche called them *dream images*. I am somewhat reluctant to use Carl Jung's term *archetypes*, but it comes close to what I am getting at. It is the nature of the image machine to rip the hide off everything, skin it, boil it down to its critical element, simplify it, narrow it.[33] What we are left with are surfaces or *templates* to be copied and marketed. In truth, the deities of ancient Greece and Rome were templates. In myth and marble the Greeks and Romans saw themselves, what they wanted to be, what they strove for—a diverse assortment of human activity and passion on a grandiose scale. Paganism can take a variety of forms, but when all is said and done, the system boils down to three simple postulates—sex, violence, and a grand identity. As Camille Paglia says, "And so to Hollywood, the modern Rome: it is pagan sex and violence that have flowered so vividly in our mass media."[34] For four centuries the Protestants tried to hold them back, but the dam was breached. The gods are back in town.

PAGAN BEAUTY

The German philosopher Friedrich Nietzsche, a student of the Greek imagination, wrote in *The Birth of Tragedy* that once the gods had been cast in their various roles and placed upon the stage of Mount Olympus, the Greeks began to emulate them. For the Greeks to glorify themselves, said the German philosopher, they had to "feel themselves worthy of glory; they had to behold themselves . . . in a higher sphere. . . . This is the sphere of beauty, in which they saw their mirror images, the Olympians."[35] The Greek gods and their Roman counterparts were exaggerated personalities, massive yet familiar to the Greek psyche. Within the pantheon one finds the unfaithful husband (Zeus/Jupiter), the jealous wife (Hera/Juno), the promiscuous lesser brother (Poseidon/Neptune), the unpitying death angel (Hades/Pluto), the homebound virgin (Hestia/Vesta), the wise daughter (Athena/Minerva), the beautiful son (Apollo) and his twin sister (Artemis/Diana), the seductress (Aphrodite/Venus), the bloody warrior (Ares/Mars), the nimble deceiver (Hermes/Mercury), the ugly kind-heart (Hephaestus/Vulcan), and the drunken carouser (Dionysus/Bacchus).

Art was the vehicle whereby the Greeks worshiped themselves. The aesthetic experience and the religious experience were one and the same. Unlike the Hebrews, who were strictly prohibited from making any type of representation of God's likeness, the Greeks, with their highly visual imagination, perfected the art of representation. To them, man was the measure of all things. The Greeks stressed *ideal* forms from a totally human-centered point of view. In polishing their technique they stumbled upon what Augustine called the *divine logos*—God's universal forms. Still, the content of their art glorified the human body. Camille Paglia says, "The Greek Kouros inherited Egypt's cold Apollonian eye, created the great western fusion of sex, power, and personality."[36] When Paglia uses the term "Apollonian eye," she is inadvertently referring to Augustine's *logos*. Paglia believes, as did Nietzsche, that the themes in Greek myth and art reflected the tension between the artist's imposition of form on the wild and chaotic forces in nature, or the Dionysian dynamic. Dionysus, the god of wine and revelry, was worshiped in cult festivals given over to sexual display, "where waves overwhelmed all family life and its venerable traditions; the most savage nature instincts were unleashed, including even that horrible mixture of sensuality and cruelty."[37]

Paglia defines pagan beauty as the "brazen pomp of sexual personae."[38] Nietzsche called it the "logic of sensuousness"[39] in which the indispensable aesthetic precondition is that of *rapture*—rapture of sexual arousal, of the feast, of daring, of movement, of nature, of cruelty, of great desire, of the will.[40] Nietzsche saw the Dionysian component as the volcanic source of art, the artist capturing the lava and molding it into an objective form. It should be said that artists and art critics who do not recognize the God of the Bible as the originator of universal forms are left with placing man at the center of bringing order to the chaos of human experience.[41] This is what Paglia and Nietzsche are doing; nevertheless, the notion that pagan beauty is a play on the tension that exists between debased human passions and the girdling of those passions by imposing form upon it is, if not an accurate observation, a highly insightful one.

According to Paglia, the Athenian cult of beauty had a supreme theme—the beautiful boy—the West's greatest sexual persona.[42] It is a theme that runs out of Egypt, through the Hellenic period into Hellenistic art, through Byzantine art into the Italian Renaissance, through European romanticism and into our own popular culture.[43] The beautiful boy is an adolescent, "hovering between a female past and a male future," "youthful bloom," a "girl-boy masculinity."[44] Archaic kouroi were vigorously masculine, says Paglia, but by the early and high classic periods these works had achieved the "perfect harmony of masculine and feminine"; then, by the time of the Hellenistic period, a definite "slide toward the feminine" can be seen.[45] One easily recognizes the style, for it is the classic youthful Greek face: high brow, strong straight nose, girlishly fleshy cheeks, full petulant mouth, and short upper lip.[46] The beautiful boy is beardless, sleek, "dreamy, remote, autistic, lost in a world of androgynous self-completion."[47] It is the face of Apollo, *The Benevento Boy*,

Cellini's *Perseus* who lifts the head of Medusa, Botticelli's *St. Sebastian*, Gainsborough's *Blue Boy*, Lord Byron, and the blonde Aryan youth in Hitler's propaganda; it is the face of Elvis Presley.

The idolization of the beautiful boy flowed out of a male-oriented Greek culture where one can find painted on everyday bowls and vases naked youths exercising with older bearded men; the elderly reclined at the drinking party or symposia caressing their favorites. Generally homosexuality—male-only relationships—was scorned; the correct term would be bisexuality, for the man who headed a family and produced many children and had a male lover was really the pattern.[48] This is not to say that Greek men did not also have female relationships outside the bonds of marriage. In Corinth, whose patron goddess was Aphrodite, temple prostitution was both accepted and utilized. Greek pottery also portrayed heterosexual relationships, males pursuing and embracing young females, and middle-aged men enjoying the company of dancing girls.[49] Apparently, Athenian women took all this in stride, but in Sparta the girls joined in with boys in athletic contests. Spartan girls were scorned by some Athenians because they paraded around town with their *chitons* (tunic-like dresses) draped open at the sides exposing their bodies and then later in the day were found racing or wrestling naked at the gym with males. Homosexuality was deeply entrenched in the Spartan military, and wives and concubines were swapped around by husbands.[50]

Although most Greek women were keepers at home, in myth and in the artist's imagination the female persona often took on masculine traits. Athena (Minerva), the goddess of wisdom, skills, and warfare, appears in cross-sexual form wearing male armor. She is motherless, having sprung from Zeus's thinking brow. Artemis (Diana) is the mirror image of her twin brother Apollo; she is the boyish huntress, the Amazon woman, the focused woman athlete, the man-hater. Paglia says Diana's militant chastity is a metaphor for her "power, freedom, and audacity."[51] She is Greta Garbo and Murphy Brown. (I am not suggesting that all Greco-Roman deities have their cinematic or telegenic equivalent, although many of them do, a correspondence Paglia eagerly points out.) So then, one sees how the Greek nude was more than just an ideal; it was also a projection of sexual power; it was a male dream machine tottering on the edge of perversity. Most of all, it was big theater. What would the Greeks have done with a camera?

The pendulum between Apollonian high form and Dionysian decadence swings back and forth. Sometime in the fourth century the Greek ideal of the male athlete swung over to a softer, gentler physique.[52] Then, when Rome embraced Greek culture, they took the softness out of the kouroi and made the male image an instrument of national propaganda.[53] Pagan beauty took on a fascist grand style. When Rome was still a republic, the Bacchus cult was entirely shocking. After promiscuity spread through the city in 186 B.C. the cult's practices were officially banned. However, "with typical Roman ambivalence," says Barry Cunliffe, "if a citizen felt particularly moved to worship the god, a magistrate could grant him permission to do so, so long as no more than five people assembled together."[54]

Imperial Rome came to permit more than the Greeks would have ever allowed. Lesbianism, public sex, and open sodomy were sins named among them. And it was not just the blatant sexual exhibitionism that marked their moral decline; it was also the boldness by which new levels of crudity were achieved. "Greek aristocratic athleticism split in two in Rome," says Paglia, one part "vulgar gladiatorship by ruffians and slaves," the other a "leisure-class sexual adventurism, a sporting life then as now."[55] For most Roman citizens the working day ended early in the afternoon, providing several hours of leisure time before supper. The public bath was a favorite place to fill the hours where one could enjoy a hot and cold bath, a rubdown, a game or two, and the conversation of friends. However, the real excitement was to be found at the circus. During the Imperial era public entertainment coincided with the feast days and multiplied so that there was some kind of state-sponsored spectacle every other day. Inaugural celebrations could last one hundred days nonstop and provided screaming audiences with hundreds of human corpses and thousands of animal carcasses. The circus games were social events that people attended to "see and be seen"; citizens decked themselves out in beautiful clothing, elaborate hairstyles, and jewelry.[56] One could also eat at the circus; and if one ate the self into oblivion so as to spoil supper, the *vomitoria* was just outside the exits of the amphitheater.

Popular performers, whether charioteers, gladiators, or actors, attracted their own fan clubs. Most of the gladiators were condemned slaves who fought to the death in hopes of one day earning their freedom, but some were freemen who put on their armor for the glory and the money. Machinery beneath the surface of the arena lifted props, scenery, and wild beasts into place while orchestrated music highlighted the action and set the mood. Those who had the animals turned on them also fought to the death but most always lost, not having the weapons of the gladiator to defend themselves. In the arena myth was transformed into visual spectacle. Even women got into the act. One account describes Minerva, half-dressed and brandishing a skewer, chasing a Tuscan wild boar around the arena.[57] Female mimes were respected more for their bodies than for their acting skills and therefore were frequently encouraged to perform a striptease in front of the crowd. Around the first century B.C. audiences lost interest in the performances of sophisticated Greek tragedy, preferring extemporaneous comedy comprised of bawdy gestures and vulgar jokes.

A show of flesh and a gush of blood were what spectators craved. Sometimes the emperors themselves managed to provide the entertainment, which was a bit unusual since actors were barred from Roman citizenship.[58] Caligula (the emperor featured on A&E's *Biography*) once paraded his wife before the army in soldier's armor. The Emperor himself made many public appearances in women's clothes. "He was eager to appear to be anything rather than a human being and an emperor," said one observer.[59] Nero, who appeared as a Greek tragedian to watch the city of Rome burn, blaming the Christians for the arson, continued Caligula's tradition of "class transvestism." On stage Nero played the roles of slave, blind man, and pregnant woman. He engaged in mock marriages with men, sometimes playing the groom, sometimes the bride. He built riverbank brothels for a show, filled them with patrician women, and solicited them from the doorways. Elagabalus did the same, only he used real Roman brothels and appeared on the other side of the doorway as a female prostitute. Likewise, Commodus appeared in public as a transvestite Hercules and "scandalized the army with his silks, jewelry . . . dancing . . . plays, pageants, and parlor games."[60] Not all the emperors stooped to so low a spectacle, but in a general sense the Dionysian dynamic prevailed in Rome when its leaders were said to be gods. Similarly, in our own culture the pendulum seems to be swinging in the direction of the god of revelry. We find ourselves under a Dionysian deluge. The beautiful boy becomes grotesque. Elvis so quickly slides to Michael Jackson.

If a culture's level of decadence can be measured by the sexual theatrics of its leaders, then our own times warn us that we are in deep trouble. Upon taking the oath of office, President-elect Clinton promised that he would have "the most ethical administration in the history of the Republic." How then did this man, who wagged his finger in the face of the American public saying, "I did not have sexual relations with that woman, Monica Lewinsky," when he full well had, manage to rank first that same year in a Gallup poll as the person Americans most admired? On the surface this seems like a great incongruity, a mind-boggling puzzle for a nation with deep Puritan roots. But when one understands the power of sexual personae in an image-saturated culture floundering in moral relativism there is little irony to be found.

When television was born, the party boss died. The personality of the candidate, intimately captured by the television screen, overwhelmed traditional political machinery. Before television one could confidently vote for a candidate's party label with little worry about whether the platform was going to be upheld. In 1996 Republican presidential nominee Bob Dole said that he had not even read his party's platform. To be elected today a candidate must do what one of Nixon's chief aides told him to do: "Break away from linear logic: present a barrage of impressions." Nixon, who had lost his first bid for President, learned his lesson.

Therefore, the second time around the campaign hired Canadian communication theorist Marshall "The Medium Is the Message" McLuhan, who went on to lecture the Nixon team that the shaping of a candidate's integral image had taken the place of discussing conflicting points of view. The 1968 campaign was based on one overriding premise: Get the voters to like the guy, and the battle's won.

Even as early as 1948, the year television cameras were introduced to the national party conventions, there were hints that the old way of doing things was about to change. The *New York Herald Tribune* ran a two-page ad that read, "Starting Today on LIFE-NBC Television: A History-Making Presentation of a Great Spectacle—The Republican Convention." The ad proclaimed that television would "bring you face to face with your favorite candidates and the important *personalities* of our time."[61] A poll of "video experts" taken before the Republican convention were asked who would be the next President if television viewers alone made the selection. Edward Murrow said Eisenhower would be because "for some reason the light doesn't seem to bounce or refract off his bald head the way it does off Stassen's."[62] Murrow, who understood the tendency of television to value image over substance, was entirely serious. Today national party conventions are little more than protracted television commercials. The 2000 Republican National Convention avoided anything that smacked of controversy. As with the Nixon campaign and all the other campaigns that have followed, the goal was to present countless feel-good images, from Bush's small-town video vignettes to the guest appearance of WWF's "The Rock," a personality best known for throwing metal chairs and sledgehammers at his opponents while screaming obscenities.

Despite lying to his staff, his wife, and all of the American people; despite the fact that he perjured himself; despite his illicit affairs; despite his impeachment (George Will wrote that Clinton was not our worst President, but rather the worst person we have had as President), President Clinton received a standing ovation at the 2000 Democratic National Convention. Late on arrival opening night, as if the whole world should wait for him, the President's appearance preceded a video tribute to himself, narrated by himself, a truly "postmodern Napoleonic moment," reflected one journalist.[63] Walking through a maze somewhere within the modern amphitheater's corridors, the television cameras followed him for what seemed like several minutes. In the background Fleetwood Mac's "Don't Stop Thinking About Tomorrow" blared away. Upon entering the stage area, the television cameras captured women crying and delegates dancing. "The roar gave way to the kind of high-pitched screaming usually reserved for rock stars," wrote Bob Jones IV in *World* magazine.[64] After a self-celebrating speech that made halfhearted references to the Democratic nominee, Al Gore, the President lingered onstage, with blushed face, enjoying every minute, not wanting to leave, soaking it all in. This was a man who several weeks earlier had posed provocatively for the cover of *Esquire*, a man whose private life became the center of public controversy, a man whose aides, it is said, affectionately called him, of all things, Elvis.[65]

CHAPTER EIGHT

On Being Postmodern

*The preservation of liberty depends upon the intellectual and
moral character of the people. As long as knowledge and
virtue are diffused generally among the body of a nation,
it is impossible they should be enslaved.*[1]

JOHN ADAMS

*I often wonder if God recognizes His own son the way we've
dressed him up, or is it dressed him down? He's a regular
peppermint stick now, all sugar-crystal and saccharine when
he isn't making veiled references to certain commercial
products that every worshiper absolutely needs.*[2]

RAY BRADBURY, FAHRENHEIT 451

POSTMODERNISM IS A TURNING FROM RATIONALITY, AND AT
THE SAME TIME AN EMBRACING OF SPECTACLE.

---

⑨

L ike many of the Founding Fathers, John Adams was a product of the Enlightenment; yet he possessed a definite Christian
conscience that he acquired from his New England Puritan forefathers. If it is possible to speak of the Enlightenment as a period
of time rather than a way of thinking, then it would also be possible to speak of, say, Jonathan Edwards as a product of the
Enlightenment as well, which he was, but not in the sense that he

was an Enlightened philosophe or a person who placed human reason above revealed Scripture. As mentioned earlier, Enlightened thinking and Christianity in eighteenth-century America formed a unique blend and did not begin to separate ways, uncomfortably, until the nineteenth century. Nevertheless, as the quotation above indicates, Adams believed that if American democracy was to work at all, two ingredients were absolutely essential—*knowledge* and *virtue*. Knowledge, Adams's first ingredient, was a quintessential Enlightenment notion as well as a Puritan ideal. One must remember that after the Puritans arrived in New England, they provided shelter for themselves, erected churches, established a government, and then built *schools*. The ingredient of knowledge carries with it the notion that liberty is dependent on an informed citizenry.

Of course, Jefferson also espoused the idea of an informed citizenry. But unlike Adams, Jefferson was an admirer of the French philosophes. Perhaps this is why Adams foresaw the dictatorship of Napoleon and Jefferson did not. Adams had a clear understanding of how the American Revolution differed from its French counterpart. While reading Mary Wollstonecraft's *French Revolution,* Adams decried many of the Enlightened writers as "fools." On a blank page beside the book's contents he scribbled: "If [the] empire of superstition and hypocrisy should be over-thrown, happy indeed will it be for the world; but if all religion and all morality should be over-thrown with it, what advantage will be gained?"[3] When Adams listed his second ingredient of liberty, that of virtue, he no doubt had in mind the concept of Christian virtue. While the Enlightenment certainly provided definitions of virtue that could be drawn from Aristotle or Cicero, virtue in eighteenth-century America derived many, if not most, of its demarcations from the Bible.

Contemporary thought strikes heavy blows at both of Adams's ingredients. Knowledge and virtue are in jeopardy because contemporary thought is both anti-intellectual *and* amoral. This chapter considers the shift in thinking and doing now coming to be called postmodernism. Specifically, I will examine the mani-

festations of postmodernism in two important cultural arenas—
the college classroom and the church sanctuary.

FROM MODERN TO POSTMODERN

Postmodernism is somewhat difficult to define because the cultural sands are still shifting beneath our feet. It is a philosophy that
some have defined as a search for novelty, momentary enjoyment,
self-indulgence, euphoria, no fixed commitments, and no rules; all
opinions are valid; differences are celebrated; personal happiness
is a supreme virtue.[4] Some see postmodernism as a culture highlighted by personal entitlement, hyperconsumerism, and an entertainment mentality.[5] Donald Wood uses the term
"post-intellectualism," for which he lists four major attributes:
"*ignorance*, a decrease in personal effectual knowledge; *dumbth*,
a decline in critical thinking and problem solving abilities; *estab-
lishmentism*, the reluctance to engage in meaningful social criticism; and *specialization*, the loss of a broad liberal arts
perspective."[6] Still others point out that postmodernism is a rejection of any notion of objective truth upon which people can manage to find agreement. Therefore, the major question is no longer,
"Is it true?" but "How does it look?" and "How does it feel?"[7]
Along these lines, Gene Veith defines postmodernism as a worldview that "assumes that there is no objective truth, that moral values are relative, and that reality is socially constructed by a host
of diverse communities."[8]

Some see postmodernism as an affront against language,
believing that language itself is delusional. French social theorist
Jean Baudrillard is such a person, but he also goes a step further,
suggesting that not only is language delusional, but so is reality
itself, the thing language is supposed to represent.[9] Baudrillard
asserts that postmodernism places the emphasis on style, splashy
spectacle, and surface detail in lieu of rational thought.[10] We are
a culture of simulations as opposed to substantialities, a culture
of copies rather than originals. Baudrillard's belief that reality is
delusional is, of course, wrong, but his observation that the image
has superseded what is behind the image is fundamental in under-

standing our times. I would therefore like to add my own definition of postmodernism to the growing heap. It is a definition that
acknowledges the powerful consequences of our new electronic
media as well as our rejection of objective truth. Simply stated,
postmodernism is a turning *from* rationality, and at the same time
an embracing *of* spectacle.

One is hard-pressed to say exactly when the modern age
ended and the postmodern age began. Sven Birkerts, author of
The Gutenburg Elegies, draws the line somewhere in the 1950s—
that moment in our history when television worked its way into
the fabric of our lives.[11] Other scholars point to the cultural
upheaval of the 1960s as a time when America turned a significant corner. But to draw a line in the sand and say that modernism
stopped here and something entirely different began there is too
simplistic. Might we say, then, that for America, postmodernism
was born in the early twentieth century at about the same time
that electronic media were making its effects known? Could it be
said that the postmodern era took its first baby steps with the
movies, started to romp around the room during the Golden Age
of radio, later enjoyed a healthy childhood during the Cold War
era with television, and is now going through a period of bemused
puberty at the dawn of the twenty-first century?

If one were to bind the last hundred years into a book, as many
publishers have done, it would not be a volume of words on a
printed page, but a photo album of mind-branding images with
each decade containing memorable moments—a spunky blonde
in sailor blues touting men from a U.S. Navy recruitment poster;
a line of flappers doing the Charleston; a mustached madman
orating how Germany's time in the sun had come; a mushroom
cloud billowing upward through the atmosphere; a Greek god
swiveling his hips on *The Ed Sullivan Show*; John and Jackie and
children on a windy beach; a farewell salute from a resigned
President boarding a government helicopter; a spacecraft exploding in midair; Clinton wagging his finger to the camera, "I did not
have sexual relations with that woman . . ."; the Twin Towers
falling down.

One distinguishing feature of the postmodern era is that human beings gain their knowledge of the world through pictures. The image has replaced modernism's dependency on the written word. Of course, there are other distinguishing features between modernism and postmodernism. As noted in Chapter Four, Neil Postman has argued that people who lived in modernism's print culture possessed a "typographical mind," having a "sophisticated ability to think conceptually, deductively and sequentially; a high valuation of reason and order; and the abhorrence of contradiction; a large capacity for detachment and objectivity; and a tolerance for delayed response."[12] However, the postmodern mind rebels against reason, has an abhorrence toward sustained inquiry, has trouble distinguishing fact from fiction, and has a remarkable ability to hold at the same time two ideas that logically contradict each other.

In many ways postmodernism is the antithesis of modernism. The table below shows the strong contrasts between the two systems. Again, one cannot say that in the year 1955 the modern era ceased and the postmodern era began. Rather, during the twentieth century one worldview began to recede and another began to come to the forefront. The proliferation of images is not the *sole* force that is pushing us out of the modern era, but I would suggest that it is a *major* factor in the shift.

TWO SYSTEMS AT A GLANCE

MODERNISM	POSTMODERNISM
Trust in reason	Tendency toward relativism
Ideal of objectivity	Ideal of subjectivity
Empirical truth	Truth created
Trust in democratic institutions	Skeptical toward authority
Design	Chance
Unity	Diversity
Progress	No deep sense of the past other than nostalgia
Forward looking	Focused on here and now
Word-oriented	Image-oriented
Concerned with depth	Fixed on surfaces
"Teach me"	"Entertain me"

Once modernism reached its logical end, the embracing of spectacle seemed natural, even convenient. Gene Veith has shown how modernism created the conditions for postmodernism.[13] The Enlightenment made human reasoning the primary vehicle for discerning truth. Out of tedious induction modern science was born. Advances in technology were shown to be so bountiful that few questioned the new god of science. Its wonders and benefits even managed to squelch the romantics who questioned what kind of meaning could be found living in a cold, mechanistic universe. To the romantics, the universe was more than a machine and man was more than just a rational creature. The romantics asked, "What about human emotion? What about intuition? What about personal experience?" Materialism—the idea that matter is the only reality—could offer no meaning for existence. It is rather depressing to think that we all evolved from a lower life-form or that we are all alone in a gigantic universe. So the romantics turned *inward*—to the self—in order to create meaning. This journey into the self is an "every man did that which was right in his own eyes" philosophy called existentialism. Today existentialism has wrapped its tentacles around our most important cultural institutions. Postmodernism is existentialism popularized.[14]

PEDAGOGY IN A POSTMODERN ERA

These are odd times. On one hand, we still believe in the laws of nature. We could not send people into outer space or begin to assume that diseases could be cured if we did not. Yet, when it comes to personal morality, Americans see truth as relative. According to George Barna, only 28 percent of American adults are certain that moral truth is absolute.[15] The great majority of Americans are either unsure about the meaning of truth or see truth as relative. The shift from universal truths to personalized truth has loosened the glue that once held our nation together. There once was a time when the United States was compared to a kind of huge container in which various metals were mixed and melted together. The melting pot metaphor said that immigrants who came to America blended together to make one culture. One became an American by assenting to a creed, namely, the U.S. Constitution. The assimilated culture was stronger than the individual cultures of which it was composed. The idea of a melting pot assumes that there is such a thing as common American values—freedom, liberty, and equality under the law. In academia today the melting pot metaphor has been thrown out and replaced with a salad bowl metaphor that claims that different cultures, like different ingredients in a salad, are combined and tossed to create a final product, but without the loss of individual texture or flavor. Such a metaphor supports the much heralded concepts of cultural diversity and cultural relativism. Under this new paradigm there is no such thing as a "composite American," only hyphenated Americans who must assert their "rights" in order not to be victimized by an older, oppressive system.

Living in a salad bowl poses real problems for public institutions. For example, it is almost impossible for tax-supported schools to latch on to any type of overarching narrative to derive meaning and purpose for their existence. In the past the tenets of Christianity provided this narrative, but now public education has no unifying ideology other than serving the needs of a technological society claiming to be socially diverse. In his book *How Should We Then Live?* Francis A. Schaeffer described what happened a number of decades ago when the purpose of education was reduced to a matter of personal peace and affluence:

> All too often when the students of the early sixties asked their parents and others, "Why be educated?" they were told, in words if not by implication, "Because statistically an educated man makes so much more money a year." And when they asked, "Why make more money?" they were told, "So that you can send *your* children to the university." According to this type of spoken or implied answer, there was no meaning for man, and no meaning for education.[16]

Reflecting society at large, the college curriculum has fragmented. Some of this fragmentation was due to the wide diversity of professions in the workplace requiring specialized skills, but this was only part of the cause. The idea of a "core curriculum" became devalued on campuses. More than a century ago John Dewey injected into the university's bloodstream a highly potent pathogen that asserted that the school's task must be to "social-ize" the student so he or she could learn how to adapt to a rapidly changing society. Dewey did not view truth as a permanent real-ity but as an ever-changing construct dependent on "progress." Throughout the first half of the twentieth century Dewey's germ spread to all organs within the American university. Increasingly, colleges adopted an "elective system" that justified just about any kind of college course in a professor's imagination.

Typically, the core curriculum a century ago consisted of English composition, literature, history, mathematics, philosophy, foreign language, social science, and physical science. But in a study conducted by the National Association of Scholars, which surveyed the curriculum of fifty leading American colleges at four points in history (1914, 1939, 1964, 1993), it was concluded that core subjects have almost disappeared. The study showed that as core courses decreased, elective courses increased. In 1997 a stu-dent could receive a B.A. from Yale with only twelve credits in lit-erature, history, or science out of a total of 1,800 course listings in the college catalogue.[17] When a student publication on the Yale campus decided to take a poke at Yale's shallow curriculum, it came up with a list of courses any student could have selected if majoring in "Women's Studies." This list represents a possible sophomore year for the major:[18]

> Redesigning the Family: Challenges from Lesbians/Gay Men
> Photography and Images of the Body
> Love Books in the Middle Ages
> Intermediate Yoruba
> Women's History: Methodical and Comparative Inquiry
> AIDS in Society
> Listening to Music
> Affirmative Action and Civil Rights in the Labor Market
> Sexual Meanings
> Troubadours and Rock Stars—a Comparison

After the Yale administration read the newspaper, named *Light and Truth* after the university's motto *Lux et Veritas*, a response was given that said that while it was not likely a student would devise such a schedule, "technically" the schedule was legitimate.[19] Author Martin Gross says our "colleges are now the ground zero of anti-intellectualism" and that what colleges are producing today are "graduates with heads full of idiosyncratic, isolated bits of knowledge," but with no "organization of thought, no plan, no basics, no foundation. . . . This gravely weakens their ability to think constructively and to distinguish truth from falsehood."[20] Indeed, Brown University's own disregard for a core curriculum led one of its deans to proclaim, "[T]he world is changing so rapidly that nobody's sure what knowledge is important anymore."[21]

Perhaps it was this inability to discern knowledge that so immobilized the administration at Brown University when irate protesters stole four thousand copies of the student newspaper, the *Daily Herald*, because of an ad placed by conservative David Horowitz denouncing the notion of paying reparations to the descendants of American slaves. The day after the theft, protesters broke into the *Herald's* office and trashed the remaining copies of the paper. Unable to tap into what kind of knowledge was appropriate for theft and burglary, the administration winked at the incident, claiming that the ad was "deliberately and deepful hurtful" and that a defining value at Brown was responding to the pain of those who were offended.[22] Despite the fact that no legal action was directed toward this "brownshirt activity" (the term editorialist John Leo now uses to describe PC campus "misbehav'n"), the university's response illustrates how what was once deemed free speech on college campuses is now often refashioned into hate speech. Leo says, "A whole vocabulary has sprung up to convert free expression into punishable behavior: hate speech, verbal assault, intellectual harassment, and nontraditional violence, a fancy term for stinging criticism."[23]

The secularization of the university, along with the unraveling of the core curriculum, has opened the floodgates for radical political entities to influence the overall mission of public education. In the 1960s universities began using the terms *diversity* and *mutual tolerance* in their mission statements, but today these same code words are heralded by groups that are often the most intolerant.[24] In the world of political correctness it would appear that the group that screams the loudest or whines the most ends up writing the university's policies.

While administrators try to figure out what constitutes knowledge and free speech, Americans in general and students in particular continue to become more stupid. At an earlier time in our history America's colleges required entering students to have mastered Greek or Latin, or both. But today colleges are lowering the academic bar on basic English proficiency. Scholastic Aptitude Test (SAT) scores, which gauge literacy skills for college-bound students, have dropped over the last several decades. To accommodate the drop, more and more colleges are redefining SAT measures or ignoring SAT scores altogether, claiming that the test discriminates against race, gender, and national origin. Others say that some students just think and learn in a different way or the test no longer fits the school's philosophical point of view.[25] In the most recent comprehensive study of adult literacy conducted in America on behalf of the Department of Education, it was found that half the nation in 1992 fell within the lowest two levels of literacy proficiency out of five levels. The study reported that almost a quarter of Americans surveyed cannot perform tasks involving a "brief uncomplicated text," such as filling out a bank deposit slip or locating information in a newspaper article.[26]

While it should concern us that a quarter of all Americans cannot read a bus schedule, use an automatic teller machine, or perhaps fill out a butterfly voting ballot, a more elusive enemy of participatory democracy is that of *aliteracy*. This is a problem not so much connected with higher education as it is with one's personal education. An aliterate person is someone who can read but does not want to. Mark Twain commented on aliteracy in this way: "The man who does not read good books has no advantage over the man who cannot read them." Even though more and

more books are being published every year, Americans are reading less and less. A 1999 Gallup poll reported that only 7 percent
of Americans can be classified as "voracious readers," and the
number of people who do not read at all has been rising for the
past twenty years.[27] One might assume that Americans like the
idea of reading books, that we frequent bookstores, buy books,
put them on bookshelves and coffee tables, and even read a page
or two in them, but that is all. Our situation seems to be
approaching that of Huxley's *Brave New World* where some
books could be had but no one actually wanted to read one.

    One reason for the decline in reading has to do with an infor-
mation environment that does not encourage book-cracking. In
an image-saturated world, where we get most of our news and
entertainment from the television, who needs reading? The astute-
ness that surrounded our once bookish culture is disappearing.
Washington Post's Linton Weeks puts her finger on our predicament when she says, "Where we once deified the lifestyles of writers such as Ernest Hemingway and F. Scott Fitzgerald, we now
fantasize about rock-and-roll gods, movie starlets or NBA super-
studs (e.g. MTV's 'Cribs'). The notion of writer-as-culture-hero is
dead and gone."[28] When the Girl Scouts of America were asked
in a survey to name their role models, less than 1 percent named
their parents. Not even ministers or teachers could get within 1
percent. On the other hand, two-thirds of the Girl Scouts named
celebrities as their favorite role models.[29] Television talk show
hosts are also among our favorite cultural heroes. While it could
be argued that Oprah Winfrey encourages reading through her
book endorsements and her own magazine (a periodical in which
she appears on the cover of every issue), other talk show hosts like
Politically Incorrect's Bill Maher says that he has not read a book
in years.[30] By his example, hero Maher is saying that reading is
irrelevant in our age. Maher might have just as easily have said,
"Reading books is not important to me because today it is television that informs the culture. We all live in TV-Land now."

    There is even a tendency for people to believe that television
awards us with certain societal gifts that at one time were always

attributed to literacy. Actor LeVar Burton made such a mistake in 1999 when he appeared before a U.S. House subcommittee protesting the cutting off of federal funds for Public Broadcasting. I hesitate to use this illustration because I believe PBS represents the best of television. Nevertheless, Burton, who is the host of the PBS children's television series *Reading Rainbow* and one-time engineer on the famed Star Trek *Enterprise*, called PBS a "shining light." "It is about the kids," he said, just before he whipped out a cellphone, flipped it open, and declared that we have such phones because "some kid grew up watching 'Star Trek' and saw Captain Kirk reach behind to that place on his hip and pull that thing out and call Scotty on the ship. That kid then grew up, became an engineer and designed a device that is as common to us today as the bread toaster."[31] Burton provided no evidence for his history of the cellphone and failed to mention that while the inspiration for the cellphone may have come from Captain Kirk, the said engineer could not have developed the skills necessary for making such a device by watching television. The engineer had to first learn how to read, write, and do arithmetic. Nevertheless, this is the type of irrationality that surrounds an irrational medium.

Not only does America face the challenges that come with illiteracy and aliteracy, but we also face the problem of cultural literacy. Our schools are producing students who are clueless about the basic tenets of our government as well as our rich national history. In his book *Cultural Literacy: What Every American Needs to Know*, E. D. Hirsch, Jr. claims that we are losing that great reservoir of knowledge that all literate Americans should possess if they wish to do such things as pick up a newspaper, read it, and make sense out of what they read in the larger context of our culture. Hirsch defines cultural literacy as that "shared body of fact, tradition, and symbol." It is that knowledge that "lives *above* the everyday levels of knowledge that everyone possesses and *below* the expert level known by only specialists."[32] It is the kind of knowledge that should be expected by all "common readers." In the past students could be expected to get this knowledge in elementary school—information about such people as John Adams,

Susan B. Anthony, and Benedict Arnold—information about such places as the Antarctic Ocean, the Arctic Ocean, and the Atlantic Ocean. The Department of Education now reports that nearly a third of our fourth-, eighth-, and twelfth-graders do not even understand the basics of the American political system, and fewer than half of high school seniors have a basic grasp of American history.[33]

And it gets worse. In a recent Roper survey of America's elite colleges and universities, it was found that only 34 percent of the respondents could identify George Washington as the American general at the battle of Yorktown, only 23 percent knew James Madison was the Father of the Constitution, and only 22 percent of college seniors could pinpoint that "government of the people, by the people, and for the people" was a line from the Gettysburg Address. Yet of those surveyed, a whopping 99 percent of students easily recognized the cartoon characters of Beavis and Butthead, and a full 98 percent were acquainted with the rap singer Snoop Doggy Dogg.[34] This should not come as a total shock, considering that 50 percent of younger voters now get most of their information about politics from late-night comedians.[35]

Not surprisingly, the general public fares little better than students in cultural literacy. So often what occurs in the halls of higher education manages to finds its way to high school and elementary classrooms, smothering the rest of the culture. In a 1997 survey of one thousand U.S. citizens commissioned by the National Constitution Center, it was found that only 5 percent of American adults could correctly answer ten fundamental questions about the U.S. Constitution. For example, only 6 percent of those polled could name all four rights guaranteed by the First Amendment. (In case you are wondering, these would include freedom of speech, freedom of the press, the right to peaceably assemble, and the right to petition the government for redress of grievances.) Almost one quarter of Americans in the survey could not even name *one* of these rights. Furthermore, about a third of the respondents did not know the number of branches in the federal government, and two-thirds could not name all three branches.[36]

198 The Vanishing Word

An important branch of cultural literacy is that of biblical literacy. When William Jennings Bryan stood before delegates at the Democratic National Convention in 1896 and declared, "you shall not crucify mankind upon a cross of gold," he was speaking to an audience accustomed to the unapologetic use of biblical metaphor in political oratory. In fact, Bryan told fellow orators that the best rhetorical devices were found in Holy Writ: "The people are more familiar with the Bible than with any other single book, and lessons drawn from it reinforce the speech."[37] Lincoln would have agreed and therefore filled his speeches with numerous biblical allusions, giving us such memorable phrases as "A house divided against itself cannot stand." One hundred years ago most American citizens were familiar with the basic content of the Scriptures, but no longer. Today public speakers run the risk of getting puzzled looks when using quotations from the Bible.

No wonder politicians now prefer to draw their one-liners from an entirely different repertoire: "Where's the beef?" (1984 national primaries); "Make my day" (Reagan in a 1985 press conference); "Don't stop thinking about tomorrow" (Clinton's theme). Andree Seu says, "We are fast approaching—let us say the handwriting is on the wall—the end of the age of biblical literacy, and the genesis of an age where every biblical allusion will have to be explained."[38] Why is this? Simply because the Bible is no longer a part of our information environment. In a recent Gallup poll, 64 percent of those questioned said they were too busy to read the Bible.[39] While the average household has three Bibles, less than half of American citizens can name the first book in the Old Testament.[40] Even Christians have difficulty recognizing basic biblical facts. In one survey, 12 percent of Christian respondents identified Noah's wife as Joan of Arc.[41]

Let me for a moment leave the subjects of irrationality and the loss of various forms of literacy and turn to another topic—that of personal entitlement and spectacle. Despite the anti-intellectual reordering of higher education, good teachers can still be found on many campuses. Unfortunately, for teachers who take their calling seriously, there exists a predicament. On one hand, there is the teacher's sincere desire to impart knowledge to the student. The predicament arises when the teacher comes to a realization that many students are indifferent to this sincere desire and could care less about the subject matter. What the students really want are good grades and an easy ride. After all, with the payment of tuition comes an "entitlement" to above-average grades. For most college students, sitting in a classroom for three hours a week per class per semester while listening to a lecturing teacher inflicts about as much pain as reading a three-hundred-word book without pictures. To ask students to do both is absurd.

Try to figure out these two seemly conflicting sets of statistics. According to the UCLA Higher Education Research Institute, which yearly conducts studies of freshman school norms, today's college freshmen are spending less time studying and doing homework than any previous year since 1987. In 1987 47 percent of freshmen reported studying six or more hours a week. Thirteen years later only 36 percent reported studying that amount of time. Ironically, while freshmen study time has gone down, high school grade averages have gone up. In 2000 42 percent of college freshmen reported earning A averages in high school compared to 18 percent in 1968. Only 7 percent reported getting C averages in 2000 compared to 23 percent in 1968.[42] So, what is one to conclude from these figures? There are only two possibilities: Either student brain size is increasing in America, causing higher averages without having to study, or it is just easier to get an A these days at school.

Newspaper journalist and Pulitzer Prize nominee Peter Sacks came to the latter conclusion when he gave up his pad and pencil (as well as higher pay) for a classroom lectern. Sacks writes that he experienced a "cultural shock" compared to his own college days twenty years earlier. Looking out upon his introductory journalism class at a community college, he quickly realized that the students had dramatically changed:

> I scanned the classroom and the unaccustomed sights before me. . . . I saw young women trying very hard to look like mod-

els in fashion magazines, with their big hair and big lips. . . . Scattered mostly in the back and far side rows were young males with professional sports baseball caps, often worn backwards. Completing the uniform of these guys was usually a pair of baggy shorts, a team T-shirt, and an ample attitude. Slumped in their chairs, they stared at me with looks of disdain and boredom, as if to say, "Who . . . cares where you worked, or what your experience is, or what you know? Say something to amuse me."[43]

This was only the beginning of Sacks's journey into the joys of teaching. Early on the administration had informed him that what was expected of a teacher was not the "actual content of learning," but whatever "worked to keep the students' attention."[44] Sacks was told that students at the college preferred working in discussion groups rather than listening to a teacher. The guiding principle seemed to be that students were to be kept busy without becoming bored.

But Sacks thought otherwise and set out to become what he perceived a proper teacher to be, and this did not include being an entertainer. After a year of teaching he was up for tenure, a status determined by a committee of peer-teachers in his own department. The committee met in a large lecture hall used for European history, which Sacks comments was all adorned with Nazi flags. When the meeting began, student evaluations were passed around. The sharpest critiques came from a newswriting class in which Sacks took a certain amount of professional pride. The students wrote comments such as, "He presents himself as God . . . Expects us to be great . . . He grades too hard."[45]

Needless to say, Sacks did not get tenure. The chairman of the committee suggested he take an acting class, and the Pulitzer Prize nominee was put on probation. Feelings hurt, but curiosity still intact, Sacks devised a survey to probe deeper into the mind-set of his students. He asked them what they thought were the most important qualities in a teacher. Forty-one percent said the teacher must be entertaining. Thirty-seven percent said the teacher must be warm and friendly. Zero percent said the teacher must be demanding.[46] Later a former student told him bluntly, "We want you guys to dance, sing, and cry. Seriously, that is what we consider to be good learning. We expect so much more from everything now because of the media. You guys can't compete."[47]

Sacks hypothesized that if he were to dumb down his instruction, make his classes more like kindergarten playtime, and teach in line with the evaluations, then he would get raving reviews and thus save his job. This he did and soon earned tenure. What Sacks says he received was an "eye-opening account of teaching in Postmodern America." The "system" rewarded coddling the students, entertaining them, and demanding little more than a mustering of mediocrity.

PIETY IN A POSTMODERN ERA

It has been claimed by some well-meaning Christians that secular journalists ignore American religious life. I do not completely agree with such an assessment. There is plenty of evidence to suggest that editors and producers constantly have their antenna up for trends and movements taking place within the church. For example, on July 16, 2001, *Newsweek* showcased the Christian entertainment industry with a feature story entitled, "The Glorious Rise of Christian Pop." I must include here the opening paragraph of the article to demonstrate how journalists are indeed sensitive to religious happenings.

> "Are you ready to rip the face off this place?" screams the lead singer of Pillar. A hyped-up crowd of teens—6,000 strong—goes nuts. The aggressive rap-rock band launches into a pummeling kickoff number, the surly singer pounding the stage with his steel-toed boot, sweating right through his baggy Army fatigues and black bandanna. He gestures like a member of some vicious street gang as he screams and roars into the mike, his arm swinging low as if on the way to the requisite crotch grab. This crude move is as integral to rap-rock as the blown kiss is to a lounge act, and is usually accompanied by a testosteroid explosion of expletives. The singer's hand slaps down hard on his thigh—and stays there. Gripping his pants leg with conviction, he screams, "Jesus Christ!" Pause. "Is he in your heart?"[48]

From this paragraph several observations can be made. The first observation concerns the subject of aesthetics. It is quite obvious that the group Pillar borrows an aesthetic found in secular rock music. The lead singer is copying a style of performance he apparently saw on a rock stage or perhaps on MTV. Those who like to defend all forms of contemporary Christian music under a banner that "all music is neutral" either have their heads in the sand or know nothing about the histories and values surrounding music forms. Second, the journalist who wrote this story *knows* the Christian band is imitating a style found in secular rock groups. When you carefully read between the lines there is a certain cynicism bleeding through here (a cynicism that is called for I might add). Journalists, even those with no religious affinity, have an innate sense toward what is irreverent. They know foolishness when they see it. But a third observation I would like to make, one that I would like to extend in the remaining part of this chapter, is that much of what is going on in our church sanctuaries falls under my definition of postmodernism—that is, a turning from rationality and an embracing of spectacle.

Now some might argue that the *Newsweek* article quoted above is only about one segment of the Christian youth culture, and that we need not concern ourselves with the stage antics of Pillar, because, after all, youthful trends usually enjoy a moment of popularity and then fizzle out—like the hula hoop. But when it comes to theatrics, it would seem that Christian adults are getting into the act as well. *The Wall Street Journal* documented some time ago the various methods churches are now using to attract their communities. One account cited a staged wrestling match of church employees.[49] Another article described the antics of a Las Vegas pastor who concluded his sermon by "ascending into heaven" via invisible wires surrounded by smoke, fire, and a light show.[50]

Robert Schuller runs the Crystal Cathedral in Garden Grove, California. When the see-through sanctuary is not being used for Schuller's weekly broadcast, it doubles as a Broadway theater during the Easter season. Every year Schuller stages an elaborate

Passion play with a cast of hundreds, complete with white Arabian horses, tigers, fireworks, and angels. (The angels fly forty feet above the heads of the gaping audience.) The technical aspects rival those at Disneyland down the road. The acting is superb, the choreography all on cue. But some have complained that what goes on inside Schuller's glass castle is mostly "smoke and mirrors."[51] Traditionally, Passion plays have sought to involve the audience in such a way that it identifies with the rowdy mob that shouts, "Crucify Him!" Not so with Schuller's show. In the Crystal Cathedral version the mob never mentions the word *crucify*. The audience is not asked, directly or indirectly, to put itself in the place of Jesus' accusers. Instead, the audience is distanced from the action—mere spectators watching a high-tech theatrical presentation. The Atonement is watered down, and the Passion story "becomes only one more tale of a suffering hero."[52] Michael R. Linton says the Cathedral's Jesus is little more than a "cosmic pixie from Never-Never Land" who counsels the crowd not to be afraid to ask for bread and safety—a Jesus who "promises anything we want, 'if we only believe.' Fairy dust for everybody, and nothing required."[53]

All the fairy dust being tossed about inside the Crystal Cathedral makes for a great show and is no doubt a factor in drawing sizable crowds. Any underlying justification for high-flying angels and preachers alike usually is not stated by the leadership, but it is nevertheless obvious to anyone who will devote two minutes to think about it. "If people want to be entertained," says the unspoken rationale, "then, by all means, let's entertain them." Subjectivism and existentialism are the dominant values in this new paradigm of worship. And sadly, it is theology that often finds itself upstaged by spectacle.

A new kind of church is in our midst. David F. Wells says these new churches are like mushrooms springing up all over the American landscape:

> Gone, very often are the familiar church buildings, and in their place are those that look more like low-slung corporate head-

quarters or country clubs. Inside, a cyclone of change has ripped out the crosses, the pews, the eighteenth-century hymns, the organs, the biblical discourses. In their place are contemporary songs, drums, cinema-grade seats, light discourses, professional singers, drama, and humor.[54]

"But there is no sense of crisis about any of this," says Wells. "Quite the reverse. The appearance is that these churches have reality by the tail."[55] Those who espouse the new paradigm argue that worship needs to be more than just "preaching at people." Generation X expects to find at church all the communication forms they experience every day in the popular culture. The church, it is said, has to be "user-friendly," or as one preacher, Pastor "Spike" Hogan, explained to a Florida newspaper, "We're dumbing down the Gospel. That's what God did when he sent his son."[56]

To use Pastor Hogan's terminology, "dumbing down the Gospel" may include a variety of new techniques to reach and keep a younger generation—rock bands, a "come-as-you-are" dress code, open-mic mornings, multimedia presentations, eating in the church services, and occasionally a little dancing here and there. Under the new paradigm, PowerPoint projections have replaced the traditional hymnbook, praise teams have replaced robed choirs, and "life lessons" have replaced Sunday sermons.

Perhaps more than we realize, contemporary Christian music (CCM) has been instrumental in altering our worship services. Christian music hits are not just consumed by the public, but are repeated through performance in local churches. There is nothing innately wrong with what is contemporary. At one point all great Christian hymns were new to the public. *New* does not always translate to mean *bad*. But we also cannot ignore the transforming impetus of what is today a very lucrative industry continually seeking to broaden its market. Unfortunately, much of what is now used in our church services imitates the simplistic, sentimental, content-free tunes of the entertainment industry, whose values I have discussed in previous chapters. Even some within the CCM industry now realize that a monster has been created.

Having attracted the attention of its secular counterpart, CCM is now mostly *owned* and *operated* by the mainstream entertainment industry. "We are no longer a maturing business, we *are* a business," says Stan Moser, a twenty-six-year veteran of the Christian music industry.[57] Moser, a former CEO for Star Song Records, became disillusioned over the movement he helped start and now candidly admits that most songs being cranked out by the CCM machine are "virtually meaningless."[58]

Perhaps Moser's word choice of "meaningless" is due, in part at least, to the fact that few (I won't say no) real hymns have been written for over seventy years.[59] I would venture to say that one stanza of a hymn like "And Can It Be" by Charles Wesley has more doctrinal content than ten songs on the Christian music market today. Traditional hymns, says pastor and author John MacArthur, have been characterized by doctrinal substance because so many of them were written by theologians. The rise of the "gospel song" at the close of the nineteenth century signaled a change in emphasis in regard to doctrinal objectivity and initiated a new form of congregational singing marked more by subjective experience.[60] MacArthur claims that the Protestant evangelical community made a mistake then and is making the same kind of mistake now "by failing to write substantial hymns while purging the old hymns from our congregational music repertoire and replacing them with trite praise choruses and pop song look-alikes."[61] Many praise choruses, sometimes called "seven-elevens" (seven words repeated eleven times), swerve abruptly from the intellect not only because they are short, but also because they are, primarily, vehicles of emotional expression. Granted, all worship has an emotional element, but the intellect is subjugated to passion the closer worship moves to a bodily experience.

And this should be a concern because pagan worship is also a bodily experience. It is my understanding that in early America drums were forbidden musical instruments except in the military. Only in one geographical pocket did drums flourish—New Orleans, the birthplace of jazz. Cut off from the mainstream

Victorian culture, the Big Easy was an incubator for a highly rhythmic music based on African singing, dancing, and drumming.[62] As the favorite music for a restless youth culture roaring through the twenties, jazz found its way into rhythm and blues and then eventually into rock and roll at mid-twentieth century. Today rock *is* mainstream, which is why so many Christian artists so casually adopt its style. I realize it might be unpopular to say it, but one cannot simply insert quasi-spiritual lyrics into a voluptuous aesthetic and call it "Christian." We should at least be as honest as most rockers, who readily admit to what their music is all about—rebellion and sex.

And of course rock music is also about celebrity. It should not come as a surprise that recording artist Michael Card says the Christian music industry is now celebrity-driven: "The song is almost irrelevant. The focus is on the person and songs have become disposable."[63] When a Christian music group adopts a rock and roll aesthetic, it naturally inherits the idolatries that come with it. Think of it as a package deal. Self-identity, self-projection, sexual personae—it's all there. Since the cult of celebrity always focuses on the details of the private life it adores, whenever a Christian artist falls into immorality, an occurrence repeated much too often, it is not only embarrassing for the Christian community, it is also big news. Big people, big audiences, and big money—these are the elements of modern show business, a force with roots extending back to the vaudeville stage. These are the same elements of the Christian music industry, a force making itself known in the local church.

Show business values are not only prevalent in church music but are also showing up at Bible study time. Those who employ themselves in publishing church-related curriculum materials realize that an epistemological shift has occurred in our culture as a result of the demise of print-based modes of learning. Whether publishers lament over this demise is another matter. Actually, publishers are successfully adapting to a post-literate society. Case in point: One of the more popular Bible studies on the market today centers around the antics of Barney Fife. The Mayberry video Bible study series, published by Thomas Nelson, is currently used by thousands of churches nationwide.[64] Now there is even a *Beverly Hillbillies* series. Certainly *The Andy Griffith Show* represents the best of old-time television entertainment, but what will Thomas Nelson market next—the spiritual dimensions of Abbott and Costello?

Nowhere is the dumbing down of Bible curricula more predominant than in youth materials. Gospel Light says it is a "sin" to bore a young person with the Gospel.[65] So it structures part of its curriculum around Bible narratives to be acted out in a daytime soap-opera format.[66] For example, a group of teens might act out Joseph receiving news that unwed Mary is with child. (If improvisations like these go anything like my old public high school drama class, I can imagine the artistic license teens might take in such an activity.) Gospel Light also encourages youth programs to use video clips from movies to bring God's Word "into focus for this media-raised generation."[67] It is suggested that young people watch the final scene from the *Raiders of the Lost Ark* to see "what a lot of people think about when it comes to the end of the world."[68]

Another organization deeply concerned about this media-raised generation is the American Bible Society. Lately the Society has been asking the question, "How can the message of the Holy Scriptures be faithfully translated and communicated from one medium to another?"[69] Or to put it another way, is it possible to make a video version of the Bible that has as much authority as a print version of the Bible? This is a rather interesting question, which the Society has answered in the affirmative. Beginning in 1989 the Society launched an experiment to test the limits and possibilities of a screen translation and has since come to the conclusion that "screen and electronic technologies could transfer and inculturate the very message of the Holy Scriptures and do so with faithfulness and integrity."[70] Operating under "dynamic equivalence theory," a theory that steers away from a belief that the very words of the Bible are inspired and therefore infallible, the Society claims that its Multimedia Translation is just as authoritative as any print translation. The Society does not yet have a complete version of the Bible in video form, but perhaps the day is coming when the preacher will not read a Scripture passage but will push a button and show a video clip dramatizing the text. Or perhaps the preacher will not be there at all, and the congregation will just watch movies.

Apparently the American Bible Society does not believe there is a huge difference between processing information from a printed page compared with processing data from a series of moving pictures—between being a reader and being a spectator. So what happens if the preacher's text is taken from the account of King David's sin with Bathsheba? Does *seeing* the passage rather than *reading* it make a difference then? Moving pictures have a way of pushing rational discourse—linear logic—into the background. As discussed in Chapter Two, there exists a long-standing and irreconcilable tension between the *Word* and the *image*. The very notion of *divine revelation*, the communication of truth that cannot otherwise be known, demands a method of documentation and preservation that goes beyond moving pictures. If each word of Scripture is "God-breathed," then each *word* originates from the mind of God, and writing becomes the preferred agency of communication, for no other medium possesses the objectivity needed to conceptualize an abstract divinity. What the Society will really have if it completes the project is not another Bible *translation*, but a visual *interpretation* of Scripture.

The revamping of Bible curricula and the Multimedia Translation are attempts to make the Scriptures more palatable for a less literate audience. Preachers are also sensitive to our postmodern needs and are therefore reshaping what has historically been the centerpiece of worship—the sermon. Commenting on where tomorrow's sermon is heading, Ed Rowell says four characteristics are emerging.[71] First, the sermon of the future will place a heavier emphasis on storytelling because, in the words of Calvin Miller, "Typical congregations nourished on years of television dramas and popular video releases have been groomed to relate to the narrative sermon."[72] In addition to a focus on narrative,

tomorrow's sermon will be integrated with multimedia technologies. Congregations will have to get accustomed to having a
screen in their face. Zipping and zapping text, church commercials, and movie clips will fill the pulpit area. Moreover, preachers will become increasingly dependent on the creative work of
others. Heavier reliance on secondary research from software programs will allow for "pop out" sermons in a matter of minutes.
Consequently, preachers will spend less time wrestling with a
Scripture passage. Finally, the new and improved sermon will sacrifice theology for relevance. The "how to" sermon will become
commonplace as ministers seek to address the felt needs of their
congregations. "If you listen to much of our preaching," quips
Duke University's Will Willimon, "you get the impression that
Jesus was some sort of itinerant therapist, who, for free, traveled
about helping people feel better."[73] To these predictions I might
also add that sermons will probably become shorter in the future.
Currently the average sermon time is about thirty minutes,[74] the
same length as Tom Brokaw's *Nightly News*. Considering that our
Puritan forefathers stayed in the pulpit for hours at a time, one
can surmise that over the last couple of centuries we have witnessed the incredible shrinking sermon.

Churches seem to be moving in a direction where anything too
cerebral is suspect. In some Christian circles it would appear that
worship has already been lobotomized. For example, some sects
belonging to the Vineyard movement now place emphasis on
spasmodic jerking, unusual visions, "holy laughing," barking like
a dog, and crowing like a chicken. In his book *Counterfeit
Revival*, Hank Hanegraaff recounts the story of one Pastor James
Ryle who during a sermon spotted a lady in the audience with the
cartoon character of Olive Oyl superimposed on her face.[75] Ryle
interpreted the cartoon image as a sign from God. As with many
of these extra-revelatory visions, an interpretation was forthcom-
ing. Ryle proclaimed to the crowd that like Olive Oyl, the lady
with the image stamped on her face (which apparently only Ryle
could see) was being fought over by a "Bluto," and that "Popeye"
was soon coming to the rescue. Ryle then turned the word *Popeye*

into a pun, saying the tattooed woman was the apple of the Father's eye or, as the preacher put it, "Pop's Eye."

Please.

It is difficult to believe that God is now using cartoon characters to make His will known; it is even more difficult to imagine an audience so gullible that it falls for such nonsense. Yet Christian magicians like Ryle abound and constitute a growing movement in evangelicalism. Hanegraaff calls this type of absurdity "a shift from faith to feelings, from fact to fantasy, and from reason to esoteric revelation."[76]

In accordance with my definition of postmodernism, today's worship is marked by a turning from rationality, and at the same time an embracing of spectacle. In the process, doctrine is watered down either from neglect or, more likely, from a willingness to compromise biblical truth to attract a following. MacArthur warns that current trends in worship only serve to weaken churches rather than to build them up:

> This modern notion of worship as a mindless exercise has taken a heavy toll in churches, leading to a decreasing emphasis on preaching and teaching and an increasing emphasis on entertaining the congregation and making people feel good. All of this leaves the Christian in the pew untrained, unable to discern, and often blithely ignorant of the dangers all around him or her.[77]

The postmodern mind has a remarkable ability to hold at the same time two ideas that logically contradict each other. Accordingly, while 60 percent of Americans believe that the Bible is totally accurate in all of its teachings, nearly 40 percent believe that while Jesus was on earth He committed sins.[78] And while 81 percent of Americans believe that Christ was born to a virgin, 40 percent deny His resurrection.[79] This is irrational. But when ministers make light of the Fall, sin, eternal punishment, grace, and the authority of Christ over our lives, when keeping everybody happy becomes a supreme virtue at church, then contradictions are bound to arise.

Francis Schaeffer reminded us a number of years ago that the great evangelical disaster is one of accommodation. "Accommodation leads to accommodation," he said, "which leads to accommodation."[80] If the church does not stand for the truth, who will? Those who have read Schaeffer's books know he had a running theme—namely, the church has historically served as a bulwark against totalitarian encroachment. What then will happen to American democracy if our meetings with God shrivel to shallow spectacles? What will happen if we continue to maintain an educational system that says it does not even know what knowledge is important anymore?

CHAPTER NINE

Formula for a Führer

*As I have pointed out in my earlier books, when the memory
of the Christian consensus which gave us freedom within
the biblical form is increasingly forgotten, a manipulating
authoritarianism will tend to fill the vacuum.*[1]

FRANCIS SCHAEFFER

*A popular government without popular information or
means of acquiring it is but a prologue to a farce
or a tragedy, or perhaps both.*

JAMES MADISON

A DANGEROUS SOUP IS COOKING.

☙

Nuremberg, September 1934. The medieval town was once
again decked out for the Third Reich's pageantry of power.
A year earlier Adolf Hitler had become Chancellor of Germany,
and so nothing stopped him now.

Nuremberg was made the heart of national unity and the site
of the annual Nazi party rallies for two reasons. It was conveniently located at a juncture of seven railway lines, allowing for
the import of thousands of labor corps, SS troops, Hitler youth,
and other spectators. But more importantly, the feudal setting
reflected the glories of Germany's ancient past. Charlemagne,

whose conquests had unified Europe well over a thousand years earlier, had fought there. To establish a psychological link between the First Empire and what was promised to be a third one, the Führer had recently presented himself with replicas of Charlemagne's crown, orb, and scepter. Everything about the Nuremberg rallies was designed to make a point.

The narrow streets, gabled roofs, and spires gave all who visited there a feeling of standing in the middle of one of the Grimms' fairy tales. The town was replete with moat and castle. There was even a torture chamber. Illuminated at night, the castle was rumored to have once been the temple of Diana as well another god, Nuoro, who, it was said, gave his name to the rituals performed there.[2] An English tourist was so impressed with the lit structure that he wrote, "And with the great fortress standing alone on its eminence and bathed in light there is much inspiration for the imagination to wander among the stories of warriors bold, fiery monsters and imprisoned maidens."[3]

But for imagination nothing quite compared to the famous "Nuremberg Maiden," a mechanical contrivance fashioned in the form of a woman with the unique ability to clasp its victim with spiked arms upon the most sensitive parts of the human body and then drop its prey upon a bed of rotating disc knives. The Maiden was a favored object of Julius Streicher, editor of the obscene *Stürmer*, who often could be found prowling around the torture chamber's dungeon, "like a pilgrim at worship."[4]

Most of the rally ceremonies took place on Zeppelin Field, a flat terrain suited for large blocs of parading soldiers and Hitler's oratorical regurgitations. Rally stage manager Albert Speer had torn down the old bleachers lining the field and had replaced them with stone ones, thirteen hundred feet long and eighty feet high. From the stands hung a multitude of red and white banners with swastikas—black spiders with an occult past—crooked crosses that eventually replaced the real crosses inside Germany's churches. The stadium was crowned with a gigantic eagle with a wingspread of one hundred feet.

Hitler had even greater plans for Zeppelin Field and had commissioned Speer to design a complex that could last for a thousand years.[5] Mussolini had the city of Rome for his backdrop—the Führer deserved even better. Therefore, Speer had placed on the drawing board plans for a more magnificent stadium, one that would be twice the size of the legendary Circus Maximus. Frankly, the goal was to create the Eighth Wonder of the World. In 1937 Speer's design won the Grand Prix at the World's Fair in Paris. Like the Temple of Diana at Ephesus and the Colossus of Zeus built by Phidias, Hitler's claim to world domination would be symbolized through "architectural megalomania." The field's name would later be changed to Marchfield after the god of war. The stands would be punctuated with great towers, twenty-four of them, each a hundred and thirty feet tall. Topping this would be a colossal sculpture of a woman whose two-hundred-foot height would dwarf Nebuchadnezzar's ninety-foot image and Nero's 119-foot colossus.

In 1934 a hundred and thirty antiaircraft searchlights intermittently were positioned around the field casting white pillars into the night sky. The beams merged into a general glow several miles up and formed a giant canopy, giving the effect of what the British ambassador called a "cathedral of ice."[6] Music played an important role in the rallies. There were bands and drums and marching. The Führer preferred Wagner, although most high-ranking party officials cared little for classical music. A year earlier the Nuremberg Opera House had been found empty; so Hitler had to pull party members from beer halls and cafés to fill the seats.[7]

Hitler descended upon Nuremberg from the clouds in his airplane—a Thor moment captured by Leni Riefenstahl, the beautiful actress and film director who documented the rally in *Triumph of the Will*. Riefenstahl had already filmed the 1933 rally, but much of the footage could not be used. Party members Ernst Rühm and Otto Strasser had shown up in too many shots and were now dead—murdered with more than a hundred other brown shirts in the "Night of the Long Knives"—a compromise Hitler made with the German military establishment to consolidate his power. Armed with a crew of a hundred and twenty personnel, Riefenstahl devised shots from planes, cranes, flagpoles, and roller skates. She caught it all—boots at ground level, strutting storm troopers, smoking torches, forests of swastika flags, thundering mock battles, two hundred thousand spectators, salutes exploding simultaneously, "Sieg Heil!" "Sieg Heil!" "Sieg Heil!" The feature-length film was shown throughout Germany and was compulsory in every cinema and school.

From the consecration of the flags to the arrival of the storm troopers for the sham battles, every display was orchestrated to stir the emotions. Alan Bullock comments in *Hitler, A Study in Tyranny* that the "sense of power, of force and unity was irresistible, and all converged with a mounting crescendo of excitement on the supreme moment when the Führer himself made his entry."[8] The crowds could hardly wait for him. Even before Hitler's keynote address, ten thousand people surrounded his hotel, the Old Rathaus, chanting, "We want our Führer!" At last Hitler appeared on the balcony to appease them. American foreign correspondent William L. Shirer commented that their faces reminded him of the crazed expressions on Holy Rollers in Louisiana.[9]

Hitler liked giving speeches around eight o'clock at night, when, he once wrote, "man's resistance is at its lowest."[10] When his time came, he entered Zeppelin Field, accompanied most often by a Wagnerian overture. Starting off in a reserved tone, he slowly worked his way into a theatrical fit. His speeches were always doctrinal, hammering the hatreds of pan-German Nazism—Versailles, Marxism, Judaism, pacifism, and democracy. No one can say the world had not been warned. "We are strong and will get stronger," he said.

"And there, in the floodlit night, jammed together like sardines, in one mass formation," wrote Shirer, "the little men of Germany who have made Nazism possible achieved the highest state of being the Germanic man knows: the shedding of their individual souls and minds . . . until under the mystic words of the Austrian they were merged completely in the Germanic herd."[11]

BEHIND THE NAZI MACHINERY

Before it was all over, five million souls among Hitler's opponents and the "racially inferior" six million Jews, three and a half million German servicemen, and millions more in the European theater were dead. As demonstrated in Fritel's painting *The Conquerors*, history's tyrants always leave us with mountains of white corpses. But Hitler never would have happened if Germany had not first been prepared for Hitler. Holocaust survivor Viktor Frankl once noted that the gas chambers were not prepared in the offices of Berlin bureaucrats, but in the lecture halls of Europe.[12] The seeds for Hitler were planted eighty years earlier when the remnants of the Reformation and the tenets of the Enlightenment faced each other on the battlefield of ideas and the Enlightenment won. German rationalist theologians like Julius Wellhausen announced to Europe that the Bible was merely a collection of human scribbles and that Old Testament monotheism was a product of evolutionary reasoning. Wellhausen's *Prolegomena to the History of Israel* (1878) was instrumental in introducing biblical criticism not only to German universities but eventually to German homes and churches. It did not take long for the methods of higher criticism to transform the Bible from a living document into a bone-dry history book.

Hitler was well aware of how liberal theology would pave the way for his movement. Even before the Nazis came to power, he boasted in a press interview that German Christianity would have little difficulty swapping the cross for the swastika:

> Will the masses ever again become Christian? Nonsense. Never again. That film is worn out. Nobody wants to see it anymore. But we'll help things along. . . . Do you really think they won't teach *our* God in their churches, these liberal priestlings who have no belief any longer, merely an office? I guarantee you that, just as they turned Haeckel and Darwin, Goethe and Stephan George into prophets of their Christianity, they will substitute our Hakenkreuz [swastika, hooked cross] for their own cross.[13]

And of course they did.

While Hitler sneered at, and at the same time was thankful for, Germany's liberal theologians, he drew his own spiritual inspiration from the wells of Hegel, Nietzsche, H. S. Chamberlain, and Wagner.[14]

From the well of George Hegel (1770-1831) Hitler drew spiritual nourishment claiming that the will of the state must take precedence over the will of the individual. The state, Hegel said, was "God walking on earth." Hegel once held the chair of philosophy at the Berlin University and believed Germany's day in the sun was coming, that what Germany needed was another Alexander, Caesar, or Napoleon to carry out the "will of the world spirit."

Friedrich Nietzsche (1844-1900) further extended Hegel's vision, although Nietzsche did not necessarily have Germany in mind when he said that what the world needed was a master race and a master to lead them. According to Nietzsche, in a world where God had died, the strong would naturally rule the weak. Of course Hitler took the super-race to be the German people and the Superman to be himself. Nietzsche's Superman would be a "genius" above the law, a beast of prey, a magnificent blond brute with his face set toward spoil and victory.

From the well of H. S. Chamberlain (1855-1927) Hitler drew the justification that the German people were the purest race on earth and ought to stay that way. Chamberlain was an Englishman by birth but a German at heart. So devoted were his writings to Teutonic superiority that the Kaiser bestowed on him the Iron Cross. His twelve-hundred-page book on race and history, *Foundations of the Nineteenth Century* (which he completed in a year and a half), claimed among other things that there were only two pure races left in the world—the Germans and the Jews. But it was the German race that was destined for greatness, having proved itself worthy by destroying the Roman Empire. The Nazi Party referred to Chamberlain as one of their spiritual founders and took his ideas to an extreme. Chamberlain was often astonished by his own work, sometimes claiming he could not even recognize what he had written. Perhaps this is because he also claimed that some of his best work occurred under the "goading of demons."[15]

Richard Wagner (1813-1883) also believed in Germany's date with destiny and indicated so in his own writings. But it was not just Wagner's political treatises that inspired Hitler; it was also the composer's visual and musical motifs. Hitler used to say, "Whoever wants to understand National Socialist Germany must know Wagner."[16] What Wagner gave Hitler, as well as the German people, was an aesthetic reaching back to a primitive ethnic *mythos*. In "Twilight of the Gods" the German people saw their old gods rising up out of the fog—barbaric, heroic, irrationally self-willed, bloody, and violent.

Hitler mounted his movement atop the rubble of World War I. Defeated, humiliated, and bankrupt, Germany lay mortally wounded. The Treaty of Versailles almost did Germany in, stripping her of territory and a sizable army, requiring her to pay huge war reparations. Nationalists and Communists gnashed their teeth on the new government. As Shirer says, from the day the Treaty was signed "Germany became a house divided."[17] In 1923, the same year Hitler led an unsuccessful revolt on the Bavarian government, the German mark plummeted to an all-time low, so that four billion marks came to equal one dollar. Morality was collapsing in on itself as reflected in the decadent cabaret spirit pervading restaurants and nightclubs.

While Hitler was sitting in prison for trying to overthrow the government, he decided to put his ideas down on paper. *Mein Kampf* synthesized all the stirrings within Hitler's demented mind—that Germany must be a pure people, that it was all the Jews' fault, that lost German territory must be reclaimed, that democracy would lead nowhere. In less than a year Hitler was out of prison and taking advantage of a momentary improvement in the German economy. Hitler immediately went back to work rebuilding his party. When the worldwide depression hit in 1929, Hitler took advantage of the crisis by once again railing against the Treaty of Versailles. The Nazi Party grew in popularity for two reasons. On one hand, brute intimidation was applied upon all perceived opponents; but that was not enough and was by nature inadequate under a democratic system. The greatest asset of the party was a sophisticated propaganda machine capable of tapping into public sentiment.

The journalist Konrad Heiden, who carefully studied Hilter's rise to power before his exile in 1933, explained the mystery of the Führer's success: "One scarcely need ask with what arts he conquered the masses; he did not conquer them, he portrayed and represented them. His speeches are day-dreams of this mass soul; they are chaotic, full of contradictions, if their words are taken literally, often senseless as dreams are, and yet charged with deeper meaning."[18] In 1928 the National Socialist German Workers Party received only 3 percent of the vote in Germany's national elections. In 1930 the party captured 18 percent of the vote. By July 1932 the Nazis constituted the largest political party in the Reichstag, receiving 37 percent of the vote, which led to Hitler's assumption of Chancellorship in January 1933.

Although today it has become fashionable for scholars of human communication and spokespeople of the entertainment industry to minimize the power of the mass media, Hitler and his minister of propaganda, Joseph Goebbels, did not minimize it. To the contrary, once Hitler became Chancellor he sought to lay his hands on every media form in Germany—art, radio, the press, and film. Whereas the propaganda of the Nuremberg rallies were like annual shots in the arm, post-1933 propaganda became total under National Socialism. Goebbels, whose doctoral thesis analyzed Romantic Drama, asserted, "In propaganda as in love, anything is permissible which is successful."[19] Two days after his appointment to the Ministry for Popular Enlightenment and Propaganda, the little sophist said, "It is not enough to reconcile people more or less to our regime, to move them towards a position of neutrality towards us, we would rather work on people until they are addicted to us."[20] Goebbels made this statement in March 1933. In May he stood before a bonfire of burning books and declared, "The age of extreme intellectualism is over . . . the past is lying in flames . . . the future will rise from the flames within our hearts."[21] Book burning was just one aspect of the anti-intellectualism associated with Nazism. This was an attitude especially cultivated among the Hitler youth. A member of the exiled Social Democratic Party observed, "[The] new generation has never had much use for education and reading. Now nothing is demanded of them; on the contrary, knowledge is publicly condemned."[22]

Goebbels's policy of addiction was pursued through gaining state control of all media outlets. Radio sets were mass-produced and sold at subsidized prices. The range of the receivers were limited to pick up broadcasts only within Germany's borders, but at least one could listen to Wagner or Hitler's speeches (fifty speeches were broadcast in 1933 alone).[23] The Nazis also controlled the content of the newspapers. Objectivity as a journalistic value was thrown out the window. "The press must not merely inform," said Goebbels, "it must also instruct."[24] Although Hitler read the newspapers, he resented journalists for being critical of him before the Nazi Party came to power. Furthermore, the Führer was of the opinion that the spoken word and pictures were more powerful to persuade than the medium of print.[25] One should not be surprised then to learn that of 1,097 German feature films produced between 1933 and 1945, one-sixth were overtly propagandist.[26] However, the majority of the films were *covertly* propagandist. As David Welch explains in *The Third Reich: Politics and Propaganda*, the strategy was to mix entertainment with political content. Goebbels held that "propaganda was most effective when it was insidious, when the message was concealed within the framework of popular entertainment."[27] The monopoly held on the film industry was a primary cog in the Nazi propaganda machine, and it paralleled America's own love affair with the cinema. Hitler arrived at a time in history when this new technological apparatus—the dream machine—lay at his disposal. Between 1933 and 1942 the number of moviegoers in Germany quadrupled.[28]

But what exactly was Nazism? What was the message Hitler wanted Germany to become addicted to? This is an important question because propaganda is more than just the art of public persuasion. It is also the art of *identification*. Propaganda cannot work unless it can reinforce existing attitudes and beliefs. This is why Hitler had to appeal to something at the subconscious level, something deep within the soul, something unspoken but felt in all of us—something dark, barbaric, and demonic—the idolizing of the creature over the Creator.

In his book *Modern Fascism: Liquidating the Judeo-Christian Worldview*, Gene Veith uncovers the true roots of Nazism when he says the "fascists sought to recover the mythological consciousness . . . the old pagan order of divine-king, the sacred community, the communion with nature, and the sacrifice of blood."[29] The "cult of the leader" was based on an interpretation of Nietzsche's "triumph of the will" through individual genius. To a large extent *the Führer myth* was a throwback to the thaumaturgic kings of the Middle Ages. Hitler was to be seen as a Messiah figure, a miracle-worker, a god. The Führer personified the state, and his power was complete. Rudolf Hess, Hitler's Deputy, often put the period on the dictator's speeches by mounting the rostrum and shouting the tautology, "The Party is Hitler! Hitler is Germany, just as Germany is Hitler!" The Nazis exploited the personal loneliness associated with modern technological societies by claiming that a return to community consciousness was the cure to urban blues. The *sacred community* was a herd with a purpose. Germany would be the glove, and Hitler would be the hand in the glove. As Veith points out, fascist theory rejected transcendent moral law for nature's law. *Communion with nature* was consistent with ancient pagan societies that drew their mythologies out of the ironies and brutalities of an unforgiving and often bloody world. It was survival of the fittest. A massive military buildup followed the Führer's acquisition of power. Hitler was a war god who called for a *blood sacrifice*. The reason he demanded absolute loyalty from the German youth was so that when they grew up, he could hurl them into the battle lines.

The Nazi regime seems like an aberration on the modern era timeline. It goes without saying that Hitler and progress are antonyms. How did one of the most educated populations on the planet become so credulous? Why would the land of Luther want to return to the Middle Ages? It is not enough to say that it was a matter of low morale or terrible economic conditions. Other modern nations also had their share of dead soldiers and depressions without succumbing to a mythological mind-set. Hitler is best explained by the circumstance of the *vanishing word*. Germany's bout with demagoguery is a story of the vanishing word with a capital *W* as well as a lower-case *w*. The rejection of the Jews, and ultimately of the dissenting Christians, was in larger scope a rejection of a transcendent God and His transcendent laws. Hitler found little merit in *the* Word or in words because it was Hitler himself who became the Word, and images naturally made him a better object of devotion. For what the *word* is to the Judeo-Christian faith, the *image* is to paganism. To solve the mystery of Adolf Hitler, one only has to look at the nature of idolatry and the vast bulk of human history. Next to God's dealing with His own people, it is the second oldest story in the world.

THE NAKED PUBLIC SQUARE

As stated earlier in this book, America was born out of a print-oriented culture. But more than that, it was born out of a print culture with a Christian conscience. The real Founding Fathers of American democracy were not Jefferson and Madison, but Luther and Calvin.[30] The Constitution was an outgrowth of Reformation thinking. Martin Luther's break from the Roman Catholic Church was motivated by the notion that both civil and church authorities are under the authority of the Scriptures. John Calvin extended this idea by insisting that man owes his obedience first to God and second to man's institutions. Along these same lines, Samuel Rutherford's work *Lex, Rex* (1644) challenged the prevailing belief of the *divine right of kings* by arguing that monarchs were under the law and not above it. In turn, Presbyterian minister and Princeton president John Witherspoon brought the principles of *Lex, Rex* directly to bear upon the writing of both the Declaration of Independence and the Constitution.

The Constitution is an acknowledgment that government must be founded on transcendent moral absolutes—that laws must be derived from the Lawgiver. There was an almost universal belief by the American colonists that majority rule would lead to totalitarianism due to man's inherent sin nature. Therefore, only a body of laws with a system of checks and balances could restrain arbitrary power. The law could not be only what the king said it was; it had to go higher. William Penn had aptly said, "If we are not governed by God, then we will be ruled by tyrants." The fixity of law had to be in the "laws of nature and of nature's God." And the predominant God in 1776 was the God of the Bible.

Dean C. Curry, in his book *A World Without Tyranny*, says that American democracy was built on four interrelated assumptions.[31] First, human rights are God-given. We are *endowed* with these rights by virtue of our humanity. If human rights are God-given, then they cannot stem from the state. To the contrary, the state has a moral obligation to see that the inalienable rights of life, liberty, and property are protected. Second, all human beings are morally, politically, and legally equal. Equality is a derivative of a just God. Third, man and government are under God's judgment and are therefore accountable to Him. Finally, liberty untempered by virtue is liberty lost. Freedom without personal moral restraint leads to excessive individualism and the infringement of these rights by others.

"How is it possible," asked Tocqueville, "that society should escape destruction if the moral tie is not strengthened in proportion as the political tie is relaxed? And what can be done with a people who are their own masters if they are not submissive to the Deity?"[32] This French historian, who observed the nation in the early 1830s, was not the only one to recognize the fragility of American democracy. The Founders clearly understood that our own form of government was insufficient if the citizens were not God-fearing and virtuous.

In his "Farewell Address" George Washington stated, "Of all the dispositions and habits which lead to political prosperity, religion and morality are indispensable supports. In vain would that man claim the tribute of patriotism who should labor to subvert the great pillars of human happiness."[33]

President John Adams later added, "[W]e have no government armed with power capable of contending with human passions unbridled by morality and religion. . . . *Our Constitution was made only for a moral and religious people. It is wholly inadequate to the government of any other.*"[34]

Even Benjamin Franklin understood the importance of personal virtue: "[O]nly a virtuous people are capable of freedom. As nations become corrupt and vicious, they have more need of masters."[35]

These voices from the past seem so foreign to us now. Such warnings today are rarely uttered unless they come from the religious right (e.g., William Bennett). What recent U.S. President has made a public statement about the moral weakness of the nation in relation to the brittleness of democracy? Most modern Presidents try to avoid saying anything about America's moral decay. The key to good politics is to be the eternal optimist despite the facts. Prosperity and technological know-how have made America the wonder of the earth, but apparently it has also created an incredible blind spot.

The truth of the matter is that political ties *have* strengthened in proportion to the loosening of moral ties. As the pillars of religion and morality have buckled, the pillars of "more government" and "judicial fiat" have propped up the nation. In the process, the Constitution, or what the Founders envisioned the Constitution to be, is vanishing. As early as 1907 Charles Evans Hughes, who later became a Supreme Court Justice, said, "[T]he Constitution is what the judges say it is."[36] As John Whitehead points out, this is not far from the assertion that the law is what the Führer says it is.[37] Largely because of the social implications of Darwinism and the rejection of transcendent truth, the Constitution has come to be seen as an "evolving document" (or as Al Gore liked to say, "a living document"). Logical positivism, which sees law as a social convention with no base of moral absolutes, is now accepted jurisprudence. A constitution without fixity in transcendent moral absolutes becomes a tyrannous tool. As Whitehead explains:

But with substitution of sociological jurisprudence for the Christian base, the doctrine of judicial review has become a tyrannous device. It places the entire government under the authority of the Supreme Court, which can void an act if in the opinion of five of the nine justices that act is unconstitutional.[38]

Logical positivism was recently demonstrated in the 2000 Presidential election as the Florida Supreme Court let the counting of ballots continue despite a definitive quantitative outcome. The Florida Court allowed subjectivity—human interpretations of whether the chads were there or not—to override the objectivity of the voting machines. What America got was a little taste of "will to power" at work as Gore and company remained bent on getting a satisfactory ruling.[39] When the Supreme Court finally made an objective application of the law, causing the outcome to go Bush's way, there were still cries of "disenfranchisement" from the political left. We can be thankful that Vice President Al Gore gave his nod to the Supreme Court ruling. Still, for some it was not until Bush "proved" himself in the aftermath of the September 11th terrorist attacks that he *earned* the right to be their President.

I have defined postmodernism as a turning *from* rationality, and at the same time an embracing *of* spectacle. Postmodern irrationality is grounded in a rejection of absolute truth that is perhaps as dangerous for us as it was for Germany. As Veith explains, when transcendent values are excluded, the political arena is reduced to sheer "will to power":

If there are no absolutes, the society can presumably construct any values that it pleases and is itself subject to none. . . . Without moral absolutes, power becomes arbitrary. Since there is no basis for moral persuasion or rational argument, the side with the most power will win. Government becomes nothing more than the sheer exercise of unlimited power, restrained neither by law nor by reason.[40]

But our postmodern irrationality is also coupled with a dependence on images. The *image* exalts itself not only against words, but ultimately against the transcendent *Logos*. Sex, violence, and the cult of celebrity fly in the face of a holy God. As Camille Paglia says, pagan Rome has been reborn in Hollywood. The letting go of transcendent truth and our love of spectacle opens the door, as it did with Germany seven decades ago, for a future führer. As Veith argues, the replacement of rational debate with media manipulation, the subordination of logic to emotionalism, and the trivialization of politics—all tenets of our popular culture—form a fertile breeding ground for fascism.[41] The *image* waits for a political life.

Richard John Neuhaus makes the observation that America is in a transitional phase that he calls "the naked public square." For the moment certain elements in our society have decreed that religion and the state must be separate. (Specifically, the Christian religion and the state must be separate.) Originally, the purpose behind the First Amendment was not to oust Christianity out of the public square but to guarantee there would be no official state religion. Today civic religion, the informing spirit at our founding and sometime thereafter, can no longer inform. Neuhaus's thesis is that the naked public square cannot remain naked. The reason for this has to do with the relationship between *law* and *laws*: "If law and laws are not seen to be coherently related to basic presuppositions about right and wrong, good and evil, they will be condemned as illegitimate."[42] Christ has been cast out, and now there is a vacuum begging to be filled with some kind of normative ethic. Neuhaus's metaphor implies that transcendence abhors a vacuum and that all societies, even democratic ones, long for some form of monism—one sovereign, one society, one law, one faith.[43] In the past Christian theism provided this normative ethic, but now that the Christian influence is disappearing, the naked public square is open to receive another god. To say that it cannot happen here, says Neuhaus, "is but a form of whistling in the dark."[44]

What Neuhaus feared when he wrote *The Naked Public Square* in 1984 was a monism more akin to communism than to fascism. Communism is less a threat today because of its failure in the former Soviet Union as well as its progressive abdication by

American intellectuals. There are more reasons to fear fascism than communism in a postmodern world. For one thing, fascism is anti-intellectual (communism is predicated on "scientific" theories). Fascism requires no rational basis other than the acceptance of a charismatic leader riding on sheer "will to power." However, it is also true that fascism likes to prey on demoralized and desperate societies. Hitler, for example, fed off desperate times that required desperate measures. While America is becoming more anti-intellectual (irrational), we are not yet demoralized or desperate. A consistently strong economy and a high standard of living has both spoiled us and kept us from danger. We seem to be safe for now, but the future arrives much faster than it used to, and the world is rapidly shrinking, and we can now blow each other up so much easier these days. Such a landscape will eventually create, I think, some extraordinary opportunities for political sophistry.

SOME MORE SUSCEPTIBILITIES

If our current slide toward irrationality is not curtailed soon, it is quite possible that many of us will not be capable of recognizing a well-dressed lie when it comes along. A dangerous soup is cooking. Our relativistic mind-set and our dependency upon images are major ingredients for a catastrophe. And there are other related susceptibilities that, taken together, form a disastrous scenario. There are four in particular that I would like to point out:

The increasing use of image manipulation in the media blurs the lines between reality and virtual reality. Certainly this is a marvelous trend for any preying despot. In the world of television, image manipulation is a natural part of the business. However, the level of sophistication and the degree of daring are reaching interesting heights. Some fear that digital engineering in the visual realm can come too close to blurring the lines between reality and virtual reality when used in unconventional ways and in conventional settings. Those who turned to watch CBS's New Year's Eve 2000 coverage may or may not have noticed the network's logo shining off a Manhattan building just right of Dan

Rather's shoulder. What viewers surely did not notice was that the logo was digitally imposed to cover up NBC's logo, the *real* one suspended above Times Square.[45] Without a shred of concern for the real, CBS restructured our reality for their own profit. The *real world* just was not suitable enough for their purposes; so they changed it.

We have come to expect images to be manipulated in high-tech, digitally enhanced movies. But what happens when journalists begin to tamper with our perceptions of reality? After O. J. Simpson was arrested for allegedly murdering his ex-wife, a villainous shadowy face of the former pro football player appeared on the cover of *Time* magazine. The major newsweekly later admitted to doctoring the photo. When NBC's *Dateline* aired a GM truck blowing up on impact with another car, General Motors filed a multimillion-dollar defamation suit against NBC. The broadcast company settled with GM and admitted to igniting the impacted car with small rocket engines. One cannot help but think of Joseph Stalin's Soviet Union where graphic artists and censors erased the party's enemies from the annals of history with paint, razors, and airbrushes. "What is to prevent image-manipulation techniques—their usefulness already established in entertainment and advertising—from crossing the line (if there still is one) into political image making?" asks Mark Slouka in his book *War of the Worlds*. "Lies, if propagated in sufficient quantity and repeated often enough will generate their own truth, as Adolf Hitler explained."[46]

The demise of the traditional family unit weakens psychological resilience. Almost half of all marriages in America end in divorce, and it has been so for three decades now.[47] Surprisingly, divorce among professed born-again believers is slightly higher than that of non-Christians.[48] We live in what family researcher and author Judith Wallerstein calls a "divorce culture." Wallerstein, who is considered a national authority on the subject, says, "[I]t's clear that we've created a new kind of society never before seen in human culture."[49] Wallerstein and others report that children of divorce are less resilient than most expected. In comparison to children of intact families, they are more aggressive, sexually active at an earlier age, suffer more depression, and are more likely to end up in a mental clinic or a hospital setting.[50] It is a vicious cycle because children *of* divorce beget children *who* divorce.

Little is being said today about the psychological repercussions, let alone the theological repercussions of our divorce culture. But if children carry with them the symbolic meaning of their parents throughout life, as Wallerstein claims,[51] when that *first-god* image is shattered through divorce, the consequences are not only horrific for the individual but also for the culture at large. Divorce is an assault against the sanctity of marriage, just as abortion is an assault against the sanctity of life. One day our divorce culture is going to come back to haunt us. As Karl Menninger says, "What is done to children, they will do to society."[52] Strong families help to guarantee a strong nation. The collapse of the family unit weakens psychological resilience and makes us more vulnerable to demagogic seduction. For example, the connection between mental stability and the susceptibility to cult induction has been documented. In one report by *The Journal of the American Medical Association*, 60 percent of the subjects studied were "substantially and chronically disturbed and unhappy for many years" before they became cult members.[53] This is not to suggest that when Hitler came to power, the people of Germany were all from broken homes or were all mentally ill. Nevertheless, Hitler did oppose the German family unit by demanding that the youth be loyal to him first, over the parent. The Führer was not only Big Brother but also a father figure. While Christ can fill the hole of the fatherless and can restore the broken God-image for a child of divorce, it also becomes easier for counter-fathers to do the same when the family is threatened.

The increasing growth of New Age religions is building a pagan ethos for the nation. The popularity of New Age religions is perhaps best demonstrated by the shelf space devoted to the movement within secular bookstores. Often the occult section dwarfs books from a Christian orthodox perspective. Charles

Colson says, "Today, New Age thinking permeates Western society, spawning a host of techniques used in medicine, business, education, the military, and even—tragically—churches."[54] Unlike Eastern mysticism, which tends to be fatalistic, Colson says the American brand of New Age religion is more optimistic and utopian.[55] Common elements of New Age spirituality include the divinity of self, the worship of nature, a tolerance for all faiths (except strict biblical Christianity), and a tolerance toward sexual permissiveness. To a large degree the New Age is nothing more than old paganism dressed up in new clothes. Colson comments:

> When people create their own religion, they create gods and goddesses in their own image. The ancient gods of mythology had limited powers, were subject to human interference, and displayed all the human weaknesses and vices. And the New Age god, who is little more than a warm feeling within or at worst a dabbling in occult powers, is merely a ratification of whatever the human ego wants.[56]

In our highly visual popular culture, New Age spirituality is often combined with a pagan aesthetic. From corny save-the-world fund-raising on MTV to the dreamy openings of Olympic festivals, pagan spectacle pervades the screen. The 2000 Super Bowl halftime show was broadcast live from Walt Disney World in an event celebrating "the magic of tomorrow." For this new-millennium extravaganza Disney entertained the audience (multiple millions of them) with a giant effigy rising into the night air as white-robed priests danced in rhythm around its base. Actor Edward James Olmos appeared between the image's feet saying, "The stage of time has returned to rekindle the human spirit and lead us in an *earthly celebration that unites the nations of the world*" (emphasis mine).

As addressed in the last chapter, pagan spectacle has also found its way into churches where parishioners run the gauntlet of seeing visions, stammering, swaying, fainting, laughing, shaking uncontrollably, barking like a dog, and crowing like a chicken. Hank Hanegraaff laments, "[W]hat was once practiced only in cults is now present in our churches, as Christians mimic the practice of pagan spirituality."[57]

The nation's susceptibility to terrorist attacks increases the likelihood of more governmental intrusion into our private lives and threatens our economic stability. Technological innovations in electronic media have thrust the issue of privacy into the public spotlight. As if the intrusion of telemarketing was not bothersome enough, now new sophisticated surveillance devices allow companies to closely track user behavior on the Internet. As television and computer technologies merge, data-gathering methods will spill over to the new evolving medium of interactive television. Already corporations like Microsoft, AT&T, Liberty Media, Proctor and Gamble, Rupert Murdoch's News Corp., Cisco, and A.C. Nielsen are gearing up for "T-Commerce" (television commerce).[58] The Center for Digital Democracy (CDD) reports that for the first time ever, companies will be able to "collect detailed information about what each user of the system is doing, what shows they watch, when and how long they watch, what advertisements they see, whether they change channels during ads or shows, and more."[59] In the near future television will be watching *you*—literally.

The telescreen technology reminiscent of George Orwell's novel *1984* now exists for commercial purposes in this country; however, with an increased effort to ward off terrorism, I-Spyism is likely to cut deeper into our personal lives. More government intrusion is almost a necessary evil, with the downside being that the infrastructure of Homeland Security will probably never be dismantled in the future.

The threat of global terrorism puts the American economy at risk. What happened on September 11, 2001, is proof that a stateside terrorist attack can put a significant dent into the nation's economy. It is a terrifying thought, but what kind of dent, economic or otherwise, would be made if a nuclear device, housed inside a three-ton pickup truck, were to be suddenly detonated in downtown Manhattan? Such a tragedy could easily send the country into a wild tailspin.

ORWELL AND HUXLEY

"It was a bright cold day in April, and the clocks were striking thirteen," begins Orwell's novel, *1984*. "Winston Smith, his chin nuzzled into his breast in an effort to escape the vile wind, slipped quickly through the glass doors of Victory Mansions, though not quickly enough to prevent a swirl of gritty dirt from entering along with him."

"A squat grey building of only thirty-four stories," begins Aldous Huxley's *Brave New World*. "Over the main entrance the words, CENTRAL LONDON HATCHERY AND CONDITIONING CENTRE, and, in a shield, the World State's motto, COMMUNITY, IDENTITY, STABILITY."

Our first smell in *1984* is boiled cabbage. In *Brave New World* it is laboratory chemicals. In *1984* there is gritty dirt. In *Brave New World* there is little dirt to be found. In *1984* almost everyone is miserable. In *Brave New World* almost everyone is happy. In Orwell's novel compliance is accomplished through pain. In Huxley's novel compliance is accomplished through pleasure. Orwell speculated that the events in his novel could come to pass in one generation. Huxley was looking six hundred years down the road (although he later said it could happen in the next century).

At first glance one might think these are entirely different prophecies. However, there are actually more similarities than differences between the two works. Foremost among those similarities is that both books are anti-utopias that envision a bleak future rather than a bright one. Both are describing the triumph of totalitarianism in a world where transcendent moral values have vanished. Both authors were attempting to address issues hotly debated in the 1930s: What would be the social implications of Darwin and Freud? What ideology would eclipse Christianity? Would the new social sciences be embraced with as much passion as the hard sciences? What would be the outcome if managerial science were taken to an extreme? What would be the long-term effects of modern peacetime advertising? Of wartime propaganda? What would become of the traditional family? How would class divisions be resolved? How would new technologies shape the future? Although these questions were on people's minds in the first half of the twentieth century, they are just as pertinent, more pertinent really, than they were seventy years ago.

The circumstances surrounding both novels are triggered by a similar set of events. In *1984* the totalitarian predicament is preluded by an atomic war, the chaos that follows, civil war, a despotic party seizing power, and finally, murderous political purges. Completed in 1948, *1984* tries to imagine what would happen if someone like Hitler succeeded. Orwell's world is geographically divided into three authoritarian states—Oceania (North America and the British Empire), Eurasia (Russia), and Eastasia (China). The three superstates are at perpetual but limited war, having chosen conventional weapons over atomic ones. Permanent war benefits the powers that be because it provides the political fodder to manipulate the masses.

In *Brave New World* there is some early talk about the relevance of biological parents—"the appalling dangers of family life," as Our Ford calls it. All is interrupted by war. (*Brave New World* was published in 1932; Hiroshima had not yet occurred.) To bring about his totalitarian predicament, Huxley uses weaponry capable of putting an "enormous hole in the ground," techniques that infect entire water supplies, and anthrax bombs (which are "hardly louder than the popping of a paper bag"). A "Nine Years' War" is followed by a "great Economic Collapse." The world is left at a crossroads. What would it be—world control or destruction? In the end the world chooses world control. Huxley believed a highly centralized and efficient totalitarian state would naturally be preferred in the face of total annihilation—that people would give up their freedom if promised stability and safety. To keep the masses content, the totalitarian state would have to maintain a culture of consumption and pleasure. To control the masses, the government would have to condition the population from birth, even before birth if technically possible, and then keep it stupid throughout adulthood. And so in Huxley's world there are human hatcheries instead of human mothers, conditioning centers instead of fathers, plenty of golf courses, lots of movie theaters or "feelies" as the novel calls them, a world where every decent girl wears a belt loaded down with ready-to-use contraceptives.

Again, the similarities between the two novels outnumber the differences. For example, *both Orwell and Huxley knew their worlds could be realized only if the past was eradicated.* In 1984 the past is a dominant theme: "Who controls the past controls the future: who controls the present controls the past." Of course, in Orwell's novel it is the Party that controls the past, and the Party has seen to it that no objective historical record exists. Books opposed to the regime are destroyed. Winston Smith, the book's protagonist, is a government bureaucrat who routinely alters written records to make them fit the Party's ideology. The past is irrelevant, as seen in Oceania's complete reversal, at the novel's midpoint, as to who is the enemy. Then comes the citizenry's complete acceptance of it: ". . . it became known, with extreme suddenness and everywhere at once, that Eastasia and not Eurasia was the enemy. . . . The Hate continued exactly as before, except that the target had been changed."

In *Brave New World*, the past is despised by everyone because the past is said to be barbaric—the past is not *progressive* like the present. After the Nine Years' War there is a "campaign against the Past." Museums are closed. Historical monuments are blown up. All books published before A.F. (After Ford) 150 are suppressed. Children are taught no history. Early in the novel Mustapha Mond, the Resident Controller for Western Europe, gathers a group of students around him and quotes the wisdom of Our Ford. "History is bunk," he says. Mond repeats the phrase slowly so everyone will get it: HISTORY IS BUNK. With a wave of the hand Mond casually brushes away Ur of the Chaldees, Odysseus, Athens, Rome, Jerusalem, Jesus, King Lear, Pascal. Whisk. Whisk.

Both Orwell and Huxley knew their worlds could be realized only if the traditional family unit was eradicated. Pulling from Hitler's Youth and the Soviets' Young Pioneers, Orwell gives us a society where the child's loyalty to the state is placed above any loyalty to parent. For example, the character of Parsons, a loyal Party member, is proud of the fact that his own seven-year-old daughter betrays him after hearing him utter in his sleep, "Down with Big Brother." Winston Smith is raised in a camp for orphans, his parents having been killed in the purges. He only has vague and guilty memories of his mother. His wife is sexually frigid, a condition considered normal by Party standards. In Huxley's novel the biological family does not exist. Prenatal development is controlled in government hatcheries via chemicals. Babies are not born but *decanted*. Only the character called Savage has been born in the natural way. Children are *conditioned* (in much the same way Pavlov's dog was conditioned) to be ferocious consumers and sexually active. In *Brave New World* "everyone belongs to everyone." Any type of familial affection is considered gross. "What suffocating intimacies, what dangerous, insane, obscene relationships between members of the family group!" says Mond to his students. "Maniacally, the mother brooded over her children (*her* children) . . . brooded over them like a cat over its kittens; but a cat that could talk, a cat that could say, 'My baby, my baby,' over and over again."

Both Orwell and Huxley knew their worlds could be realized only if rational thinking was eradicated. In 1984 "war is peace," "freedom is slavery," and "ignorance is strength." "Doublethink" is the ability to hold simultaneously two opinions that cancel each other out. Indeed, orthodoxy in 1984 is *not* thinking—not needing to think—unconsciousness. According to the character Syme, by 2050 all literature would be pure Newspeak. Orwell knew that if you limited and altered a people's language—their public discourse—you would also be limiting and altering their culture. The problem with Winston Smith is that he thinks too much. At his day job he systematically erases the truth from public memory, but at night all he can think about is knowing the real truth. In the end Winston's powers of reasoning are destroyed through Electro-Convulsive Therapy, which makes him believe two plus two equals five. The Therapy even makes him love Big Brother. In

Brave New World, it is Bernard Marx who thinks too much, which makes his associates think his brain was damaged when too much alcohol was administered to him as a fetus. Bernard is contrasted with the character of Lenina Crowne, a true material girl whose deepest affections lie in vibro-vacuum massage machines, new clothes, synthetic music, television, flying, and *soma*. Whenever Lenina is confronted with a perplexing dilemma, all she can do is recite trite government phrases: "The more stitches, the less riches," "Ending is better than mending," "Never put off tomorrow the fun you can have today." Bernard tries to get Lenina to think about individual freedom, but she will have none of it and can only reply, "I don't understand." In the end the characters that think the most, Bernard and Savage, are isolated from the rest of society as misfits.

Both Orwell and Huxley knew their worlds could be realized only if religious inclinations could be rechanneled. In *1984* Big Brother is omnipresent. His image is found on coins, stamps, books, banners, posters, and cigarette packets. There is a certain religious fervor in the required Two Minutes of Hate and Hate Week, rituals that Orwell models after the Nuremberg rallies. The Two Minutes of Hate is a kind of secular church service where the devil (Goldstein) is railed against and God (Big Brother) is worshiped. The assembly is worked up into a frenzy, jumping up and down and screaming at the tops of their voices at Goldstein until the face of Big Brother appears "full of power and mysterious calm" and so vast that it almost fills the screen. In *Brave New World* all crosses have been cut off at the tops of churches to create Ts. Religious ritual is found in Solidarity Services and in Orgyporgy. At the start of each Solidarity Service the leader makes the sign of the T, turns on the synthetic music, and passes the communion cup of *soma*. As the service continues the music gets louder and the drumbeat becomes more pronounced. The congregation chants, "Ford, Ford, Ford." Everyone dances around the room in a linked circle until the assembly falls into a pagan-style debauch.

Both Orwell and Huxley knew their worlds could be realized only if technology was used as a means to an end. In Orwell's novel technology is used as a means of control. There are two-way telescreens, snooping helicopters, and hidden microphones. In Huxley's novel technology is used as a means of conditioning. There are hatcheries, feelies, contraceptives, and *soma.* In both books efficiency is highly valued. In *1984* total control is possible because technology has made it possible. In *Brave New World* society has surrendered to the god of technology—technology with a capital T.

Finally, and perhaps most importantly, both Orwell and Huxley are describing totalitarian states where an elite ruling class controls the masses. In *1984* the Inner Party, comprised by 2 percent of the population, wields absolute power. Below this autocratic iceberg 13 percent are trained technicians, and the rest, the Proles, are slave workers. In Orwell's novel the ruling class grabs power and maintains power for the sake of power alone. O'Brien tells Winston, "The Party seeks power entirely for its own sake. We are not interested in the good of others; we are interested solely in power." "If you want a picture of the future," says Winston's torturer, "imagine a boot stamping on a human face— forever." In *Brave New World* classes have to be created—Alphas, Betas, Deltas, Gammas—to perform the various tasks within society. No one objects to their rank because people have been conditioned to think their particular class is the happiest. Nevertheless, Huxley's world is an authoritarian one even if the conditioning is conducted through repetitive suggestions with such techniques as "sleep teaching." As the Director of the hatchery reminds us, "But all these suggestions are *our* suggestions!" When Savage realizes that Mustapha Mond also knows lines from Shakespeare, we are told that it is Mond who makes the laws and can therefore break them as he pleases, something no one else is allowed to do. And it is Mond who sends Bernard off to the islands—islands that the Controller says are fortunate because otherwise people who wanted to do such things as think and read Shakespeare would have to be sent to the "lethal chamber."

The worlds of Orwell and Huxley are only fiction, but they are reasonable speculations about the future based on real conditions that existed in the twentieth century—Hitler, Stalin, weapons of mass destruction, the burgeoning social sciences, advances in biology, and electronic media. The double-barrel threat of tyranny and technology with a capital T is just as acute now as it was then. And which prophecy is more probable? The author of this book does not have a definitive answer to that question. Orwell thought *Brave New World* implausible because he maintained that hedonistic societies do not endure, that they were too boring, and that Huxley had not created a convincing ruling class.[60] Perhaps. I think there are other questions to think about—questions that seek to address the probability of either anti-utopia occurring.

For example, if humans hold weapons of mass destruction, will they ever actually use them on each other? Also, are western nations capable of resisting the temptation to exercise sheer "will to power" over each other, abandoning democracy, in the absence of transcendent moral values? And what will happen if we lose our word-based modes of learning? And what type of religion will seek to replace Christianity? These were the questions Orwell and Huxley were addressing, and they are the questions that plague us now. It is quite possible that a *Brave New World* could lead to a *1984*—that a tyranny with a happy face could produce a tyranny with a sad face. Or it could happen the other way around, as Huxley envisioned it. Ideally, a formula for a führer would encompass both tragedy and comedy, pain as well as pleasure. The German people loved Hitler up to the edge of the abyss. He gave them a good show while seducing them to wage war against the world.

Of course there are other scenarios that contain elements found in Orwell and Huxley. In Ray Bradbury's *Fahrenheit 451*, books are burned, malcontents are chased down by robot dogs, and the masses stay glued to large television screens. In E. M. Forster's "The Machine Stops," the main character is a woman who lives her life in a room below the surface of the earth. She occupies herself with giving lectures through a looking glass, her electronic connection to a world of other people living inside little rooms below the surface of the earth. All life is plugged into the Machine—a ubiquitous hum. Everything goes well until her son decides he no longer wants to talk to his mother through a screen but wants to see her face to face. When the mother comes to visit the son, he confesses to her that he has journeyed to the surface, beyond the life of the Machine, where there are stars, rocks, and wind. This is too much for the mother, who prefers virtual reality to reality itself. The story ends with the Machine breaking down, which is to say, life support for everyone below the surface is suddenly and violently unplugged.

And then there is the biblical scenario of the last days—of wars and rumors of war, of love waxed cold, of abounding antichrists, of 666, and of the image of the beast. Compared to the events found in the book of Revelation, Hitler's antics were only a dress rehearsal for something much larger. Of all the scenarios about the future, this is the one Christians should give the closest attention because it is the true one. However, we know not the day or hour of His coming. I have deliberately chosen not to make this a book about biblical prophecy. We already have plenty of those, and I saw no reason to add another one. My main concern has been with America and what could happen to us *before* the end of the world. As far as I can tell, the Bible has little to say about America and the end times. But I know that some people reading this book will inevitably see Apocalypse between my lines. So as not to sound too much like a gloom-and-doomster (I am really an optimist by nature), let me end by offering some reasonable suggestions. For I really do believe America is at two roads diverged and that choosing the right road can make all the difference.

CHAPTER TEN

Conclusion: Making Waves

Let your moderation be known unto all men.

PHILIPPIANS 4:5

*Those who speak about this matter must often raise their voices
to a near-hysterical pitch, inviting the charge that they
are everything from wimps to public nuisances to Jeremiahs.
But they do so because what they want others to see
appears benign, when it is not invisible altogether.*[1]

NEIL POSTMAN

IF WE KNOW WHAT LIES BEHIND A PARTICULAR MEDIUM,
ARE ABLE TO POINT OUT HOW IT WORKS AND WHY IT SWAYS
PEOPLE THE WAY IT DOES, THEN WE CAN LESSEN ITS POWER
OVER US.

Since it would be cruel to paint such a bleak picture and then
leave the reader pondering what should be done about the
questions raised in this book, let me offer some remedies for our
idolatrous predicament. Starting with the individual and then
moving outward to the home, church, and finally school, these
solutions would form the strongest assault against the triumph of
idolatry if accomplished cumulatively. Each area of resistance
becomes more difficult as the ripples widen because it requires a

larger collective response. But even one or two ripples are better than no ripples. Making one little wave is at least a start.

PERSONAL RESISTANCE

The triumph of idolatry is possible because we are all pagans at heart. Man is a religious creature by nature and therefore must worship *something*. Blake recalls in his poem "Marriage of Heaven and Hell" that when the poets of old animated the objects of nature and made gods out of them, a religious system was formed, and in time people pronounced that the gods had ordered the system all along. "Thus men forgot that All deities reside in the human breast," Blake says. Just as idolatry was the natural inclination of the soul five thousand years ago, so it is today. Living in a high-tech society does not make us any less susceptible to the trappings of pagan idolatry and all the tyrannous auxiliaries that go along with it. My main point throughout the book has been that technological innovations in communications media, coupled with a rejection of biblical truth, is ironically pulling us back to a pagan past.

Keeping ourselves from idols—making sure that we do not become participants in society's idolization process—is the incipient ripple and is a matter of personal holiness. The epistle of First John admonishes believers not to set their affections on all that glitters in this present world: "For all that is in the world, the lust of the flesh, and the lust of the eyes, and the pride of life, is not of the Father, but is of the world" (1 John 2:16). The world of which the apostle speaks is not necessarily the created abode we live in (rocks and trees, skies and seas); rather, it is the *world system* that is hostile to God and under Satan's dominion. Believers are to turn away from sensual desires and resist the pull of Vanity Fair. Idolatry is predicated on the eye-gate. The pagan walks by sight, whereas the Christian is to walk by faith based upon the revealed *Logos*.

RESISTANCE AT HOME

The second ripple of resistance originates from the first one and encompasses the home. Keeping ourselves from idols also means that parents must control life under the roof. So many elements of our culture wage war against domestic tranquillity. Corporate life cuts into home life with long working hours and long commutes. Negative media content is so pervasive that concerned parents have a difficult time monitoring what their children see and hear. The temptation to keep up with the Joneses compels many households to live outside their budgets. The market no longer merely tells us what products are available—it now persuades us to have more and more—the newest computer, a $40,000 SUV, a $500,000 home.

Some people have had enough. The decade-old simplicity movement is a conscious attempt to opt out of the corporate rat race. These people know that even if you win the rat race, you are still a rat. Under the banner of "less is more," anticonsumerists intentionally scale down their material wants for a more simple way of life. For some, living simple means taking a cut in pay and moving to a small town with a slower pace. For others it might mean downsizing to a smaller house so the wife can be at home with the kids. For Henry Thoreau it meant retreating to the woods to live on Walden Pond.

Of course, some people retreat from the rat race not because they want to re-prioritize their values but because they are paranoid. Those who join a compound, put on army fatigues, and build up an arsenal of weapons are usually motivated by hate or fear of the government or some aspect of society they realize they cannot change by rational means. Therefore, they bury their heads in the sand (the Luddite stance) or prepare for war (the commando stance). Neither of these attitudes end up simplifying one's life but rather complicate it. Balance is the key.

Resistance at home does not have to mean moving the family to the woods. Resistance might mean keeping things simple at home by altering media consumption habits. For over half a century now the American home has wrapped itself around the television set. There is no law that says the TV has to be the nucleus of the home—that all life has to be centered around a flickering screen. It might cause waves with the children at first, but some thought needs to be given to the idea of downsizing the set to ten inches and putting it in the kitchen, or better still, the bathroom. Not owning a television set is a viable option as well. I know people who do not own a set and have managed to maintain their sanity and live respectable lives. For others, controlling *what* is watched and *how much* is watched is a step in the right direction. Discernment, discretion, and denial should not be household dirty words when it comes to choosing what movies to watch. Ultimately, parents are responsible for the environment they create for their children. Television watching and Internet surfing should never be done haphazardly. Parents should organize and monitor the use of electronic media in the home. Other forms of leisure should be sought—reading a book, taking a hike, inviting someone over for a well-prepared meal and stoking the dying art of conversation. If we can bring ourselves to place television and other forms of electronic media in a more remote corner of our lives, we might find that there would be more time for reflection, more time for family, and more time for God.

RESISTANCE AT CHURCH

A third but more difficult area of resistance is to be found in the waves one must be willing to make at church. Churches must return to the Word as their final authority and practice. Francis Schaeffer believed that the weight given to the full authority of Scripture was the determinate watershed issue for theology, doctrine, and the Christian life. Like the melting snow on the Swiss Alps, where half of the snow ends up in the North Sea and half of it ends up in the Mediterranean, Schaeffer claimed that a loose view toward biblical inspiration and authority will end up a thousand miles apart from a conservative view. Returning to the Word means adopting a worldview in regard to what the Bible teaches about the cosmos, human nature, and history. It means preserving older forms of worship that are *logos*-centered—maintaining Scripture reading and keeping the sermon the centerpiece of the service. It also means taking off our pragmatic eyeglasses whereby all things are viewed under a success-oriented paradigm: Does it work? How does it look? Will it draw a crowd? It means asking tough questions in loving confrontation: What is wrong with the older hymnals? Do we really need both a contemporary service and a traditional one? What are we saying by having two services? Is it such a good idea to have the church staff wrestle each other during the Sunday night service? These kinds of questions are not always easy to ask, but they get at the root of what are most often shallow motivations to be attractive to those outside of the church or those with one foot in the door.

RESISTANCE AT SCHOOL

By design, schools are wave-making machines and can be just as potent as the home or the church in resisting the idolization process. But if schools fall under the same spell that has mesmerized the rest of the culture—namely, that all technological progress is for our *good* no matter where it takes us—then we might as well surrender to the binary bullies right now and let them start searching for the safest way to implant computer chips in our brains. Schools must take new media technologies seriously for altogether different reasons than have been suggested thus far. The computer has ushered us into the information age. There was a time when we perceived ourselves as having an information scarcity. Our greatest need, or so they told us, was to increase the amount of information, make it more available, and of course make it arrive faster. Through wires and light waves, satellites and silicon chips, we poured the information in until we were flooded in facts. We no longer have a scarcity of information.[2] What we have is information glut. Information has been reduced to the level of meaningless garbage because there is so much of it. Parents, educators, and community leaders need to understand that our real problem is not providing Johnny at school with a computer (chances are he already has one at home); our real problem is knowing what information is essential for Johnny to live a sensible life.

Resistance at school means that educators must make a dis-

tinction between *knowledge* and *wisdom*. More value should be
placed on the latter. In the midst of a growing trend to rethink
public education, Christians and conservatives in general should
not be afraid to suggest at school board meetings that the wisdom that serves the community best is the wisdom that served
the nation for almost two centuries. After all, classical western
thought, and more specifically the Judeo-Christian heritage, is
our oldest educational tradition. This may sound like a radical
idea, but the only alternative is more irrationality and relativism.
I am *not* suggesting that public education be Christianized. I *am*
suggesting that schools look to the past rather than to the future
to find their purpose for educating children. It is entirely possible for public schools on the local level to embrace a classical
education without becoming sectarian. Parents should take a
proactive stance in influencing the content of the curriculum.
Civility, virtue, abstinence, creationism, and religion in general
do not have to be anathema in the public square. This is a fight
worth fighting.

Christian schools are in the unique and privileged position of
being able to act on the culture's slide toward stupidity. Taken
together, the home, the church, and the Christian school present
a powerful trilateral force against the triumph of idolatry. It is
time once again to be a "people of the Book." But two dangers
must be recognized. First, if Christian communities accommodate
or ape the culture they are seeking to win, then their effectiveness
is seriously reduced or even lost. Second, Christian communities
should not withdraw from the culture but rather engage it head-
on. As Jesus taught, we must be *in* the world but not *of* it.
Enclaves are not necessarily bad things—plants grow best inside
hothouses; but if the triangle of the home, church, and Christian
school becomes a monastery, then we are hiding our light under
a bushel.

Finally, public, private, and home-bound schools need to add
a new subject to their curriculum—media ecology. The term *ecology* is borrowed from biology to signify a desire for balance in the
information environment. It carries the idea that a degree of har-

mony can be achieved between human beings and their inventions. Sometimes referred to as media literacy, the subject of media ecology views how various forms of communication shape the cultural institutions for good or ill. The study of communication itself—how symbols, codes, and media shape discourse—is an ancient one extending all the way back to Athenian democracy. Classical education has traditionally placed human communication at the center of the curriculum. The Trivium consisted of grammar, logic, and rhetoric. Of course, any study of human communication today should also include electronic media because of the tremendous influence of radio, cinema, television, and the Internet. For schools to say nothing about the influence of these inventions upon our culture is to say they do not influence our culture when we instinctively know that they do. Media ecology is multidisciplinary because it touches upon other subjects like philosophy, history, technology, rhetoric, education, political science, and religion.

Rather than asking what technology can do *for* us (the question that is most always asked now), the discipline of media ecology asks what technology is doing *to* us. The subject can be geared to the needs of elementary, secondary, or college students in a number of different ways. As a college course, media ecology can stand alone in the curriculum as a required social science and may be studied under the headings of Media Literacy, Media and Society, or Communication History. I would suggest that it be taught outside of the Broadcasting Department, if possible, since professors who encourage students to pursue careers in radio and television might be reluctant to comment on the downside of their field, whereas an education, English, or history professor may have no such hesitations. Since we know that young children watch twenty thousand television commercials a year, it might be a good idea for them to know *how* commercials are made and *why* they are made. High school students need to know how to read a newspaper as well as how to properly watch television news. They need to know what goes on behind the news camera, why most news anchors are beautiful people, and why the television news industry depends on ratings. Teenagers need to know that celebrities are packaged and marketed like candy bars, that NBA athletes have difficulty holding on to their money and finding a job when they retire, and that childhood stars have high rates of suicide after they grow up or become ugly.

To grapple with issues like these demystifies television and other forms of electronic media. In the words of Neil Postman, it "breaks the spell" of powerful media technologies.[3] If we know what lies behind a particular medium, are able to point out how it works and why it sways people the way it does, then we can lessen its power over us.

Selected Bibliography

Barna, George. *Boiling Point: It Only Takes One Degree: Monitoring Cultural Shifts in the 21st Century*. Ventura, CA: Regal Books, 2001.

Birkerts, Sven. *The Gutenburg Elegies: The Fate of Reading in an Electronic Age*. Boston: Faber and Faber, 1994.

Bloom, Allan. *The Closing of the American Mind*. New York: Simon and Schuster, 1987.

Boorstin, Daniel. *The Image: A Guide to Pseudo-Events in America*. New York: Harper and Row, Colophon Books, 1961.

Carey, James W. *Communication as Culture: Essays on Media and Society*. New York: Routledge, 1989.

Collier, James Lincoln. *The Rise of Selfishness in America*. New York: Oxford University Press, 1991.

Crowley, David and Paul Heyer, eds. *Communication in History: Technology, Culture, Society*, 3rd ed. New York: Longman, 1999.

Czitrom, Daniel J. *Media and the American Mind: From Morse to McLuhan*. Chapel Hill, NC: University of North Carolina Press, 1982.

Eisenstein, Elizabeth L. *The Printing Revolution in Early Modern Europe*. New York: Cambridge University Press, 1983.

Ewen, Stuart. *All Consuming Images: The Politics of Style in Contemporary Culture*. New York: Basic Books, 1988.

Gabler, Neal. *Life: The Movie, How Entertainment Conquered Reality*. New York: Vintage Books, 1998.

Hanegraaff, Hank. *Counterfeit Revival: Looking for God in All the Wrong Places*. Nashville: Word Publishing, 2001.

Hirsch, E. D., Jr. *Cultural Literacy: What Every American Needs to Know*. Boston: Houghton Mifflin Company, 1987.

Howe, Daniel Walker, ed. *Victorian America*. University of Pennsylvania Press, 1976.

Lasch, Christopher. *The Culture of Narcissism: American Life in an Age of Diminishing Expectations*. New York: Warner Books, 1979.

Lockridge, Kenneth A. *Literacy in Colonial New England*. New York: W. W. Norton & Company, 1974.

MacMullen, Ramsay. *Christianity & Paganism in the Fourth to Eighth Centuries*. New Haven, CT: Yale University Press, 1997.

Manchester, William. *A World Lit Only by Fire: The Medieval Mind and the Renaissance*. Boston: Little Brown and Company, 1992.

Marsden, George M. *The Soul of the American University: From Protestant

Establishment to Established Nonbelief. New York: Oxford University Press, 1994.

McLuhan, Marshall. *The Gutenberg Galaxy: The Making of Typographic Man*. Toronto: University of Toronto Press, 1962.

Morris, Henry M. *The Long War Against God*. Grand Rapids, MI: Baker Book House, 1989.

Neuhaus, Richard John. *The Naked Public Square: Religion and Democracy in America*. Grand Rapids, MI: William B. Eerdmans, 1984.

Paglia, Camille. *Sexual Personae: Art and Decadence from Nefertiti to Emily Dickinson*. London and New Haven, CT: Yale University Press, 1990.

Postman, Neil. *Teaching as a Conserving Activity*. New York: Delacorte Press, 1979.

——. *Amusing Ourselves to Death: Public Discourse in the Age of Show Business*. New York: Penguin Books, 1985.

——. *The Disappearance of Childhood*. New York: Vintage Books, 1992.

Riesman, David, Nathan Glazer, and Reuel Denney. *The Lonely Crowd*. New York: Doubleday Anchor Books, 1950.

Sacks, Peter. *Generation X Goes to College: An Eye-Opening Account of Teaching in Postmodern America*. Chicago and LaSalle, IL: Open Court, 1996.

Schaeffer, Francis A. *How Should We Then Live? The Rise and Decline of Western Thought and Culture*. Wheaton, IL: Crossway Books, 1976.

——. *The Great Evangelical Disaster*. Wheaton, IL: Crossway Books, 1984.

Seznec, Jean. *The Survival of the Pagan Gods: The Mythological Tradition and Its Place in Renaissance Humanism and Art*. Trans. B. F. Sessions. New York: Princeton University Press, 1981.

Veith, Gene Edward, Jr. *Modern Fascism: Liquidating the Judeo-Christian Worldview*. Saint Louis: Concordia Publishing House, 1993.

——. *Postmodern Times: A Christian Guide to Contemporary Culture*. Wheaton, IL: Crossway Books, 1994.

Welch, David. *The Third Reich: Politics and Propaganda*. New York: Routledge, 1993.

Whitehead, John W. *The Second American Revolution*. Wheaton, IL: Crossway Books, 1982.

Wykes, Alan. *The Nuremberg Rallies*. New York: Ballantine Books, 1970.

Notes

Chapter One: Introduction: Tomorrowland

1. Leonard Mosley, *Disney's World* (Chelsea, MI: Scarborough House Publishers, 1990), p. 290.
2. Dennis McCafferty, "New Frontiers: Changing the Way We Play," *USA WEEKEND*, May 28-30, 1999, p. 4.
3. Lewis Mumford, *Technics and Civilization* (New York: Harcourt, Brace and World, 1934), p. 85.
4. John Costello, *The Pacific War* (New York: Rawson, Wade Publishers, 1981), p. 581.
5. Ibid., p. 582.
6. Peter Wyden, *Day One: Before Hiroshima and After* (New York: Simon & Schuster, 1984), p. 135.
7. Roger Burlingame, *Henry Ford: A Great Life in Brief* (New York: Alfred A. Knopf, 1966), p. 3.
8. Ibid., pp. 3-7.
9. Robert S. Lynd and Helen Merrell Lynd, *Middletown: A Study in American Culture* (New York: Harcourt, Brace and World, 1929), p. 257.
10. Ibid., p. 7.
11. James Lincoln Collier, *The Rise of Selfishness in America* (New York: Oxford University Press, 1991), p. 151.
12. Lynd and Lynd, *Middletown: A Study in American Culture*, p. 258.
13. David Gelernter, *1939: The Lost World of the Fair* (New York: The Free Press, 1995), p. 13.
14. Ibid., pp. 168-169.
15. Ibid., pp. 36-37.
16. Ibid., pp. 167-168.
17. Quoted in ibid., p. 167.
18. Quoted in ibid., p. 354.
19. Lynn Spigel, "Making Room for TV," in D. J. Crowley and Paul Heyer, eds., *Communication in History: Technology, Culture, Society*, 3rd ed. (New York: Longman, 1999), p. 269.
20. "New Study Finds Kids Spend Equivalent of Full Work Week Using Media," Kaiser Family Foundation press release, November 17, 1999. See http://www.kff.org/content/1999/1535pressreleasefinal.doc.html (accessed August 8, 2001).
21. "Adult Literacy in America," National Center for Educational Statistics, U.S. Department of Education, 1993.
22. This is the definition for literacy used in the survey, "Adult Literacy in America."
23. George Barna, *Virtual America* (Ventura, CA: Regal Books, 1994), p. 34.
24. Ibid., pp. 34-35.
25. See Sven Birkerts, *The Gutenburg Elegies: The Fate of Reading in an Electronic Age* (Boston: Faber and Faber, 1994), p. 127.
26. Byron T. Scott and Ann Walton Sieber, "Remaking *Time, Newsweek*, and *U.S. News and World Report*," in Philip S. Cook, Douglas Gomery, and Lawrence W. Lichty, eds., *The Future of News: Television, Newspapers, Wire Services, Newsmagazines* (Washington, D.C.: The Woodrow Wilson Center Press, 1992), p. 201.
27. See Daniel Boorstin, "From Hero to Celebrity: The Human Pseudo-Event," in *The Image* (New York: Harper and Row, Colophon Books, 1961), pp. 45-76.
28. Julia Lieblich, for the Associated Press, "Southern Baptists Urged to Avoid New Methods of Worship," *The Leaf-Chronicle*, Clarksville, TN, June 16, 1999, p. B3.
29. George Barna, *Virtual America*, p. 147.
30. Neil Postman, *Amusing Ourselves to Death: Public Discourse in the Age of Show Business* (New York: Penguin Books, 1985), pp. 155-156.
31. Kenneth Burke, *The Philosophy of Literary Form* (Berkeley, CA: University of California Press, 1973), p. 191.
32. The phrase, "high-tech version of the Dark Ages" was used by Robert Bork in *Slouching*

Towards Gomorrah: Modern Liberalism and American Decline (New York: Regan Books, 1997), p. 4.

Chapter Two: Tables of Stone

1. This is how Camille Paglia begins her book *Sexual Personae: Art and Decadence from Nefertiti to Emily Dickinson* (London and New Haven, CT: Yale University Press, 1990), p. 1.
2. Ibid., p. 139.
3. See Mal Couch, ed., *Dictionary of Premillennial Theology* (Grand Rapids, MI: Kregel, 1996), p. 61.
4. Henry M. Morris, *The Long War Against God* (Grand Rapids, MI: Baker Book House, 1989), p. 255.
5. *Halley's Bible Handbook* (Grand Rapids, MI: Zondervan, 1965), p. 65.
6. Couch, ed., *Dictionary of Premillennial Theology*, p. 62.
7. See Gene Edward Veith, Jr., *Modern Fascism: Liquidating the Judeo-Christian Worldview* (Saint Louis: Concordia Publishing House, 1993), p. 146.
8. "Humiliation of the word" is a phrase borrowed from Jacques Ellul's book *The Humiliation of the Word* (Grand Rapids, MI: William Eerdmans, 1985).
9. Paglia, *Sexual Personae: Art and Decadence from Nefertiti to Emily Dickinson*, p. 59.
10. For an ardent description of Egyptian art see Paglia, "The Birth of the Western Eye," in ibid., pp. 40-71.
11. Daniel J. Boorstin, *The Creators: A History of Heroes of the Imagination* (New York: Random House, 1992), p. 155.
12. Will Durant, *Our Oriental Heritage* (New York: MJF Books, 1992), pp. 198-199.
13. Ibid., p. 163.
14. Paglia, *Sexual Personae: Art and Decadence from Nefertiti to Emily Dickinson*, p. 59.
15. Boorstin, *The Creators: A History of Heroes of the Imagination*, p. 161.
16. See Neil Postman and Camille Paglia, "Two Cultures—Television Versus Print," in D. J. Crowley and Paul Heyer, eds., *Communication in History: Technology, Culture, Society*, 3rd ed. (New York: Longman, 1999), p. 290. This chapter is a lively discussion of the separate worlds of image and print.
17. Walter H. Ong, *Orality and Literacy: The Technologizing of the Word* (New York: Methuen, 1982), pp. 78-83.
18. I. J. Gelb, *A Study of Writing* (Chicago: The University of Chicago Press, 1963), p. 221.
19. Ibid., pp. 221-222.
20. Ibid., p. 232.
21. See Jack Goody and Ian Watt, "The Consequences of Literacy," in Crowley and Heyer, eds., *Communication in History: Technology, Culture, Society*, p. 47.
22. Neil Postman, *Amusing Ourselves to Death: Public Discourse in the Age of Show Business* (New York: Penguin Books, 1985), p. 13.
23. See Harold Innis, "Media in Ancient Empires," in Crowley and Heyer, eds., *Communication in History: Technology, Culture, Society*, p. 28.
24. C. H. Kraeling and R. F. Adams, *City Invincible*, 1960, quoted in A. R. Millard, "The Practice of Writing in Ancient Israel," in *The Biblical Archaeologist* 4 (December 1972), p. 102.
25. Innis, "Media in Ancient Empires," p. 24.
26. Postman, *Amusing Ourselves to Death: Public Discourse in the Age of Show Business*, p. 13.
27. Eric Havelock, *Origins of Western Literacy* (Toronto: Ontario Institute for Studies in Education, 1976).
28. Carroll Atkinson and Eugene T. Maleska, *The Story of Education* (Philadelphia: Chilton Company, 1962), p. 11.
29. William Barclay, *Educational Ideals in the Ancient World* (Grand Rapids, MI: Baker Book House, 1959), pp. 13-14. Also see the conclusion reached by James L. Crenshaw, "Education in Ancient Israel," in *Journal of Biblical Literature* 4 (December 1985), p. 614.
30. *Kiddushin 30b*, quoted in Barclay, *Educational Ideals in the Ancient World*, p. 16.
31. See Alan R. Millard, "The Practice of Writing in Ancient Israel," in *The Biblical Archaeologist* 4 (December 1972), pp. 98-111.
32. Ibid., p. 108.
33. Ibid., p. 111.
34. Ibid., p. 110.
35. William G. Dever, "Save Us from Postmodern Malarkey," *Biblical Archaeology Review* (March/April 2000), p. 34.

36. Alan R. Millard, "The Question of Israelite Literacy," in *Bible Review* 3 (Fall 1987), p. 29.
37. See John J. Davis and John C. Whitcomb, *A History of Israel: From Conquest to Exile* (Winona Lake, IN: BMH Books, 1981), pp. 48-49.
38. See ibid. for reasons God punished the Canaanite cities.
39. See Leon Wood, *A Survey of Israel's History* (Grand Rapids, MI: Zondervan Publishing House, 1970), p. 208.
40. Durant, *Our Oriental Heritage*, pp. 296-297.
41. Ibid., p. 245.
42. William Barclay, *Educational Ideals in the Ancient World*, pp. 24-25.
43. *Josephus: Against Apion*, quoted in ibid., p. 12.
44. *Sayings of the Jewish Fathers*, quoted in ibid., p. 34.
45. Ibid., p. 13.
46. Ibid.
47. G. H. Box, *E.B. 2. 1190*, quoted in ibid., p. 14.
48. Ibid., p. 32.
49. See Marvin R. Wilson, "The Jewish Concept of Learning: A Christian Appreciation," in *Christian Scholar's Review* 5 (1976), pp. 359-360.
50. See Jack Goody and Ian Watt, "The Consequences of Literacy," in Crowley and Heyer, eds., *Communication in History: Technology, Culture, Society*, p. 46.
51. Ibid.
52. Gene Edward Veith, Jr., *Postmodern Times: A Christian Guide to Contemporary Culture* (Wheaton, IL: Crossway Books, 1994), p. 30.
53. Boorstin, *The Creators: A History of Heroes of the Imagination*, p. 164.
54. Ibid., p. 170.
55. Ibid., p. 172.
56. Ibid., p. 178.
57. Ibid., p. 117.
58. See "Did You Know?" in *Christian History*, Vol. 17, No. 1, 1998.
59. Paglia, *Sexual Personae: Art and Decadence from Nefertiti to Emily Dickinson*, p. 25.
60. Francis A. Schaeffer, *How Should We Then Live? The Rise and Decline of Western Thought and Culture* (Wheaton, IL: Crossway Books, 1976), p. 26.
61. Paglia, *Sexual Personae: Art and Decadence from Nefertiti to Emily Dickinson*, p. 139.
62. *Augustine De Doctrina Christiana 40*, quoted in Barclay, *Educational Ideals in the Ancient World*, p. 231.

Chapter Three: When Night Fell

1. C. E. Stancliffe, *St. Martin and His Hagiographer. History and Miracle in Sulpicius Severus* (Oxford, 1983), quoted in Ramsay MacMullen, *Christianity & Paganism in the Fourth to Eighth Centuries* (New Haven, CT: Yale University Press, 1997), p. 146.
2. See Bob Scribner, "Heterodoxy, Literacy and Print in the Early German Reformation," in *Heresy and Literacy, 1000-1530*, eds. Peter Biller and Anne Hudson (New York: Cambridge University Press, 1996), p. 255.
3. This account is based on Edward Gibbon's *The Decline and Fall of the Roman Empire*, Vol. 3 (London: Everyman's Library, 1976).
4. Ibid., p. 222.
5. Ibid., p. 226.
6. Ibid., p. 228.
7. J. B. Bury, *The Invasion of Europe by the Barbarians* (New York: W. W. Norton & Company, 1967), p. 16.
8. Gibbon, *The Decline and Fall of the Roman Empire*, Vol. 3, p. 253.
9. Ibid.
10. Ferdinand Lot, in Norman F. Cantor, ed., *The Medieval World: 300-1300* (New York: Macmillan, 1963), p. 12.
11. Bruce Shelly, "The Emperor's New Religion," *Christian History*, Vol. 17, No. 1, 1998, p. 40.
12. MacMullen, *Christianity & Paganism in the Fourth to Eighth Centuries*, p. 2.
13. Ibid., p. 152.
14. Ibid., p. 72.
15. Ibid., pp. 21-22.
16. Ibid., pp. 8-10.
17. Ibid., pp. 151-152.
18. Ibid., p. 33.
19. Ibid., p. 58.

20. John O. Gooch, "The Emperor Strikes Back," *Christian History*, Vol. 17, No. 1, 1998, p. 41.
21. MacMullen, *Christianity & Paganism in the Fourth to Eighth Centuries*, p. 72.
22. William Manchester, *A World Lit Only by Fire: The Medieval Mind and the Renaissance* (Boston: Little Brown and Company, 1992), p. 11.
23. MacMullen, *Christianity & Paganism in the Fourth to Eighth Centuries*, p. 43.
24. Ibid., p. 66.
25. Ibid., p. 154.
26. Manchester, *A World Lit Only by Fire*, p. 12.
27. Ibid., p. 13.
28. Jean Seznec, *The Survival of the Pagan Gods: The Mythological Tradition and Its Place in Renaissance Humanism and Art*, trans. B. F. Sessions (New York: Princeton University Press, 1981), pp. 319-320.
29. MacMullen, *Christianity & Paganism in the Fourth to Eighth Centuries*, p. 96.
30. G. G. Coulton, *The Medieval Village* (New York: Dover Publications, 1989), p. 65.
31. James Burke, "Communication in the Middle Ages," in D. J. Crowley and Paul Heyer, eds., *Communication in History: Technology, Culture, Society*, 3rd ed. (New York: Longman, 1999), p. 71.
32. Barbara W. Tuchman, *A Distant Mirror: The Calamitous 14th Century* (New York: Alfred A. Knopf, 1978), p. 134.
33. Manchester, *A World Lit Only by Fire*, p. 55.
34. Harry J. Gaff, "Literate and Illiterate; Hearing and Seeing: England 1066-1307," in Harry J. Gaff, ed., *Literacy and Social Development in the West: A Reader* (New York: Cambridge University Press, 1981), p. 16.
35. Kenneth Clark, *Civilisation: A Personal View* (New York: Harper & Row Publishers, 1969), p. 17.
36. See Gaff, "Literate and Illiterate; Hearing and Seeing," pp. 14-29.
37. Ibid., pp. 16-17.
38. The points about the fading of literacy during the Middle Ages are discussed in Neil Postman's insightful work, *The Disappearance of Childhood* (New York: Vintage Books, 1992), pp. 11-14. Postman argues there was no such thing as childhood in the Middle Ages because childhood is not as much a biological state as it is a social one, formed by the demands of education.
39. Eric A. Havelock, *Origins of Western Literacy* (Toronto: Ontario Institute for Studies in Education, 1976), p. 65.
40. Postman, *The Disappearance of Childhood*, pp. 11-12.
41. Ibid., p. 12.
42. Burke, "Communication in the Middle Ages," p. 71.
43. Ibid., p. 77.
44. Ibid., p. 75.
45. MacMullen, *Christianity & Paganism in the Fourth to Eighth Centuries*, p. 90.
46. Postman, *The Disappearance of Childhood*, p. 14.
47. Neil Postman, *Conscientious Objections: Stirring Up Trouble About Language, Technology, and Education* (New York: Random House, Vintage Books, 1988), p. 153.
48. Manchester, *A World Lit Only by Fire*, p. 6.
49. Ibid.
50. Ibid.
51. Ibid.
52. J. H. Plumb, "The Great Change in Children," *Horizon*, Vol. 13, No. 1, Winter 1971, p. 7. The quote here is also noted in Postman, *The Disappearance of Childhood*.
53. Philippe Ariès, *Centuries of Childhood*, trans. Robert Baldrick (New York: Random House, Vintage Books, 1962), p. 103. The quote here is also noted in Postman, *The Disappearance of Childhood*.
54. Manchester, *A World Lit Only by Fire*, p. 66.
55. MacMullen, *Christianity & Paganism in the Fourth to Eighth Centuries*, p. 153.
56. "Did You Know? Little Known or Remarkable Facts About Everyday Faith in the Middle Ages," *Christian History*, Vol. 15, No. 1, pp. 2-3.
57. See Burke, "Communication in the Middle Ages," pp. 78-79.
58. R. I. More, "Literacy and the Making of Heresy, c.1000-c.1150," in *Heresy and Literacy, 1000-1530*, p. 20.
59. See Water H. Ong, *Orality and Literacy: The Technologizing of the Word* (New York: Methuen, 1982).
60. Lori Ramos, "Understanding Literacy: Theoretical Foundations for Research in Media

Ecology," in *The New Jersey Journal of Communication*, Vol. 8, No. 1, Spring 2000, p. 53.
61. See Neil Postman, *Teaching as a Conserving Activity* (New York: Delacorte Press, 1979).
62. Gene E. Veith, Jr., *Postmodern Times: A Christian Guide to Contemporary Thought and Culture* (Wheaton, IL: Crossway Books), pp. 183-184.
63. Stephen Carter, *Civility: Manners, Morals, and Etiquette of Democracy* (New York: Basic Books, 1998), pp. 14-15.
64. See John Leo, "A Lovely Day for Haranguing," *U.S. News and World Report*, November 13, 1995, p. 33.
65. Carter, *Civility: Manners, Morals, and Etiquette of Democracy*, pp. 6-7. The song was "Necroebophile," from the album *The Tomb of the Mutilated.*
66. Allan Bloom discusses rock music in *The Closing of the American Mind* (New York: Simon and Schuster, 1987), p. 74.
67. C. S. Lewis, *Screwtape Letters* (New York: Macmillan, 1976), p. 29.
68. Robert Bork, *Slouching Towards Gomorrah: Modern Liberalism and American Decline* (New York: Regan Books, 1997), p. 263.
69. Richard Carliss, "A Star Trek into The X-Files," *Time*, April 7, 1997, p. 42.
70. Todd Halvorson of *Florida Today*, "HD119850 Signal Was Loud and Clear," in *Pensacola News Journal*, October 24, 1999, p. 2A.
71. Charles Strohmer, "The Future—Your Call?: The Commercialization of Psychics and Astrology," *Christian Research Journal*, Vol. 22, No. 1, 1999, p. 34.
72. Veith, *Postmodern Times*, p. 200.
73. Bork, *Slouching Towards Gomorrah*, p. 250.
74. Ibid., pp. 264-265.
75. Myron Gilmore, *The World of Humanism, 1453-1517* (New York: Harper and Row, 1952), p. 186.

Chapter Four: The Fiery Word

1. See Neil Postman and Camille Paglia, "Two Cultures—Television Versus Print," in D. J. Crowley and Paul Heyer, eds., *Communication in History: Technology, Culture, Society*, 3rd ed. (New York: Longman, 1999), p. 291.
2. Francis A. Schaeffer, *How Should We Then Live? The Rise and Decline of Western Thought and Culture* (Wheaton, IL: Crossway Books, 1976), p. 79.
3. E. R. Chamberlin, *The Bad Popes* (New York: Dorset Press, 1986), p. 164.
4. David Freedberg, "The Power of Images: Studies in the History and Theory of Response," in John Hale, *The Civilization of Europe in the Renaissance* (New York: Atheneum, 1994), p. 435.
5. Chamberlin, *The Bad Popes*, p. 161.
6. William Manchester, *A World Lit Only by Fire: The Medieval Mind and the Renaissance* (Boston: Little Brown and Company, 1992), p. 79.
7. Ibid., p. 71.
8. See David S. Schaff, *History of the Christian Church*, Vol. 6 (Grand Rapids, MI: William B. Eerdmans, 1910), p. 766.
9. The account of Johann Tetzel is taken from the following sources: Will Durant, *The Reformation: A History of European Civilization from Wycliffe to Calvin: 1300-1564* (New York: MJF Books, 1992), pp. 338-339; H. G. Hail, *Luther: An Experiment in Biography* (New York: Doubleday & Company, 1980), p. 251; and Manchester, *A World Lit Only by Fire: The Medieval Mind and the Renaissance*, pp. 133-136.
10. See Durant, *The Reformation*, p. 344.
11. Elizabeth L. Eisenstein, *The Printing Revolution in Early Modern Europe* (New York: Cambridge University Press, 1983), p. 153.
12. See quote by Maurice Gravier in ibid., pp. 153-154.
13. See *D. Martin Luther's Werke: Kritische Gesamtausgabe*, 58 vols. in Hail, *Luther: An Experiment in Biography*, p. 170.
14. J. A. Froud, *Life and Letters of Erasmus* (New York, 1894) in Durant, *The Reformation*, p. 388.
15. See quote by A. G. Dickens, in Eisenstein, *The Printing Revolution in Early Modern Europe*, p. 148.
16. See S. H. Steinberg, *Five Hundred Years of Printing* (Baltimore, MD: Penguin Books, 1955), p. 123.
17. Eisenstein, *The Printing Revolution in Early Modern Europe*, p. 157.
18. The highlights of Tyndale's life are based primarily on A. N. S. Lane, "William Tyndale

and the English Bible," in *Great Leaders of the Christian Church*, ed. John D. Woodbridge (Chicago: Moody Press, 1988).

19. John Foxe, *Foxe's Book of Martyrs* (North Brunswick, NJ: Bridge-Logos Publishers, 1997), p. 98.
20. Eisenstein, *The Printing Revolution in Early Modern Europe*, pp. 162-163.
21. David Daniel, *William Tyndale: A Biography* (London and New Haven, CT: Yale University Press, 1994), p. 3.
22. Eisenstein, *The Printing Revolution in Early Modern Europe*, p. 157.
23. Ibid., p. 143.
24. Marshall McLuhan, *The Gutenberg Galaxy: The Making of Typographic Man* (Toronto: University of Toronto Press, 1962), p. 153.
25. Leland Ryken, *Worldly Saints: The Puritans as They Really Were* (Grand Rapids, MI: Academie Books, Zondervan, 1986), pp. 2-7.
26. Cassandra Niemczyk, "Did You Know? Little-known or Remarkable Facts About American Puritans," *Christian History*, Vol. 13, No. 1, 1994, p. 3.
27. D. M. Lloyd-Jones, *The Puritans: Their Origins and Successors* (Carlisle, PA: The Banner of Truth Trust, 1996), pp. 240-241.
28. Cotton Mather, *Cares About the Nurseries* (Boston, 1702), in Edmund S. Morgan, *The Puritan Family* (New York: Harper & Row, 1966), p. 89.
29. James D. Hart, *The Popular Book: A History of America's Literary Taste* (New York: Oxford University Press, 1950), p. 8.
30. Kenneth A. Lockridge, *Literacy in Colonial New England* (New York: W. W. Norton & Company, 1974), p. 99.
31. Ibid., pp. 69-71.
32. Alden T. Vaughan, *New England Frontier: Puritans and Indians: 1620-1675* (Boston: Little, Brown and Company, 1965), pp. 326-327.
33. Ibid., p. 333.
34. Cotton Mather, *Magnalia* (1702), Book IV, in Samuel Eliot Morison, *The Intellectual Life of Colonial New England* (New York: New York University Press, 1956), p. 28.
35. See the discussion in Ryken, *Worldly Saints*, p. 159.
36. Iain Murray, *Jonathan Edwards: A New Biography* (Carlisle, PA: The Banner of Truth Trust, 1987), pp. 68-69.
37. Ibid., p. 332.
38. Ibid., p. 86.
39. Ibid., pp. 214-215.
40. This quote is from a proposal letter written by Edwards in 1723 to Massachusetts Supreme Court Justice Paul Dudley, for the possible publication of "Spiders," in ibid., p. 64.
41. Ibid., p. 138.
42. See ibid., p. 189. Edwards stopped writing out his sermons in 1741, and there are no eye-witness accounts of him actually "reading" a sermon on record.
43. Harry S. Stout, *The New England Soul: Preaching and Religious Culture in Colonial New England* (New York: Oxford University Press, 1986), p. 228.
44. "A Dawning in the New World," *Christian History*, Vol. 8, No. 3, 1989, p. 9.
45. D. Martyn Lloyd-Jones, *Preaching and Preachers* (Grand Rapids, MI: Zondervan, 1971), p. 97.
46. See Ryken, *Worldly Saints*, pp. 103-104.
47. Jonathan Edwards, *Religious Affections*, ed. James M. Houston (Minneapolis: Bethany House, 1996), p. 7.
48. See "In the Wake of the Great Awakening," *Christian History*, Vol. 8, No. 3, 1989, pp. 18-19.
49. Stout, *The New England Soul*, p. 210.
50. Ibid., p. 310.
51. Neil Postman, *Teaching as a Conserving Activity* (New York: Delacorte Press, 1979), p. 29.
52. Lawrence A. Cremin, *American Education: The Colonial Experience (1607-1783)* (New York: Harper & Row, 1970), p. 545.
53. Ibid., p. 551.
54. Unless otherwise noted, the information on the Founding Fathers is taken from David Barton, *Education of the Founding Fathers* (Aledo, TX: WallBuilders, 1992), video-recording.
55. Hart, *The Popular Book*, p. 47.

56. Noah Webster, *History of the United States* (New Haven, CT: Durrie & Peck, 1832), in David Barton, *Original Intent: The Courts, the Constitution, & Religion*, 2nd ed. (Aledo, TX: WallBuilders Press, 1997), p. 6.
57. Benjamin Franklin, *The Autobiography of Benjamin Franklin*, ed. John Bigelow (Roslyn, NY: Black's Readers Service Company, 1932), pp. 56-57.
58. See William David Sloan, James G. Stovall, and James D. Startt, eds., *The Media in America: A History* (Scottsdale, AZ: Publishing Horizons, n.d.), p. 36.
59. Ibid., p. 39.
60. David Ramsay, *The History of the American Revolution*, Vol. II (Philadelphia, 1789), in ibid., p. 55.
61. In James R. Wilson and S. Roy Wilson, *Mass Media, Mass Culture: An Introduction*, 5th ed. (New York: McGraw-Hill, 2001), p. 101, emphasis added.
62. Hart, *The Popular Book*, p. 25.
63. Ibid., p. 18.
64. Neil Postman, *Amusing Ourselves to Death: Public Discourse in the Age of Show Business* (New York: Penguin Books, 1985), p. 63.
65. Barton, "Education of the Founding Fathers."
66. Schaeffer, *How Should We Then Live?*, p. 110.

Chapter Five: Something in the Air

1. Martin Green, *The Armory Show and the Paterson Strike Pageant* (New York: Charles Scribner's and Sons, 1988), p. 181, in James Lincoln Collier, *The Rise of Selfishness in America* (New York: Oxford University Press, 1991), p. 125.
2. This story and others about the beginning of the telegraph can be found in Tom Standage, *The Victorian Internet: The Remarkable Story of the Telegraph and the Nineteenth Century's On-line Pioneers* (New York: Walker and Company, 1998), pp. 1-2.
3. Daniel J. Czitrom, *Media and the American Mind: From Morse to McLuhan* (Chapel Hill, NC: University of North Carolina Press, 1982), p. 12.
4. Perry Miller, *The Life of the Mind in America* (New York: Harcourt, Brace, and World, 1965), p. 48.
5. James W. Carey, *Communication as Culture: Essays on Media and Society* (New York: Routledge, 1989), p. 15.
6. Ibid.
7. This definition of culture is used by Quentin J. Schultze, *Communication for Life: Christian Stewardship in Community and Media* (Grand Rapids, MI: Baker Academic, 2000), p. 20.
8. Collier, *The Rise of Selfishness in America*.
9. Daniel Walker Howe, "Victorian Culture in America," in Daniel Walker Howe, ed., *Victorian America* (Philadelphia: University of Pennsylvania Press, 1976), p. 3.
10. Ibid., p. 4.
11. Collier, *The Rise of Selfishness in America*, pp. 8-18.
12. Collier elaborates on three of these factors in *The Rise of Selfishness in America*, p. 8.
13. See John Tebbel, *George Washington's America* (New York: E. P. Dutton and Company, 1954), pp. 264-265.
14. Collier, *The Rise of Selfishness in America*, p. 6.
15. Howe, "Victorian Culture in America," in ed. Howe, *Victorian America*, p. 9.
16. Nathan O. Hatch, *The Democratization of American Christianity* (New Haven, CT: Yale University Press, 1989), p. 4.
17. Ibid., p. 3.
18. Ibid.
19. Howe, "Victorian Culture in America," in ed. Howe, *Victorian America*, p. 12.
20. Ibid., p. 16.
21. Collier, *The Rise of Selfishness in America*, p. 9.
22. For the change in alcohol consumption rates, see Joseph R. Gusfield, "Prohibition: The Impact of Political Utopianism," in John Braeman, Robert H. Bremner, and David Brody, eds., *Change and Continuity in Twentieth Century America: The 1920s* (Athens, OH: Ohio State University Press, 1968), pp. 272-273, in ibid., p. 14.
23. Howe, "Victorian Culture in America," in ed. Howe, *Victorian America*, p. 26.
24. See "American Magazines, 1740-1900," in David Sloan, James G. Stovall, and James D. Startt, eds., *The Media in America: A History*, 2nd ed. (Scottsdale, AZ: Publishing Horizons, 1989), pp. 261, 264-265.
25. Ages Repplier, "American Magazines," *Yale Review* 16 (1926-1927): 261-274, in ibid., p. 276.

26. Collier, *The Rise of Selfishness in America*, p. 15.
27. *Historical Statistics of the United States, Colonial Times to 1970*, Part 1. Bureau of the Census (Washington, D.C., September 1975), Table H, pp. 664-668.
28. Collier, *The Rise of Selfishness in America*, p. 19.
29. Ibid., p. 35.
30. Ibid., p. 33.
31. Ibid., p. 39.
32. See David Riesman, Nathan Glazer, Reuel Denney, *The Lonely Crowd* (New York: Doubleday Anchor Books, 1950).
33. Collier, *The Rise of Selfishness in America*, p. 48.
34. Jib Fowles, "Mass Media and the Star System," D. J. Crowley and Paul Heyer, eds., *Communication in History: Technology, Culture, Society*, 3rd ed. (New York: Longman, 1999), p. 196.
35. Bernard Sobel, *Burleycue: An Underground History of Burlesque Days* (New York: Farrar & Rinehart, 1931), p. 202.
36. Ibid.
37. Collier, *The Rise of Selfishness in America*, p. 58.
38. Ibid., p. 61.
39. Ibid., p. 66.
40. Francis A. Schaeffer, *How Should We Then Live? The Rise and Decline of Western Thought and Culture* (Wheaton, IL: Crossway Books, 1976), p. 121.
41. Ibid., p. 122.
42. Ibid., p. 124.
43. Jacques Barzun, *From Dawn to Decadence; 500 Years of Western Cultural Life; 1500 to the Present* (New York: Harper Collins, 2000), p. 470.
44. Ibid., emphasis mine.
45. See George M. Marsden, "The Christian Legacy in the Epoch of Science," *The Soul of the American University: From Protestant Establishment to Established Nonbelief* (New York: Oxford University Press, 1994), pp. 113-122.
46. D. H. Meyer, "The Victorian Crisis of Faith," in ed. Howe, *Victorian America*, p. 76.
47. Marsden, *The Soul of the American University*, p. 326.
48. Ibid., p. 329.
49. Howe, "Victorian Culture in America," in ed. Howe, *Victorian America*, p. 19.
50. Collier, *The Rise of Selfishness in America*, p. 105.
51. Green, *The Armory Show and the Paterson Strike Pageant*, p. 181, in ibid., p. 125.
52. James Leuba, *The Belief in God and Immortality: A Psychological, Anthropological and Statistical Study* (Chicago, 1921 [1916]), pp. 280, 282, in ibid., p. 295.
53. Robert S. Lynd and Helen Merrell Lynd, *Middletown: A Study in American Culture* (New York: Harcourt, Brace and World, 1929), p. 139.
54. Collier, *The Rise of Selfishness in America*, pp. 158-159.

Chapter Six: The Machines of Show Business

1. Alvin Toffler, *The Third Wave* (New York: Bantam Books, 1980), p. 158.
2. Kathy Peiss, *Cheap Amusements: Working Women and Leisure in Turn-of-the-Century New York* (Philadelphia: Temple University Press, 1986), p. 142.
3. For a fuller account of the development of vaudeville see James Lincoln Collier, *The Rise of Selfishness in America* (New York: Oxford University Press, 1991), pp. 74-82 and Albert F. McLean, Jr., *American Vaudeville as Ritual* (Lexington, KY: University of Kentucky Press, 1965).
4. McLean, *American Vaudeville as Ritual*, p. 72.
5. Collier, *The Rise of Selfishness in America*, pp. 74-82.
6. Daniel J. Czitrom, *Media and the American Mind: From Morse to McLuhan* (Chapel Hill, NC: University of North Carolina Press, 1982), pp. 11-12.
7. Neil Postman, *Amusing Ourselves to Death: Public Discourse in the Age of Show Business* (New York: Penguin Books, 1985), p. 69.
8. James W. Carey, *Communication as Culture: Essays on Media and Society* (New York: Routledge, 1989), p. 211.
9. Graham Clarke, *The Photograph* (New York: Oxford University Press, 1997), p. 41.
10. Oliver Wendell Holmes, "The Stereoscope and the Stereograph," *The Atlantic Monthly*, June 1859, reprinted in Beaumont Newhall, ed., *Photography Essays and Images* (1980), pp. 53-54, in Stuart Ewen, *All Consuming Images: The Politics of Style in Contemporary Culture* (New York: Basic Books, 1988), p. 24.

11. Quoted in Ewen, *All Consuming Images*, p. 25.
12. Holmes, "The Stereoscope and the Stereograph," p. 60, in ibid.
13. See Postman, *Amusing Ourselves to Death: Public Discourse in the Age of Show Business*, pp. 73-75.
14. Ibid., p. 77.
15. Tino Balio, ed., *The American Film Industry* (Madison, WI: The University of Wisconsin Press, 1976), p. 30.
16. Quoted in Eric Rhode, *A History of the Cinema: From Its Origins to 1970* (New York: Hill and Wang, 1976), p. 4.
17. Jason E. Squire, ed., *The Movie Business Book* (New York: Simon & Schuster, 1983), p. 3, in Shirley Biagi, *Media Impact: An Introduction to Mass Media*, 3rd ed. (Belmont, CA: Wadsworth, 1998), p. 189.
18. Daniel J. Czitrom, *Media and the American Mind: From Morse to McLuhan*, pp. 41-42.
19. Ibid., p. 43.
20. See Jib Fowles, "Mass Media and the Star System," D. J. Crowley and Paul Heyer, eds., *Communication in History: Technology, Culture, Society*, 3rd ed. (New York: Longman, 1999), p. 199.
21. Thomas Doherty, *Pre-Code Hollywood: Sex, Immorality, and Insurrection in American Cinema, 1930-1934* (New York: Columbia University Press, 1999), p. 2.
22. Ibid., p. 261.
23. Ibid., p. 262.
24. Fowles, "Mass Media and the Star System," Crowley and Heyer, eds., *Communication in History*, p. 201.
25. James R. Wilson and S. Roy Wilson, *Mass Media, Mass Culture: An Introduction*, 5th ed. (New York: McGraw-Hill, 2001), p. 228.
26. Fowles, "Mass Media and the Star System," Crowley and Heyer, eds., *Communication in History*, p. 202.
27. Wilson and Wilson, *Mass Media, Mass Culture*, p. 229.
28. See Christopher Lasch, *The Culture of Narcissism: American Life in an Age of Diminishing Expectations* (New York: Warner Books, 1979), p. 38.
29. Wilson and Wilson, *Mass Media, Mass Culture*, p. 236.
30. Ibid.
31. Jonah Goldberg, "Violent Fantasy: It's Not the Hollywood Gore That's the Problem," *National Review*, October 23, 2000, p. 64.
32. Ibid.
33. Kenneth Turan, "*Apocalypse Now* Review," National Public Radio's *Morning Edition*, national broadcast, August 6, 2001; also see www.npr.org/archives.
34. Quoted in Archer Gleason, *History of Radio to 1926* (New York: American Historical Society, 1938), in Wilson and Wilson, *Mass Media, Mass Culture*, p. 256.
35. Roland Gelatt, *The Fabulous Phonograph, 1877-1977* (New York: Collier Books, 1977), p. 32, in Collier, *The Rise of Selfishness in America*, p. 96.
36. Quoted in Marshall McLuhan, "Understanding Radio," in Crowley and Heyer, eds., *Communication in History*, p. 252.
37. Wilson and Wilson, *Mass Media, Mass Culture*, p. 262.
38. McLuhan, "Understanding Radio," in Crowley and Heyer, eds., *Communication in History*, p. 252.
39. Ibid., p. 254.
40. Jim Zarroli, "All or Nothing at All," National Public Radio's *Morning Edition*, national broadcast, November 28, 2000; also see www.npr.org/archives.
41. Wilson and Wilson, *Mass Media, Mass Culture*, p. 281.
42. Don Dixon, "NRP 100," National Public Radio's *Morning Edition*, national broadcast, November 3, 2000; also see www.npr.org/archives.
43. John Podhoretz, "Id TV: On MTV It's Always Spring Break," *National Review*, October 23, 2000, pp. 33-34.
44. Ibid., p. 34.
45. Ibid.
46. Ibid.
47. J. Bottum, "The Soundtracking of America," *The Atlantic Monthly*, March 2000, p. 70.
48. C. S. Lewis, *The Screwtape Letters* (West Chicago, IL: Lord and King Associates, 1976), p. 75.
49. Ibid.
50. Norm Goldstein, *The History of Television* (New York: Portland House, 1991), p. 19.
51. Quoted in ibid., p. 15.

260 ℒ♥ The Vanishing Word

52. Quoted in ibid., p. 10.
53. Quoted in Robert D. Putnam, *Bowling Alone: The Collapse and Revival of American Community* (New York: Simon & Schuster, 2000), p. 217.
54. Goldstein, *The History of Television*, p. 15.
55. Table in ibid., p. 217.
56. Biagi, *Media Impact*, p. 158.
57. This figure is based upon Nielsen Media Research in "What a Difference a Decade Makes: A Comparison of Prime Time Sex, Language, and Violence in 1989 and '99," a Special Report by Parents Television Council, www.parentstv.org/publications/reports/Decadestudy/decadestudy.html, page 1 of 20 (accessed August 8, 2001).
58. Neil Postman, *Building a Bridge to the Eighteenth Century: How the Past Can Improve Our Future* (New York: Alfred A. Knopf, 1999), p. 49.
59. *New York Times*, October 16, 1990, p. C8.
60. Patricia Palmer, "The Social Nature of Children's Television Viewing," in Phillip Drummond and Richard Patterson, eds., *Television and Its Audience: International Research Perspectives* (London: BFI Books, 1988), pp. 143-144.
61. "What a Difference a Decade Makes," Parents Television Council, www.parentstv.org/publications/reports/Decadestudy/decadestudy.html, page 4 of 20 (accessed August 8, 2001).
62. "More TV Shows Include Sexual Content; Safer Sex Messages Most Common When Teen Characters or Sexual Intercourse are Involved," Kaiser Family Foundation press release, February 6, 2001, www.kff.org/content/2001/3087/SexonTVPR.htm, page 1 of 3 (accessed August 8, 2001).
63. Karl Zinsmeister, "Wasteland: How Today's Trash Television Harms America," *The American Enterprise*, March-April 1999, p. 34.
64. Lynn Rosellini, "Pro Wrestling: Lords of the Ring," *U.S. News & World Report*, May 17, 1999, p. 55.
65. David Grossman, "What the Surgeon General Found; As Early as 1972, the Link Was Clear Between Violent TV and Movies and Violent Youths," *Los Angeles Times*, October 21, 1999, p. B11, in "What a Difference a Decade Makes," Parents Television Council, www.parentstv.org/publications/reports/Decadestudy/decadestudy.html, page 2 of 20 (accessed August 8, 2001).
66. Ibid.
67. John Leo, "A Lovely Day for Haranguing," *U.S. News and World Report*, November 13, 1995.
68. David Bauder for the Associated Press, "Jenny Jones Is a Hit—At Least on the Witness Stand," *Pensacola News Journal*, April 19, 1999.
69. Arian Campo-Flores and Yuval Rosenberg, "A Return to Wilding," *Newsweek*, June 26, 2000, p. 28.
70. Linda Wertheimer, "Central Park—News Coverage," National Public Radio's *All Things Considered*, national broadcast, June 19, 2000; also see www.npr.org/archives.
71. Brian Winston, *Media Technology and Society, A History: From the Telegraph to the Internet* (New York: Routledge, 1998), pp. 156-157.
72. *Time*, "The Future of Technology," cover issue, June 19, 2000.
73. Ray Kurzweil, "Will My PC Be Smarter Than I Am?" *Time*, June 19, 2000, pp. 82-85.
74. Jon Swartz, "Sex Called a Big Deal On Internet; Poll Says Women Talk, Men Look," *San Francisco Chronicle*, June 10, 1998, p. A1, in Wilson and Wilson, *Mass Media, Mass Culture*, p. 57.
75. Randy Hammer, "Getting Back to Election Basics," *Pensacola News Journal*, August 20, 2000, p. 11A.
76. Holman W. Jenkins, Jr., "Pornography, Main Street to Wall Street," *Policy Review*, February & March 2001, p. 9.
77. George Barna, *Boiling Point: It Only Takes One Degree: Monitoring Cultural Shifts in the 21st Century* (Ventura, CA: Regal Books, 2001), p. 223.
78. Gene Edward Veith, "The Pornographic Culture," *World*, April 7, 2001, p. 17.
79. John Leland, "More Buck for the Bang: How Sex Has Transformed the Porn Industry," *Newsweek*, September 20, 1999, p. 61, in Gene Edward Veith, Jr. and Christopher L. Stamper, *Christians in a .com World: Getting Connected Without Being Consumed* (Wheaton, IL: Crossway Books, 2000), p. 129.
80. Jenkins, "Pornography, Main Street to Wall Street," p. 8.

Chapter Seven: The Image

1. Camille Paglia, *Sexual Personae: Art and Decadence from Nefertiti to Emily Dickinson* (London and New Haven, CT: Yale University Press, 1990), p. 32.
2. See Neil Postman and Camille Paglia, "Two Cultures—Television Versus Print," in D. J. Crowley and Paul Heyer, eds., *Communication in History: Technology, Culture, Society*, 3rd ed. (New York: Longman, 1999), p. 298.
3. *The Random House Dictionary of the English Language: The Unabridged Edition* (New York: Random House, 1973).
4. James Montgomery Boice, *Romans*, Vol. 1 (Grand Rapids, MI: Baker Book House, 1991), p. 156.
5. Robert Brow, *Religion: Origins and Ideas* (Chicago: InterVarsity Press, 1966), as discussed in ibid., p. 172.
6. Ibid., pp. 172-173.
7. F. Godet, *Commentary on St. Paul's Epistle to the Romans*, trans. A. Cusin, Vol. 1 (Edinburgh: T. & T. Clark, n.d.), p. 184, in Boice, *Romans*, Vol. 1, p. 191.
8. John Boardman, Jasper Griffen, Oswyn Murry, eds., *The Oxford History of the Classical World* (New York: Oxford University Press, 1986), p. 261.
9. See Neal Gabler, *Life: The Movie, How Entertainment Conquered Reality* (New York: Vintage Books, 1998), pp. 174-175.
10. Ibid., p. 176.
11. Christopher Lasch, *The Culture of Narcissism: American Life in an Age of Diminishing Expectations* (New York: Warner Books, 1979), pp. 96-97.
12. James R. Wilson and S. Roy Wilson, *Mass Media, Mass Culture: An Introduction*, 5th ed., (New York: McGraw-Hill, 2001), p. 344.
13. Ibid., p. 361.
14. Ibid., p. 49.
15. Shirley Biagi, *Media Impact: An Introduction to Mass Media*, 3rd ed. (Belmont, CA: Wadsworth, 1998), p. 217.
16. Vance Packard, *Harper's Bazaar*, August 1957, in "The Ad and the Id," Fredric Rissover and David C. Birch, eds., *Mass Media and the Popular Arts* (New York: McGraw-Hill, 1971), p. 9.
17. For a further discussion of these characteristics of American advertising see Daniel Boorstin, "The Rhetoric of Democracy," in Robert Atwan, Barry Orton, and William Vesterman, eds., *American Mass Media: Industries and Issues*, 3rd ed. (New York: Random House, 1986).
18. Vance Packard, *Harper's Bazaar*, August 1957, in "The Ad and the Id," p. 15.
19. Kathleen Hall Jamieson, *Packaging the Presidency: A History and Criticism of Presidential Campaign Advertising*, 3rd ed. (New York: Oxford University Press, 1996), p. xxiii.
20. Ibid., p. 517.
21. See Kathleen Hall Jamieson's insightful *Eloquence in an Electronic Age: The Transformation of Political Speechmaking* ((New York: Oxford University Press, 1988), pp. 238-255.
22. Jamieson, *Packaging the Presidency*, p. 521.
23. Daniel Boorstin, *The Image: A Guide to Pseudo-Events in America* (New York: Vintage Books, 1961), p. 207.
24. Dennis L. Wilcox, Phillip H. Ault, and Warren K. Agee, *Public Relations: Strategies and Tactics*, 4th ed. (New York: Harper Collins College Publishers, 1995), p. 43.
25. Boorstin, *The Image*, p. 3, emphasis mine.
26. Ibid., p. 58.
27. Ibid., p. 60.
28. Ibid.
29. Stuart Ewen, *All Consuming Images: The Politics of Style in Contemporary Culture* (New York: Basic Books, 1988), p. 93.
30. "Quotable Quotes," *Reader's Digest*, June 2001, p. 73.
31. Ewen, *All Consuming Images*, pp. 95-96.
32. Ibid., p. 101.
33. See ibid., p. 96 and Boorstin, *The Image*, pp. 37-38 for further discussion of media stereotyping.
34. Paglia, *Sexual Personae: Art and Decadence from Nefertiti to Emily Dickinson*, p. 33.
35. Friedrich Nietzsche, *The Birth of Tragedy*, trans. and ed. Walter Kaufmann (New York: The Modern Library, 1992), p. 44.
36. Paglia, *Sexual Personae*, p. 112.

262 ✑ The Vanishing Word

37. Nietzsche, *The Birth of Tragedy*, p. 39.
38. Paglia, *Sexual Personae*, p. 139.
39. See Martin Heidegger, *Nietzsche: The Will to Power as Art*, Vol. 1, trans. David Farrell Krell (San Francisco: Harper San Francisco, 1991), p. 83.
40. Ibid., pp. 96-97.
41. For further discussion of these critics see Gene Edward Veith, Jr., *State of the Arts: From Bezalel to Mapplethorpe* (Wheaton, IL: Crossway Books, 1991), pp. 137-138.
42. See Paglia, *Sexual Personae*, pp. 109-110.
43. This is one of the major themes in ibid.
44. Ibid., p. 115.
45. Ibid., p. 123.
46. Ibid., p. 115.
47. Ibid., p. 121.
48. William Harlan Hale, ed., *The Horizon Book of Ancient Greece* (New York: American Heritage Publishing Co., 1965), p. 272.
49. Ibid., p. 262.
50. See ibid., pp. 263-266.
51. Paglia, *Sexual Personae*, p. 80.
52. Ibid., p. 124.
53. See ibid., p. 127.
54. Barry Cunliffe, *Rome and Her Empire* (New York: McGraw-Hill, 1978), p. 114.
55. Paglia, *Sexual Personae*, p. 131.
56. Anna Maria Liberati and Fabio Bourbon, *Ancient Rome: History of a Civilization That Ruled the World* (New York: Stewart, Tabori & Chang, 1996), pp. 69-70.
57. Ibid., p. 74.
58. The scandalous information on the lives of Roman emperors is taken from Paglia, *Sexual Personae*, pp. 133-137.
59. *Dio's Roman History*, trans. Ernest Cary (London, 1927), 7:347, in ibid., p. 134.
60. Paglia, *Sexual Personae*, p. 135.
61. Roger Simon with Art Samuels, "Philadelphia Story," *U.S. News & World Report*, August 7, 2000, p. 33, emphasis mine.
62. Ibid., p. 34.
63. Wladyslaw Pleszczynki, "Hymn to Him," *The American Spectator*, October 2000, p. 78.
64. Bob Jones IV, "Can't Stop Thinking About Yesterday," *World*, August 26, 2000, p. 17.
65. "Washington Whispers," *U.S. News & World Report*, June 18, 2001, p. 6.

Chapter Eight: On Being Postmodern

1. Quoted in David McCullough, *John Adams* (New York: Simon & Schuster, 2001), p. 70.
2. Ray Bradbury, *Fahrenheit 451* (New York: Ballantine Books, 1953), p. 81.
3. Quoted in McCullough, *John Adams*, p. 619.
4. This summary definition of postmodernism is taken in part from Denis McQuail, *Mass Communication Theory: An Introduction*, 3rd ed. (Thousand Oaks, CA: Sage Publications, 1994), p. 59.
5. This is how Peter Sacks summarizes postmodernism in "The Postmodern Revolt," in *Generation X Goes to College: An Eye-Opening Account of Teaching in Postmodern America* (Chicago and LaSalle, IL: Open Court, 1996), pp. 107-121.
6. Donald Wood, *Post-Intellectualism and the Decline of Democracy: The Failure of Reason and Responsibility in the Twentieth Century* (Westport, CT: Praeger, 1996), p. 36.
7. See Kirk Hallahan, *The Consequences of Mass Communication: Cultural and Critical Perspectives on Mass Media and Society* (New York: McGraw-Hill, 1997), p. 45.
8. Gene Edward Veith, Jr., *Postmodern Times: A Christian Guide to Contemporary Thought and Culture* (Wheaton, IL: Crossway Books, 1994), p. 193.
9. See Neil Postman's discussion of Jean Baudrillard and language in *Building a Bridge to the Eighteenth Century: How the Past Can Improve the Future* (New York: Alfred A. Knopf, 1999), p. 8.
10. See Hallahan, *The Consequences of Mass Communication*, p. 45.
11. See Sven Birkerts, *The Gutenberg Elegies: The Fate of Reading in an Electronic Age* (Boston: Faber and Faber, 1994), p. 214.
12. Neil Postman, *Amusing Ourselves to Death: Public Discourse in the Age of Show Business* (New York: Penguin Books, 1985), p. 63.
13. Veith, *Postmodern Times: A Christian Guide to Contemporary Thought and Culture*, pp. 35-41.
14. In *Postmodern Times* Veith explains how existentialism provided a rationale for con-

temporary relativism: "Existentialism began in the nineteenth century, but by the middle of the twentieth century, it emerged as a major philosophical movement. . . . It has become the philosophy of soap operas and television talk shows. Its tenets shape political discourse and are transforming the legal system. Existentialism is the philosophical basis for postmodernism"; p. 38.

15. George Barna, *Boiling Point: It Only Takes One Degree: Monitoring Cultural Shifts in the 21st Century* (Ventura, CA: Regal Books, 2001), p. 42.
16. Francis A. Schaeffer, *How Should We Then Live? The Rise and Decline of Western Thought and Culture* (Wheaton, IL: Crossway Books, 1976), pp. 205-206.
17. See Martin Gross, *The End of Sanity: Social and Cultural Madness in America* (New York: Avon Books, 1997), p. 112.
18. List of courses for Yale's "Women Studies" taken from ibid., p. 113.
19. Ibid.
20. Ibid., p. 115.
21. Ibid., p. 110.
22. John Leo, "Ivy League therapy: Free Speech and Hurt Feelings Collide at Brown," *U.S. News & World Report*, April 2, 2001, p. 14.
23. Ibid.
24. See George M. Marsden, *The Soul of the American University: From Protestant Establishment to Established Nonbelief* (New York: Oxford University Press, 1994), pp. 423-424.
25. See "This is Just a Test," *The American Spectator*, August 1999, p. 16; "No SAT Scores Required," *Time*, September 11, 2000, pp. 52-53; Marcia Yablon, "The Scam Behind SAT-bashing," *The New Republic*, October 30, 2000, pp. 24-25.
26. "Literacy Statistics from the Most Recent National Adult Literacy Survey—1992," The American Literacy Council, www.americanliteracy.com/literacy_figures.htm, pages 1 and 2 of 3 (accessed September 29, 2001).
27. See Linto Weeks, "The No-Book Report: Skim It and Weep," *Washington Post*, May 14, 2001, p. C1.
28. Ibid.
29. L. Brent Bozell, III, "A Poisoned Culture: Television Launches an All-out Assault on the American Family," *The American Legion*, December 2001, p. 15.
30. Weeks, "The No Book Report: Skim It and Weep," p. C1.
31. Quoted in George Will, "No Longer a Need for Public Broadcasting," *Pensacola News Journal*, August 4, 1999, p. A12.
32. E. D. Hirsch, Jr., *Cultural Literacy: What Every American Needs to Know* (Boston: Houghton Mifflin, 1987), p. 19.
33. "America for Dummies? Evidence of Growing Ignorance Abounds; That's Not the Whole Story," *U.S. News & World Report*, April 30, 2001, p. 8.
34. Susan Salai, "Hollywood History Lessons; Who's Imitating Whom?" *Campus*, Fall 2001, p. 21.
35. Steve Bell, "The Media and Politics: It's More Than the News," *Mass Media Annual Editions*, 9th ed. (Guilford, CT: McGraw-Hill/Dushkin, 2002), p. 87.
36. "School Reform News: New Poll and Paper Show How Schools Fail to Teach Civics," The Heartland Institute, www.heartland.org/education/nov97/poll.htm, pages 1 and 2 out of 2 (accessed January 7, 2001).
37. Quoted in Kathleen Hall Jamieson, *Eloquence in an Electronic Age: The Transformation of Political Speechmaking* (New York: Oxford University Press, 1988), p. 28.
38. Andree Seu, "The Word Stands Forever: But It's Lost in the Minds of the Biblically Illiterate," *World*, special issue, May/June 2001, p. 44.
39. David C. McCasland, "Let's Read It!" *Our Daily Bread*, December-February 2001-2002, December 31.
40. Ibid.
41. Ibid.
42. Statistics taken from the UCLA Higher Education Research Institute, "The American Freshman: 2000 Executive Summary," www.gseis.ucla.edu/heri/00_exec_summary.htm, page 3 out of 7 (accessed September 29, 2001).
43. Sacks, *Generation X Goes to College*, p. 9.
44. Ibid., p. 12.
45. Ibid., pp. 48-49.
46. Ibid., p. 55.
47. Ibid., p. 144.
48. Lorraine Ali, "The Glorious Rise of Christian Pop," *Newsweek*," July 16, 2001, p. 40.

49. Gustav Niebuhr, "Mighty Fortresses: Megachurches Strive to Be All Things to All Parishioners," *The Wall Street Journal*, May 13, 1991, p. A5.
50. Robert Johnson, "Heavenly Gifts: Preaching a Gospel Of Acquisitiveness, a Showy Sect Prospers," *The Wall Street Journal*, December 11, 1990, p. A1.
51. Assertions about the theological shallowness of Schuller's annual Easter show is taken from Michael R. Linton, "Smoke and Mirrors at the Crystal Cathedral," *First Things*, June/July 1997, pp. 12-13.
52. Ibid., p. 13.
53. Ibid.
54. David F. Wells, "Introduction: The Word In The World," in John H. Armstrong, gen. ed., *The Compromised Church* (Wheaton, IL: Crossway Books, 1998), p. 20.
55. Ibid.
56. Mary Maraghy, "That Modern Religion: Contemporary Approach Sparks Debate Among Churchgoers," *Florida Times Union* (Jacksonville), January 31, 2001, p. A13.
57. Jim Long, "We Have Created a Monster: Industry Veteran Stan Moser Reflects on How a Movement of the Spirit Became a Wall Street Success Story," *Christianity Today*, May 20, 1996, p. 27.
58. Ibid.
59. See John MacArthur, "With Hearts and Minds and Voices," *Christian Research Journal*, Vol. 23, No. 2, p. 38.
60. Ibid.
61. Ibid., p. 40.
62. Robert Palmer, *Rock & Roll: An Unruly History* (New York: Harmony Books, 1995), p. 21.
63. Jim Long, "Who's the Leader of This Band? Michael Card and Steve Taylor Wonder What the Industry Won't Do for Money," *Christianity Today*, May 20, 1996, p. 12.
64. Corrie Cutrer, "What Would Andy Do? Fictional Mayberry Is Setting for Hit Bible Study," *Christianity Today*, September, 2000, p. 27.
65. *The Word on the New Testament: Youth Builders Group Bible Studies*, ed. Jim Burns (Cincinnati: Gospel Light, 1977), p. 12, in Cathy Mickels and Audrey McKeever, *Spiritual Junk Food: The Dumbing Down of Christian Youth* (Mukilto, WA: Winepress Publishing, 1999), p. 20.
66. Ibid., p. 65, in *Spiritual Junk Food*, p. 20.
67. *Case Studies, Talk Sheets and Discussion Starters*, gen. ed. Jim Barnes (Cincinnati: Gospel Light, 1977), p. 103, in *Spiritual Junk Food*, p. 21.
68. *The Word on the New Testament*, p. 161, in *Spiritual Junk Food*, p. 21.
69. Robert Hodgson, "Introduction: An Urgent Need: God's Word in a Post-Literate World," Robert Hodgson and Paul A. Soukup, eds., *From One Medium to Another: Basic Issues for Communicating the Scriptures in New Media* (New York: The American Bible Society, 1997), p. 3.
70. Ibid., p. 6.
71. Ed Rowell, "Where Preaching Is Headed: 4 forces Shaping Tomorrow's Sermon," *Leadership*, Winter 1997, pp. 95-98.
72. Quoted in ibid., p. 96.
73. Quoted in ibid., p. 98.
74. Barna, *Boiling Point*, p. 239.
75. James Ryle, *Hippo in the Garden* (Orlando, FL: Creation House, 1993), p. 13, in Hank Hanegraaff, *Counterfeit Revival: Looking for God in All the Wrong Places* (Nashville: Word Publishing, 2001), p. 82.
76. Hanegraaff, *Counterfeit Revival*, p. 286.
77. MacArthur, "With Hearts and Minds and Voices," p. 39.
78. Barna, *Boiling Point*, pp. 190-191.
79. Ibid., p. 191.
80. Francis A. Schaeffer, *The Great Evangelical Disaster* (Wheaton, IL: Crossway Books, 1984), p. 146.

Chapter Nine: Formula for a Führer

1. Francis A. Schaeffer, *The Great Evangelical Disaster* (Wheaton, IL: Crossway Books, 1984), p. 23.
2. Alan Wykes, *The Nuremberg Rallies* (New York: Ballantine Books, 1970), p. 88.
3. Ibid., p. 51.
4. Ibid., p. 50.

5. See Albert Speer, "Architectural Megalomania," *Inside the Third Reich: Memoirs by Albert Speer*, trans. Richard and Clara Winston (New York: Macmillan, 1970), pp. 50-70.
6. Ibid., p. 59.
7. Ibid., p. 60.
8. Alan Bullock, *Hitler, A Study in Tyranny* (New York: Harper Colophon Books, 1964), p. 379.
9. Quoted in John Toland, *Adolf Hitler* (Garden City, NY: Doubleday, 1976), p. 361.
10. Quoted in Wykes, *The Nuremberg Rallies*, p. 46.
11. Ibid., p. 145.
12. Viktor Frankl, *The Doctor and the Soul: Introduction to Logotherapy* (New York: Knopf, 1982), p. xxi.
13. Hermann Rauschning, *Talks with Hitler*, in *Memoirs of Alfred Rosenberg*, with commentaries by Serge Lang and Ernst von Schenck, trans. Eric Posselt (New York: Ziff-Davis Publishing Company, 1949), p. 89.
14. Summaries on Hegel, Nietzsche, Chamberlain, and Wagner are taken from William L. Shirer, *The Rise and Fall of the Third Reich* (New York: Simon and Schuster, 1960), pp. 97-113.
15. Ibid., p. 105.
16. Ibid., p. 101.
17. Ibid., p. 59.
18. Quoted in Michael Burleigh, *The Third Reich: A New History* (New York: Hill and Wang, 2000), pp. 100-101.
19. Quoted in David Welch, *The Third Reich: Politics and Propaganda* (New York: Routledge, 1993), p. 17.
20. Quoted in ibid., p. 24.
21. Quoted in ibid., p. 28.
22. Quoted in ibid., p. 63, based on a Sopade report that included underground communications of the Social Democratic Party.
23. Ibid., p. 33.
24. Quoted in ibid., p. 35.
25. Ibid., p. 39.
26. Ibid., p. 46.
27. Ibid., p. 48.
28. Ibid.
29. Gene Edward Veith, Jr., *Modern Fascism: Liquidating the Judeo-Christian Worldview* (St. Louis: Concordia Publishing House, 1993), p. 18.
30. These comments about the influence of Luther and Calvin on American democracy are taken from John W. Whitehead, *The Second American Revolution* (Wheaton, IL: Crossway Books, 1982), pp. 201-202.
31. See Dean C. Curry, *A World Without Tyranny: Christian Faith and International Politics* (Wheaton, IL: Crossway Books, 1990), p. 145.
32. Alexis De Tocqueville, *Democracy in America*, Book I, Chapter XVII.
33. George Washington, *Address of George Washington, President of the United States . . . Preparatory to his Declination* (Baltimore: George and Henry S. Keatinge, 1796), pp. 22-23, in David Barton, *Original Intent: The Courts, the Constitution, & Religion*, 2nd ed. (Aledo, TX: WallBuilders Press, 1997), p. 319.
34. Emphasis mine. John Adams, *The Works of John Adams, Second President of the United States*, ed. Charles Frances Adams, Vol. IX (Boston: Little, Brown, and Company, 1854), p. 229, to the Officers of the First Brigade of the Third Division of the Militia of Massachusetts on October 11, 1798, in Barton, *Original Intent*, p. 319.
35. Benjamin Franklin, *The Works of Benjamin Franklin*, ed. Jared Sparks, Vol. X (Boston: Tappan, Whittemore and Mason, 1840), p. 297, to Messrs. The Abbés Chalut and Arnaud on April 17, 1787, in Barton, *Original Intent*, p. 321.
36. David J. Danelski and Joseph S. Tulchin, eds., *The Autobiographical Notes of Charles Evans Hughes* (Cambridge, MA: Harvard University Press, 1973), p. 143, in Whitehead, *The Second American Revolution*, p. 20.
37. Whitehead says, "Such an attitude is not that far removed from the 1936 decree of the Third Reich Commissar of Justice: 'A decision of the Fuhrer in the express form of law or decree may not be scrutinized by a judge. In addition, the judge is bound by any other decisions of the Fuhrer, provided that they are clearly intended to declared law.'" From Ernst van Hippel, "The Role of Natural Law in the Legal Decisions of the Federal German Republic," Natural Law Forum 4 (1959): 106, p. 10, in Whitehead, *The Second American Revolution*, p. 20.

38. Whitehead, *The Second American Revolution*, p. 54.
39. See Gene Edward Veith, "Politics Without Truth," *The Christian Research Journal*, Vol. 23, No. 4, pp. 60-61.
40. Gene Edward Veith, Jr., *Postmodern Times: A Christian Guide to Contemporary Thought and Culture* (Wheaton, IL: Crossway Books, 1994), p. 159.
41. Veith, *Modern Fascism*, pp. 12-13.
42. Richard John Neuhaus, *The Naked Public Square: Religion and Democracy in America* (Grand Rapids, MI: William B. Eerdmans, 1984), p. 80.
43. Ibid., p. 85.
44. Ibid., pp. 83-84.
45. "A Trick of the Eye," *Time*, January 24, 2000, p. 67.
46. Mark Slouka, *War of the Worlds: Cyberspace and the High-tech Assault on Reality* (New York: Basic Books, 1995), p. 121.
47. Walter Kirn with Jeanne McDowell, Timothy Padgett, Andrea Sachs, and David E. Thigpen, "Should You Stay Together for the Kids?" *Time*, September 25, 2000, p. 76.
48. George Barna, "Christians Are More Likely to Experience Divorce Than Are Non-Christians," Barna Research Group, http://www.barna.org (accessed August 2000), in George Barna and Mark Hatch, *Boiling Point: It Only Takes One Degree: Monitoring Cultural Shifts in the 21st Century* (Ventura, CA: Regal Books, 2001), p. 42.
49. Judith S. Wallerstein, Julia M. Lewis, Sandra Blakeslee, *The Unexpected Legacy of Divorce: A 25 Year Landmark Study* (New York: Hyperion, 2000), p. 295.
50. Ibid., p. xxiii.
51. Ibid., p. 79.
52. Quoted in ibid., p. 294.
53. John G. Clark, Jr., MD, *The Journal of the American Medical Association*, July 20, 1979, p. 279.
54. Charles Colson and Nancy Pearcey, *How Now Shall We Live?* (Wheaton, IL: Tyndale House, 1999), p. 266.
55. Ibid., p. 264.
56. Ibid., p. 271.
57. Hank Hanegraaff, *Counterfeit Revival: Looking for God in All the Wrong Places* (Nashville: Word Publishing, 2001), p. 71.
58. Frank Beacham, "Is ITV the Next I-Spy?" *TV Technology*, August 8, 2001, p. 35.
59. Center for Digital Democracy report, "TV That Watches You: The Prying Eyes of Interactive Television" (2001), quoted in ibid.
60. See Valerie Meyers, "*Nineteen Eighty-Four*: An Anti-Utopia," *Modern Novelists: George Orwell* (New York: St. Martin's Press, 1991), p. 118.

Chapter Ten: Conclusion: Making Waves

1. Neil Postman, *Amusing Ourselves to Death: Public Discourse in the Age of Show Business* (New York: Penguin Books, 1985), p. 156.
2. See Neil Postman, "Science and the Story That We Need," *First Things*, January 1997, p. 29.
3. Postman, *Amusing Ourselves to Death: Public Discourse in the Age of Show Business*, p. 161.

General Index